Acclaim for Tim Cahill

"Tim Cahill is the working-class Paul Theroux. . . . He delights in finding stories too peculiar to be labeled merely off-beat." —*The New York Times*

"Cahill writes in an agreeably off-the-wall fashion; he has a way with anecdotes, and he can be quite funny." —*Washington Post*

"Cahill [has] the what-the-hell adventuresomeness of a T. E. Lawrence and the humor of a P. J. O' Rourke." —*Condé Nast Traveler*

"Tim Cahill is one of those rare types whose fun quotient seems to increase in direct proportion to the diceyness of the situation." —*San Francisco Examiner*

"You might call him crazy. You might call him reckless. But you'll definitely call him hilarious. Adventure-travel crash-dummy Tim Cahill is to travel writing what P. J. O'Rourke is to political commentary." —*Hartford Courant*

Tim Cahill

Jaguars Ripped My Flesh

Tim Cahill is the author of five books. He lives in Montana and is currently *Outside* magazine's editor-at-large and a contributing editor to *Esquire* and *Rolling Stone*.

Jaguars
Ripped
My Flesh

Tim Cahill

Vintage Departures
Vintage Books
A Division of Random House, Inc.
New York

FIRST VINTAGE DEPARTURES EDITION, APRIL 1996

Copyright © 1987 by Tim Cahill

Library of Congress Cataloging-in-Publication Data
Cahill, Tim.
Jaguars ripped my flesh / Tim Cahill.
p. cm. — (Vintage departures)
ISBN 0-679-77079-8
1. Adventure stories, American.
2. Travelers' writings, American. 3. Voyages and travels. I. Title.
PS3553.A365J3 1996
813'.54—dc20
95-46721
CIP

Author photograph © Marion Ettlinger

Printed in the United States of America
10 9 8 7 6 5 4 3 2 1

To Richard J. and Elizabeth Cahill:
the first lucky thing that ever happened to me.

Acknowledgments

All stories originally appeared in *Outside* magazine except: "The Lost World," "Gorilla Tactics," and "Eruption," which appeared in *GEO*; "Shark Dive," which appeared in the *Los Angeles Times Magazine*; "Fear of Falling," which appeared in *West*; and "The Underwater Zombie," which appeared in *Sport Diver*.

Contents

Introduction

When I was growing up in the late 1950s and early '60s, there was very little in the way of literate adventure writing. Periodicals that catered to our adolescent dreams of travel and adventure clearly held us in contempt. Feature articles in magazines that might be called *Man's Testicle* carried illustrations of tough, unshaven guys dragging terrified women in artfully torn blouses through jungles, caves, or submarine corridors; through hordes of menacing bikers, lions, and hippopotami. The stories bore the same relation to the truth that professional wrestling bears to sport, which is to say, they were larger-than-life contrivances of an artfully absurd nature aimed, it seemed, at lonely bachelor lip-readers, drinkers of cheap beer, violence-prone psychotics, and semiliterate Walter Mitty types whose vision of true love involved the rescue of some distressed damsel about to be ravaged by bikers, lions, or hippopotami.

I was reminded, quite viscerally, of genre a few years ago while scuba diving on the barrier reef near Whitsunday Island just off the coast of Far North Queensland in Australia. Hooker's Reef was a typical coral atoll, an ovoid shape from the air, the ring of reef almost completely exposed during low tide. Inside the wall was a shallow lagoon populated by crabs, shellfish, squid, remoras, and the odd marine turtle. Larger, more predatory organisms lived outside the reef, where the wall sloped down into a disconcerting darkness. I like diving big walls—the sensation, gliding over the purple darkness of abysmal depths, is that of dream flight—so I was diving outside the lagoon, in the realm of the predators.

The living reef had been trying to grow out from the wall, and it was building fastest near the surface, where there is the most light. This process had created some impressive overhangs: great expanses of golden brown antlerlike elkhorn coral stretched out perpendicular to the vertical wall twenty feet and more. In places these cantilevered coral platforms had collapsed, forming vast rubble heaps on the sloping wall below. There, spikes of elkhorn lay white, bleached in death, so that these amalgamated colonial organisms looked like the tangled bones of thousands of small children.

My diving partner was a New Zealand man who liked to be called The Kiwi. Together we had figured out the current, and were letting it carry us under the coral platforms and against the kaleidoscope of color that was the reef wall. At forty feet, there were tube sponges growing on yellow ledges like impossible purple cacti; we saw pink plating corals in the shapes of miniature pagodas; there were banks of fire coral and stands of soft corals: lacy blue-green sea fans and velvety golden sea whips that bent with the current so that in places the wall looked like some sloping meadow alive with alien wildflowers. Swimming against this mosaic of color was a teeming chaos of small, brightly colored aquarium fish that divers call scenics—blue-green wrasse; red parrot fish; bright yellow long-nosed butterfly fish; and several solitary Moorish idols, an aloof black-and-white fish of immense dignity designed, apparently, by a creator entirely fascinated with the art deco style.

When we hit the largest of the rubble slopes, there was no life at all.

It was about seven in the morning and the sun was still low in the sky. It slanted through the water in rippling, purely religious shafts, through which planktonic matter glittered and shifted like dust motes in the light from an attic window. The rubble slope was ash gray in color, and the entire effect, in contrast to the palette of the living wall, was one of devastation: the white broken branches of skeletal elkhorn coral, the sandy rubble, the smoky light. It looked like the aftermath of some hideous saturation bombing raid, the fires still smoldering. The eerie sense of dread was intensified by the total lack of fish on a reef that was otherwise a celebration of marine life.

This was ominous: there had been fish enough on the other rubble slopes. The Kiwi and I anxiously scanned the water ahead. We saw them below at about eighty feet: three sleek tiger sharks, on the feed.

They were forty feet away and the current was going to drive us directly over them. Tiger sharks are nasty fellows—certified man-eaters—the Australian divers refer to them as "munchies"; harmless lagoon-dwelling sharks such as black tips and white tips are called "reefies." We drifted over this trio of munchies, and one rose, languidly, to greet us. He looked to be about seven or eight feet long.

We were not, at this point, being attacked by tiger sharks. We were being *menaced* by tiger sharks, and it is not precise to say that my entire life flashed before my eyes. What I found myself thinking about were four peculiar magazines I had purchased earlier. They were printed in Australia by Page Publications, but they seemed to be reprints from older American magazines with roughly similar names: *Action for Men, Men's Challenge, Amazing Men's Stories,* and *Fantastic Men's Stories.* The titles alone produced an odd sense of subliterary déjà vu.

These magazines were all of a type and it was difficult to tell one from another. Each carried a story about a single brave man who stands up to blood-crazed horror bikers: "I Battled Georgia's Terror Bikers (Two years in prison had turned them into a pack of mindless animals!)" and "Vengeance Feud with the 'Rat-Pack' Cycle Gang (They came at him like a tornado whirling into a Midwest town at dawn!)." Three of the magazines had a cave story: "We found Mussolini's $60 Million Treasure Cave (A freak cave-in trapped them and left them at the mercy of a horde of vampire bats!)."

Another staple story seemed to be the jungle trek. I was particularly fascinated by "Our Death Race with Snake-Worshipping Headhunters of New Guinea" and "Prisoner of the Legendary 'Leper Army' Jungle Bandits." Guys escaping from headhunters or leprous guerrillas generally dodge flesh-ripping jaguars in South America and rhinos in Africa. These men are invariably accompanied by one or more "nymphos." The jungles seem to be full of women suffering from this provocative disorder. As a former editor of such magazines once put it, "Even the rhinos were nymphos."

For all of this, the stories that came most immediately to mind as we drifted over the tiger sharks were the ones about animal attacks. In these magazines, the most inoffensive animals imaginable suddenly become horror-movie material. "I Fought Off Montana's Blood-Crazed Coyotes" is a case in point— "The razor-toothed beasts had come for one thing: human flesh!" In another article, a group was savaged by (I'm not making this up) "the nightmare giant condors of the Chilean Andes!"

In *Action For Men* many of the animal-attack stories happen *now*, as you read them, right here in the present tense. "A Monster Ape Is Ripping the Town Apart!" Or, more to the point, "My God, We're Being Attacked by Tiger Sharks!" In this rousing effort, a commercial diver named Jack Sturges and his crew are working to repair a ruptured line under a floating oil rig in the Gulf of Mexico when they're attacked by two twenty-foot-long tiger sharks. Sturges stabs one of the tigers in the belly with his knife. The other shark turns on its bleeding companion and tears it apart in a blood-crazed razor-toothed feeding frenzy. The divers escape through dark torrents of flowing shark blood. Praised by his employers for his courage and quick thinking, Sturges modestly replies, "Danger, sunken shipwrecks, sharks—they're all part of a day's work!"

Right, sure, Jack.

The tiger sharks confronting me weren't even in the *Action For Men* league. They looked to be a mere eight feet long. Adjusting for adrenaline magnification, I was probably trembling before a trio of mere six-footers. Little fellows. Sissy sharks: a couple of minutes' worth of light, bare-hand work for your basic *Man's Testicle* kind of guy.

The truth is that actual human beings, as opposed to *real men*, experience genuine terror in such situations. And if these human beings know anything at all about *real sharks*, they do not draw their knives. The only use for a knife during a shark attack is pure treachery: stab your buddy, swim like hell, and hope the munchies take him.

The nearest of the tiger sharks passed within four feet of my mask and eyed us curiously. The others coasted below, a foot or two above the smoking rubble. Blake's line about "fearful symmetry" rang through my mind. The closest shark rolled and dived back down into the smoldering broken coral. In two minutes, no more, the current had driven us well past the now disinterested sharks.

I felt a jolt of fully explicable exhilaration—a sense of the world reborn—followed by a kind of professional glee. Here was something I could write about: something I had, in fact, predicted years earlier.

Back a decade ago, in 1976, Jann Wenner, the editor of *Rolling Stone*, assigned a group of his editors the task of designing a new outdoor magazine to be called *Outside*. Michael Rogers wrote up a prospectus. Harriet Fier and I helped fine tune the outline that was to become *Outside*.

We weren't going to try to take on the venerable hunting and fishing magazines or any of the lesser hook-and-bullet efforts. We didn't feel we could compete with special-interest books that told the reader how to paddle a canoe or buy a backpack twelve times a year. *Outside* would cover an entire spectrum of outdoor activities, and the emphasis, in the feature well, would be on good reporting and literate writing. It was, at the time, a unique concept.

Early on, I argued for a travel-adventure piece in each issue. There was some small dissension. Adventure stories were the stuff of *Action For Men*, hardly the sort of literate writing Rogers and Fier wanted to see in *Outside*. I pointed out that there was a tradition of outdoor adventure and travel writing in American literature—James Fennimore Cooper, Herman Melville, Mark Twain—and that the tradition was not well served by the stories in *Men's Challenge*. "If you're diving and see a shark, a real man-eater, that's enough for a story right there," I argued. "Just seeing a certain kind of shark is an adventure." I suggested that we find men and women who could report the facts and who could write an evocative English sentence about, say, shark diving, without a lot of gratuitous chest pounding.

We would be dealing, I said, with dreams, and dreams are immensely fragile. Most of us abandoned the idea of a life full of adventure and travel sometime between puberty and our first job. Our dreams died under the dark weight of responsibility. Occasionally the old urge surfaces, and we label it with names that suggest psychological aberrations: the big chill, a midlife crisis. *Outside*, as I saw the new magazine, should be in the business of giving people back their dreams. The tough assignments would go to writers, not adventurers. "We don't want supermen and -women," I argued. "We want physically ordinary folks. The reader should think, 'Hey, if this clown can do it, so can I.' If the writer's sort of incompetent and easily frightened, all the better."

The last thought gave Harriet Fier an idea. "You do it," she said.

Terry McDonell was hired as *Outside's* managing editor and Will Hearst became the publisher. Each endorsed the idea that adventure-travel writing didn't have to be moronic drivel, and I enjoyed their unqualified financial and moral support. Which isn't to say McDonell, Hearst, and the entire *Outside* staff didn't enjoy making some fun of the latest expedition. Was I going to the cloud forests of Peru to look for ancient cities buried in the foliage? Better call *Action For Men* for one of their old titles. Something like: *Jaguars Ripped My Flesh.*

The fact that Frank Zappa had recently released an album titled *Weasels Ripped My Flesh* probably figured, unconsciously, in what was to become the generic title for all my stories. At the time, however, we were thinking in terms of pulp men's magazines. "Get some blood in there and use a lot of exclamation points," McDonell counseled, and what he meant was, "I don't want to see any blood or any exclamation points."

Jaguars ripped my flesh for two more years!

In October 1978, Larry Burke of Burke Communications purchased *Outside* and the offices were moved from San Francisco to Chicago. John Rasmus was named editor of the new magazine. A sure, steady editor, John's vision of what *Outside* could be paralleled that of the original editors, right on down to the odd adventure-travel story.

During that decade, the adventure-travel business has boomed, and outdoor adventure stories have become, well, almost fashionable. I have written them, over the past few years, for many national magazines. And *Outside*, a magazine that usually carries one adventure-travel piece per issue, is frequently nominated for and has once won the National Magazine Award for General Excellence.

* * *

Occasionally, in the course of my travels, I have been slapped in the face with some particularly egregious example of ecological rape—"The Shame of Escobilla" is a case in point—and have felt compelled to report upon it. Similarly, the account of what happened in the aftermath of the eruption of Mount Saint Helens is a dark one. In general, however, the stories that follow were conceived in fun and are meant to be read for pleasure.

One final truth: savage blood-crazed razor-toothed jaguars have been ripping at my flesh without surcease for over ten years now, and I have yet to see one in the wild.

Tim Cahill
Montana, 1986

1

Tracking Snipe

The Book on Survival

Two fourteen-year-old rock climbers, Jim Deering and Ryan Angus, were stranded. They had been climbing in Bell Canyon, not far from Salt Lake City, when one of those dense, dirty fogs that bedevil the western front of the central Rockies rolled in and left the two stuck on a high ledge. It was late—6:00 P.M.—and the fog, thick as cotton candy, muffled and muddied the fading sun. Just for a moment, before the light died altogether, the sky glittered with the color of steel wool. Then the world purpled down into absolute blackness, with the dank inevitability of an Edgar Allan Poe poem.

Deering and Angus kept their wits about them. They didn't try to descend in the darkness, which, on that frigid night, is one of the things they did right. The temptation to "go for it" must have been great. The idea of shivering through fifteen hours or more of below-freezing temperatures generates a sense of anxiety that, in its effects, is sometimes indistinguishable from pure panic.

I've felt it often enough myself: this unhealthy urge to push on past the safety point rather than bivouac in uncomfortable circumstances.

Once, in Peru, three of us spent twelve hours climbing up through the rain forest on the jungled eastern flanks of the Andes. We were looking for a long ledge of rock rising above the tangled vegetation where, we had been told, there were human remains and funeral urns. The ledge was called the "City of the Dead," and we couldn't find it anywhere. When the sun began to set, we were exhausted and angry, still somewhere around the eight-thousand-foot level, while our tents and sleeping bags were down on the river bottom at about five thousand feet. All we had with us were day packs, rain gear, about two handfuls of trail mix apiece to eat, and a climbing rope we had brought with us in case we had to lower ourselves down into the City of the Dead.

The stream we'd been following down to the river had become a waterfall, and the sheer cliff face below us dropped for what looked to be about forty feet. It was hard to judge the extent of the drop because of all the vegetation and the darkness that was pooling up at the base of the cliff. One of our number suggested we uncoil the rope and go for it. The thought of the warm bags below and the frozen night ahead made this seem like an eminently sensible idea. It was a forty-foot drop. We had eighty feet of rope: Why not double the rope around the tree, rig up a carabiner brake bar, rappel down, retrieve the rope, crash through the dark jungle for another couple of hours, and sleep warm? What a good idea.

The end of the rope disappeared in the darkness below, and something I'd read in some woodsy survival book somewhere began snapping away at the periphery of my resolve. The book said that a smart hiker never jumps, ever. You might be standing on a fallen tree trunk, and the ground is right there, two feet below, but how do you know there isn't some ankle-twisting vine skulking just out of sight? Some leg-breaking badger hole covered over with grass? A rattlesnake? According to the survival manual, you should sit on the tree and lower yourself gently all that two feet to the ground. This advice had always seemed overly cautious to me, like the diet books that tell you to "consult your doctor before beginning this or any other weight-reduction program." Still, rappelling into inky blackness without knowing precisely how long a drop it was suddenly seemed stupid, if not suicidal. "A smart hiker," I told my companions, "never jumps into the whirling darkness of abysmal depths." Or words to that effect. So we spent a night huddled around a gasping, half-choked fire, wishing it was five degrees colder so that the rain would turn to snow. In the morning, the sun rose on the face of the cliff. Jungle rock glowed, as if from within, in the pastel pinks and rose-petal reds of a Monet painting. The drop was more than 150 feet. We all stood there, looking down, thinking how close we had come to finding the City of the Dead the hard way.

Angus and Deering, trapped on the fogged-in ledge above Bell Canyon, knew better than to even think about making a descent in the darkness. What they needed was a fire: a fire for physical and psychological comfort; a fire to ward off hypothermia; a fire to summon rescuers. There were plenty of twigs on the ledge, but they were thin and wet, soaked through, hard to light. The young climbers had a limited supply of matches and a wilderness survival book with them. Survival books are full of good advice—a smart hiker never jumps, for example—and people fogged in on high, rocky ledges find them especially interesting reading. When their first attempts to light the twigs failed, Angus and Deering made their second smart move of the night. They settled back and consulted the book. Carefully following instructions, the boys spent two hours trying to light their fire. It was now 8:00 P.M. Twenty rescuers from the Salt Lake City sheriff's office were searching for the stranded climbers: helicopters clattering helplessly through the fog and darkness. Below, the boys were still following instructions, still trying to light a fire by the book. Their lives, if it came to that, depended on the fire, on the book.

I find this story fascinating, because I am a man who sits around at home reading wilderness survival books the way some people peruse seed catalogues or accounts of classic chess games.

Philosophically, I like Paul Petzoldt's *The Wilderness Handbook*. Petzoldt, former director of the National Outdoor Leadership School, isn't big on the challenge of the wilderness, confronting and overcoming fears outdoors so as to become more confident in business or interpersonal relationships. The wilderness Petzoldt loves is its own reward, to be enjoyed—here's the part I like—in comfort. There are plenty of challenges out there, he seems to be saying, but they ought to be thought out and self-imposed, not thrust upon one by circumstances, or worse, by guides with drill-instructor mentalities. Accordingly, the first chapter of *The Wilderness Handbook* is titled "Survival: Avoiding Survival Situations." It is full of sane and sensible advice.

Emotionally, though, I like books that foster personal wilderness-survival fantasies. Generally, my light plane goes down somewhere in the Amazon or Alaska. Occasionally I crash in Nepal, Africa, or Patagonia. I'm seldom seriously injured in the crash, but with my knowledge of wilderness survival lore, it's my job to save the lives of at least six people. I've got a Swiss Army knife, some strong monofilament, a pocket full of fishhooks, and my waterproof set of five Survival Cards, produced by Lee Nading of Bloomington, Indiana. If the plane goes down in the Arctic, the Survival Cards warn that there is "QUICKSAND at stream junctures," and that "FOOT TRAVEL is risky, exhausting, useless; travel by RAFT no matter how long it takes to build. . . . Most towns are on rivers." If the fantasy turns nasty, I sometimes have to perform a field amputation while referring to the Survival Cards, a full paragraph of which starts by warning me not to make the decision to lop off someone's arm or leg "lightly . . . sever the muscles at the new skin line . . . the muscle will promptly retract, leaving the bone exposed . . . Then cut the bone . . ."

Two of the best books I've found for extended outdoor survival daydreams are *Bushcraft* by Richard Graves and *Outdoor Survival Skills* by Larry Dean Olsen. Both books suppose the reader is going to be stranded for days or weeks or even months in the wilderness. I can barely hang a picture, but after going over either of these texts, I am capable of building a crude shelter, making a rope out of vines, trapping rabbits for dinner, and assembling a proper salad out of rude weeds.

How to Survive on Land and Sea by Frank and John Craighead was first written in 1943 for the U.S. Navy, and it is still one of the best books on survival in unusual environments. It contains information on hunting and gathering (if the monkey eat, you probably can too), mountain travel, ocean navigation, cooking, food preservation, vermin, and predators. The section on dealing with native peoples avoids common errors of cultural superiority ("your own fate . . . may depend on your treating native peoples well"), though I disagree with the Craigheads' contention that "if you can outdo the natives in feats of strength or skill, you will be held in esteem. . . ." Once, on the island of Man-hat-tan, I sat in a waterfront bar and defeated all comers in wrist-wrestling until several of the natives gathered around my table and suggested, in their quaint island dialect, that "either you get outta here or we kick youse ass."

Perhaps Jim Deering and Ryan Angus were beginning to get similarly annoyed with their own wilderness survival manual after following its instructions and still failing to light a fire after two hours. At 8:00 P.M., just as the sheriff's search party got off the ground, the boys made their third smart decision of the night. "It was so hard to start the fire," Angus said later, "so we started ripping out the pages and it started right up." Searchers spotted the flaming survival book, and the two climbers were evacuated by helicopter.

Pombe Wisdom

No one who lives in France is ever referred to as a "native,"
no matter how far back he can trace his ancestry. Natives,
so we imagine, are folks who live along the banks of tea-
colored rivers that flow through impenetrable jungles that are
located in amorphous countries with unpronounceable names.
Natives wear loincloths, have bones in their noses, dine on root
crops, and roast lizards for lunch.

The word is one with more meaning than its stated definition
allows. Because natives are technologically primitive, we also
suppose them to be intellectually and emotionally barren. People
who don't know the difference between a Buick and New York City
are not capable of simple human accomplishments such as the put-
on.

Or are they?

Carl Sagan, in *Broca's Brain*, asked anthropologists if they
could ever be certain that "the natives are not pulling your leg." He
wasn't sure, for instance, that Bronislaw Malinowski had actually
discovered a people on the Trobriand Islands who had not worked
out the connection between sexual intercourse and childbirth.

Babies, the people told Malinowski, were the result of complicated interrelationships between the stars and various gods. Malinowski responded with the birds and bees, and the natives listened politely until he got to the business about a nine-month gestation period.

"Hardly possible, my dear Professor Malinowski," they said, or words to that effect; and by way of proof, they pointed to a woman holding a newborn child. The woman's husband, Malinowski learned, had been away for *more than two years.*

"Prescientific people," Sagan points out, "are people. Individually, they are as clever as we are." Sagan thought that these natives might have been having a little fun with Malinowski. "If some peculiar-looking stranger came into my town and asked *me* where babies came from," Sagan wrote, "I'd certainly be tempted to tell him about storks and cabbages."

The supposition that people who don't know a Buick from New York are necessarily stupid can be a costly mistake. Back in the seventies, a famous French research vessel was chugging about Truk lagoon in the Caroline Islands, looking for the *Shinohara*, a Japanese submarine sunk in World War II. The crew confined itself to science and did not socialize with the local people. It never found the *Shinohara.*

A few years later, an American research team arrived at Truk and set up a search for the sub. The Americans were more gregarious than the French, and, during the course of one long night of drinking and talking, a local Micronesian fellow said he remembered the *Shinohara* and knew where it had gone down. The Americans gave it a go, and the Micronesian succeeded where magnetometers had failed. The find resulted in a popular ABC-TV special. More important, the men who had gone down with the *Shinohara* were finally given a proper Shinto burial by their relatives.

I like to think that the American success in finding the *Shinohara* had something to do with faith in the intelligence of the natives, a faith that was fueled by the consumption of alcoholic beverages. A man has reason to justify his own vices, of course, but it has been my experience that nothing more quickly transforms natives into people than a couple of beers, a few jars of jugo de caño, a bottle of pombe, or several cups of chuba.

Jugo de caño is the fermented juice of sugar cane, a kind of sickly sweet wine that tastes a bit like orange soda. It goes down easy after a long walk, and it sneaks up on you like a mugger in the night. I drank quite a lot of it in certain chicken-scratch villages in the eastern foothills of the Andes, drank jar after jar up there in the cold, green cloud forests overlooking the sprawling immensity of the Amazon jungle. It is a fact, little studied by science, that after five jars of jugo, previously unilingual Americans are capable of speaking perfect Spanish and that Peruvian Indians will forsake Quechua and speak English with the facility of the entire Yale debating team.

Jugo is not kind to one in the morning, and this too affirms the humanity of all involved: Men who suffer much together are forever brothers.

In the Philippines, the language of instruction is English and the medium of communication may be rum—Anejo and Manila are good—or malloroca, a coconut wine flavored with anise. Green Parrot brand comes in a clear bottle, and the cork under the cap is usually black and crumbly from contact with the wine. You can drink this stuff at the Hobbit bar in Manila. All the waiters are dwarfs or midgets, and the entertainment consists of good Philippine folk singers crooning tragic songs about finally earning a gold record, only to have their pancreas (yes, pancreas) fail on them. The Hobbit draws a mixed crowd, tinged Graham Greeneish, and no one there, from the dwarfs on up to the smugglers, could rightly be considered a native.

For that, you'd have to go to some remote area of the country: Go thirty miles north of Bogo, to the foreboding northern tip of the island known as Cebu. There the most popular fermented refreshment is known as chuba, pronounced "tuba." It is made from the rapidly fermenting sap of the coconut palm and colored with mangrove bark. In the morning, chuba gatherers bring in the sap, which is sweet and orange and has a white froth on top. The longer it is aged, the more sour and alcoholic it becomes. Properly aristocratic chuba is as bitter as lemon juice, but it will drop you to your knees and set you to howling at the jungle moon.

I was staying in this remote corner of the world with five other American men, and the people of the dusty little village called us all Joe. In the weeks I was there, I spent two nights sitting out on the beach demolishing jugs of chuba with various locals, and for this I earned a new and distinct nickname: Chuba Joe. One of those locals was the schoolteacher. He impressed me, and the feeling must have been mutual, because I was asked to speak before his students: Chuba Joe, Doctor of Fermented Communication.

Pombe is a product of the tiny African country of Rwanda. I'm not really sure how pombe is made, but what I do know is consistent with its revolting taste: It involves mashing up rotten bananas with bare feet and burying the resultant mess in a cask for an undetermined amount of time. After the pombe is exhumed, it is poured into liter bottles that once contained beer. You get a wooden straw with the bottle—give it back after you're done—because an unappetizing black sludge forms at the bottom of the bottle and along the sides. The stuff tastes like death, and even the most dedicated pombe enthusiasts avoid it.

One of my drinking buddies in Rwanda was a guide and guard in the Virunga National Park, a refuge for the last two hundred mountain gorillas in the world. Big May was a taciturn sort, given to brief rages and prolonged sulks. He often carried a short stick, like a riding crop, which he banged on tables when making a point. He bullied his peers, sometimes poking them in the chest with his stick and backing them across rooms. He was a bad drinker.

There were small wooden homes all along the trails to the mountains where the gorillas lived, and if the people had pombe to sell, they'd put fresh flowers by the front door. Pombe vendors who saw Big May walking by in the morning stationed spies along the trail in the evening. When Big May was spotted, runners sprinted back to the houses to remove the flowers.

Sometimes the runners were slow. Sometime Big May took a back trail. Sometimes he got to a home before the flowers could be hidden, and then the people were in for a night of table-banging and intimidation.

It was easy to see Big May as a "mean native," which is to say, a man with an inscrutably ugly soul. The truth was something else again. Several pombe-soaked nights with Big May convinced me that he had, like Mark Twain, taken a philosophical and biting dislike to the whole "damned human race." We had swum around the language barrier in a sea of pombe. Big May seemed a familiar sort. The wells of gentleness and compassion in him were entirely reserved for animals, and animals of one peculiar sort—gorillas. These gorillas were threatened by the land-lust of the people Big May bullied in his pombe-generated rages.

Big May seemed to like me. I wasn't interested in growing potatoes in the Virungas, and there were things he could teach me. He liked people who listened intently and didn't interrupt with their own senseless opinions. And after several hours of pombe, the rage would dissipate, for moments, into softness.

One day while patrolling the mountains, Big May found a baby gorilla, Mtoto by name, with her hand caught in a poacher's wire trap. If she couldn't extricate herself, she'd die. The silverback, Mrithi, a four-hundred-pound male, crouched by his daughter, angry and agitated. Mrithi howled at Big May. The gorilla's teeth were coated with black tartar and were the size of small carrots.

Big May dropped to his belly and made the double-belching sound that signifies lack of aggressive intent among gorillas. He crawled forward carefully, risking a charge by Mrithi. Such a charge could be deadly, but Big May got to Mtoto and managed to twist the wire off her hand while Mrithi hooted and pounded his chest. It was an act of incredible bravery.

One of my traveling companions was amazed that Big May, of all people, had done this thing. "Big May cares," he said, incredulous.

Anybody who'd spent a night sucking pombe out of a bottle with Big May would have known that. He was a disagreeable man who couldn't tell you the difference between a Buick and New York City, but he possessed sensitivity and rare courage. It took only the proper circumstances, or sufficient pombe, to see that in him.

Getting Lost

I seem to have spent a lot of time lost: I've been lost in the jungles of South America and Africa, lost in the Arctic, lost at sea, lost in the caves of Kentucky, and even lost atop a mountain I can see from my front door. I'm a master of inept bushwhacking, of erroneous orienteering. Give me two roads converging in the woods on a snowy evening, and I'll take the one most bivouacked.

The first time, it happened in a department store during the Christmas shopping rush. I was perhaps four years old, and my mother had dressed me up for my interview with the Santa who presided there. A picture taken at the time shows a skinny child bundled up in a large jacket with mittens on strings dangling from the sleeves. I was sitting there on Santa's lap wearing a red beret and a look of complete terror. "Ho, ho, ho," this albino Sasquatch said, and all I could think about was the giant in the story "Jack and the Beanstalk."

Sometime later during that trip, probably while my mother was paying for some purchase, I wandered off. There were more people than I had ever seen before, and the place was full of shiny stuff that a kid could play with or examine or ignore as the mood struck. I was a cliché. A child lost in a department store during the Christmas crush. But it was like a dream of flight, this small exploratory foray, a heady, soaring sensation combined with the vague impression that everything—the toys, the people, the half-price sofas, the Philco radios, and the blinking lights—somehow belonged to me. When an adult holds a child's hand, the world belongs to the adult. But for those few minutes, all of it—the wholy shiny new world—was mine.

As my mother tells the story, she spent half an hour "frantic with worry" looking for me. She was riding up an escalator, about to search another floor, when she looked over toward the adjacent escalator and saw a red beret sticking up above the moving rail. She called to me, shouted out my name—"Tim, Tim"—and I glanced over as if to say, in utter surprise, "*moi?*" I am told that I looked at my mother with the sort of vague, disinterested curiosity one usually reserves for people who make a spectacle of themselves in public. I was captured at the bottom of the escalator and scolded in such a way that I felt absolutely loved. It is a sweet memory, this tearful reunion, but I also recall a sense of some small disappointment: It would have been nice to have been lost just a little while longer.

Not every directional misadventure, however, has been my fault. Sometimes, as Bogart said about the waters in *Casablanca*, I have been misinformed. South America is a good place for this sort of thing. When asked, a typical South American male is likely to rattle off detailed directions to your desired destination. The fact that he has no idea where it is that you want to go will not deter him in the least.

I have discussed the matter with veteran South American travelers and with members of the South American Explorers Club, and we have come up with three possible explanations for this behavior. It may have something to do with the tradition of macho: A man may feel somehow less of a man if he cannot give directions to a stranger. (Likewise, American males find it difficult to admit they are lost. "Why don't we just pull into the gas station and ask," she says. "Naw," he replies, teeth clenched, "it's gotta be just around the corner." This can go on for hours.)

A second explanation may have something to do with the

courtly Latin tradition of courtesy. How rude to reply "I don't know" to a guest in one's country.

A third explanation: In the mountainous hinterlands, say in the eastern foothills of the Andes, Indians, who generally speak Spanish as a second language, often give directions like "above" or "below." When the traveler arrives above or below to find that he has been misinformed, he seldom has the energy to climb back to the source of the misinformation for a bit of clarification. Better to simply push ahead and ask again at the next village.

Something like this happened to Gonzalo Pizarro back in 1541. A decade before that, Gonzalo's half brother, Francisco, had led the Spanish conquest of the Incas. In the ten years that followed, I am certain the news of the conquest then gradually floated up over the Andes and into the cloud forests at 10,000 feet, where the Chachapoyas and other peoples lived. Gonzalo and his expedition of 200 Spaniards were looking for cities of gold and groves of cinnamon trees. The people must have known that these strangers carried sticks that killed from afar, that they were great ones for rape and robbery, for pillage and murder, not to mention wholesale enslavement of the locals.

"Oh yeah," the native people told Pizarro, "a city of gold—you bet. It's about a ten-day march over that range of mountains on the horizon there." The expedition staggered around for more than a year, certain that the gold and spices were just over the next rise. Some Spaniards deserted the expedition. Many died of disease or fatigue and malnutrition. Eventually the survivors ate their dogs and horses. Only a few of the Spanish managed to stumble back into Quito in August of 1542.

The Indian people east of Quito were left in peace for centuries due to this policy of misdirection. And I think the impulse survives in the folk who live there today. "Who knows what the strangers want? Let's send them out to the nasty land where no one goes, send them so far away they'll never come back."

In Africa, in a remote central equatorial country, the people I met seemed eager to be of help, but I had mistakenly bought and studied a Swahili phrase book under the impression that the language was used in business and social intercourse. And it was, everyplace in the country except under the Virunga volcanoes, where I happened to be. There, people spoke Kinyarwanda, and only a few spoke a smattering of Swahili, which, in any case, I spoke ungrammatically, one painful word at a time, from the dictionary, rather like Tarzan speaks English. "Where . . . trail . . . Ruhengeri?" (*"Mahali . . . wapi . . . utambaazi . . . Ruhengeri?"*)

Sometimes, however, it's all my fault. Given my sloppy technique with compass and topo map, I generally stroll into camp or back to the trailhead several days overdue. I believe that I can read a map pretty well if I take my time and really concentrate, but I am like those accident-prone people who, according to psychiatrists, want to punish themselves by bouncing off speeding semis or falling down stairs. I want to get lost. I like to get lost. I am creative in my ineptitude.

The survival and woodcraft books I own all caution the traveler to sit and think when disoriented. "DON'T PANIC," they scream— the sort of admonition that makes a person consider running off into the bush, hands in the air, screaming and gibbering. How come no one ever tells you to relax and enjoy it? My rules for the lost and inept—my kind of people—are simple. When backpacking, never run your food supply too low. Be entirely self-sufficient. Never, but never, leave your pack to see if the trail ahead seems to be the right one. You want to be able to sleep comfortably and eat to maintain your strength; you can't do either if you've managed to lose your pack as well as yourself. If all else fails, you can go on half-rations and wander around for a few days until you find your back trail and—humiliation!—go back the way you came.

Finally, consider your predicament a privilege. In a world so shrunken that certain people refer to "the global village," the term "explorer" has little meaning. But exploration is nothing more than a foray into the unknown, and a four-year-old child, wandering about alone in the department store, fits the definition as well as the snow-blind man wandering across the Khyber Pass. The explorer is the person who is lost.

When you've managed to stumble directly into the heart of the unknown—either through the misdirection of others or, better yet, through your own creative ineptitude—there is no one there to hold your hand or tell you what to do. In those bad lost moments, in the times when we are advised not to panic, we own the unknown, and the world belongs to us. The child within has full reign. Few of us are ever so free.

"How in the hell did you manage to get lost half an hour from camp?" my backpacking companions ask.

"Dumb luck," I tell them.

Bad Advice

Recently, I came across a survival manual issued to American troops in the South Pacific during World War II. The book contained a section on sharks that shimmered with falsehoods and sparkled with bad advice. At the time, soldiers and sailors had been hearing horror stories of shark attacks in the aftermath of several South Pacific maritime disasters. For instance, when the troop carrier *Cape San Juan* was torpedoed by a Japanese submarine, the merchant ship *Meredith* managed to rescue only a third of the fifteen hundred men who went down. The majority of those who died, according to eyewitness reports, were torn to shreds by sharks in a feeding frenzy. One rescuer, quoted in Michael Jenkinson's book, *Beasts Beyond the Fire*, said, "I heard soldiers scream as the sharks swept them off the rafts. Sometimes the sharks attacked survivors who were being hauled to the *Meredith* with life ropes."

In what Jenkinson thinks was an effort to "dispel shark fears among American troops," the survival manual stated flatly that sharks are "frightened by splashing" and easy to kill: Just stab the "slow-moving, cowardly" attacking shark in the belly. And, hey, why waste the chance to have a little fun in the bargain. . . . Swim out of line of his charge, grab a pectoral fin as he goes by, and ride with him as long as you can hold your breath."

This is real bad advice, and I was mulling it over early in October while camping and kayaking on the southeastern coast of Alaska. Specifically, I was thinking about the comforts of bad advice, and wondering what well-informed people do when confronted by an Alaskan brown bear.

These fellows weigh as much as fifteen hundred pounds and can stand nine feet tall. Your basic inland grizzly, by contrast, reaches a maximum height of seven feet and weighs about nine hundred pounds. For a time, the Alaskan brown was thought to be a separate species, but biologists are now satisfied that browns and grizzlies are different races within the same species, *Ursus arctos*. In other words, bad-news bears, because *Ursus arctos* of any race are aggressively unpredictable. Their fight-or-flight response leans heavily toward fight: The beasts evolved on the high plains and tundras, in competition with wolves, saber-tooths, and the like; with nowhere to hide, their best defense was a good offense. The American black bear, by contrast, evolved in the mountains and forests, in plenty of cover. With the exception of a sow with cubs, a black bear is likely to flee a threatening situation. Merely startle a grizzly, however, and instinct may launch him into an attack. And sometimes it seems to take even less than that.

In Yellowstone National Park, not far from where I live, it was an unusually bad year for grizzly attacks. On July 30, a grizzly dragged a young woman from her tent and killed her. In August, a Yellowstone grizzly mauled a twelve-year-old boy, and another injured a park naturalist and her husband. On September 4, two California campers survived a mauling in Glacier Park.

No one knows what caused the attacks, but some biologists studying Yellowstone grizzlies speculate about a lack of food: This was a lean year for high-country berries and white bark pine cones, they say, and the grizzlies may have been driven down into campsites in search of food. Others think that Yellowstone bears have become too accustomed to hikers and have lost their fear of man because firearms are not allowed in the park. Still others think that bears previously tranquilized with PCP—a drug that can cause violence in humans—have suddenly gone berserk on the drug. My own theory, which I began to develop as I thought about going up to Alaska, involves revenge. The Yellowstone bear population is declining disastrously. Soon it will be too small to support a self-sustaining population. I suspect that the few remaining beasts there can feel the black suction of extinction and are showing an existential rage beyond the capacity of their species. Perhaps they would be more benign where they were less threatened. Native Alaskans I talked to before my kayaking trip pointed out that there had been no maulings and no deaths all year in the area where I was going.

Still, my kayaking partner, photographer Paul Dix, and I found it hard to be casual about the big browns. We had agreed before the trip that we wouldn't carry any fatty or odorous foods. Bears don't see particularly well, and their hearing isn't very keen, but they can apparently smell bacon several miles away. We cooked on the wave-washed intertidal zone—in accord with Park Service regulations—and stored our food a quarter-mile from the tent, along with the clothes we wore for cooking. We had been told not to camp on an obvious game trail, which seemed like a pretty self-evident piece of information until a friendly ranger advised us that our campsite—the beach just above the high-tide line—was in fact the prime game trail. So we camped in the tangled bush beyond the sand. In the mornings, when we hiked inland to find our food, we never failed to see tracks, mostly moose and wolves. Then one day: the track of a bear so huge it seemed prehistoric.

The alder breaks above the sand were jungle-thick and just high enough to obscure our vision. With an offshore wind blowing our scent out into the ocean, we could easily stumble onto some crabby, nearsighted, half-dead brownie. We tried to make plenty of noise, tried to give some bear ample warning that we were coming. We shouted as we walked. I adopted the dominant voice of unquestioned authority.

"Clear out, you pathetic wimps!"

Paul, who is a gentle soul, added, "He doesn't really mean that, guys. We like bears."

After a few minutes of apologizing for me, Paul took to long explanations of why he wasn't actually with me.

All this seemed to be sensible enough, but what if we had the bad luck to stumble onto a bear anyway? Neither of us seemed to know what to do for certain. There were no trees within miles, and the head-high alder bushes would hardly support the weight of a man. Not much protection from a bear that stands nine feet tall on its hind legs. We needed a strategy.

Some people, I know, advocate playing dead. There is, for instance, a Montana rancher who was attacked by a grizzly two decades ago. The bear ripped most of this man's collarbone from his chest with one swipe. The rancher fell over and lay still, as if dead, all the while feeling the grizzly's hot breath on the back of his neck. "I could smell her," he said. "She stunk like anything."

On the other hand, I had just read a new and authoritative book, *The Grizzly Bear*, by Thomas McNamee, who thinks that "playing dead may be a good idea once an attack is initiated. But I tend to think that playing dead before the bear exhibits any aggressive tendencies may in fact be an invitation." And then there was an old cartoon I remembered on the subject: Two bears were sitting around after dinner, picking their teeth and chatting. There was a backpack and hiking boot on the ground. One bear was saying, "Don't you just love it when they play dead?"

A privately published guidebook to the local trails carried the suggestion that we attempt to intimidate a bear by putting our arms around each other, in order to look like one big animal. Lumped together in this manner, we should speak to the bear in loud, dominant, and commanding voices. Somehow, this had the ring of riding sharks as long as you could hold your breath. Besides, Paul and I were philosophically divided as to what should be said. Suppose I had Paul sit on my shoulders so we looked like some great tall animal. I'd be screaming, "You pathetic wimp!" while Paul would be trying to explain that, although he was sitting on my shoulders and all, we weren't really together.

And if that didn't work, it'd be pretty tough to run. I'd have to try psychology on the bear, all the while backing off slowly with Paul teetering on my shoulders. Maybe a little Freud would give the bear pause: "Uh, have you ever studied defense mechanisms? Like projection? Like, if I called you a pathetic wimp, see, it's not really you, it's me that's the pathetic wimp. . . ."

"I'm not with him!"

McNamee knows of cases where the one-big-animal approach has worked, but he has reservations about it. "I'd say Doug Peacock's method would be a better one. I can't think of anyone who's been closer to more grizzlies than Doug."

Peacock, who lived ten seasons with grizzlies in Yellowstone and Glacier parks, has been charged by more than a dozen different bears. "I stand my ground," he says. "I'm not saying this is foolproof or even recommending it. It's just always worked for me. So far."

Peacock bases his response on studies of interactions between the bears themselves. He's almost certain, for instance, that running will provoke an attack. Peacock tries to act like a self-confident bear who just doesn't feel like fighting today. "I stand sideways because I think confronting them full front is aggressive. I try not to look them in the eye for the same reason. I speak to them in a quiet voice. For some reason, I hold my arms out. I suppose it makes me look like a bigger animal, but I do it because it feels right."

McNamee thinks Peacock's method is sound, but adds, "There could be something Doug hasn't figured into the equation. It could be as simple as the confidence he has in himself that someone else might lack. Then again, there could be something in that old Hemingway stuff about animals smelling fear."

When you're standing in the alder breaks after stepping over a monstrous bear track on the beach; when it's getting dark and there are suspicious . . . sounds . . . out in the bush; when there's no place to run or climb or hide; the fact that no one knows for sure how a human should act when confronted by a brown bear is not reassuring. Suddenly, I longed for something that would deliver supreme confidence. What we really needed here was some truly bad advice.

2

News of the World,

Such As It Is

Going South

Strange Translations

In Spanish, the word for "now" is *ahora*. In the Peruvian state of Chachapoyas, on the eastern foothills of the Andes, overlooking the immensity of the Amazon basin, a fellow who wants the metal skid plate bolted back onto the frame of his Volkswagen might use the word *ahorita*, "a very short right now." The mechanic is likely to get to it in a week or so. He has two or three trucks belonging to regular customers that he must deal with first, and he works at a stately and dignified pace. The mechanic is a man of honor, impervious to bribes, and the phrase *ahorita, y no más*—"a very short right now, and no more"—strikes him as a very good joke. The word *hoy*, "today," is cause for hilarity unequaled in the whole lugubrious history of Peru. The mechanic slaps his forehead, pounds his knee, rolls about on the ground clutching his belly and spluttering, very like a man suddenly seized with intolerable abdominal cramps.

"*Ahorita y no más*," he giggles. "*Madre de Dios, hoy.*"

Mañana, of course, is the feast of San Fermín, or somebody, and then there is the weekend, and the mechanic does not work on Saturday or Sunday. The men of his family, he explains, live long and well. To rush about with a red face and shaking hands, this is bad for the heart . . . for the soul. The mechanic would be honored if the gringo would forget about his skid plate and join him and his family for the feast celebrating the birth of San Fermín.

The mechanic lives in a wood-frame house with a dirt floor and a tin roof. There are 857 people in his family, all of whom have lit votive candles, which give the house an air of elegance, like the altar of a cathedral on Easter morning. The gringo will please stand here, in the place of honor, so that all 1,923 members of the mechanic's family may meet him. The entire family is very proud of one man, a young fellow wearing a cardigan sweater from Lima. He is smiling in a sick, terrified manner, pushed forward by a lava flow of humanity.

"Goo-by berry mush," he says, extending a shaking hand.

"Goo-by," shout dozens of children.

"How is ju nome?" the young man asks in a quavering voice. All 2,429 members of the family stand in silence, swollen with pride.

"My name is Tim," the gringo says. "Timoteo."

"Timoteo," the young man repeats. There is some strange plea in his eyes, and he seems near tears.

The mechanic can bear it no longer. In Spanish, he explains that the young man is his brother, a teacher. He learned English in Lima, and English is one of the subjects he teaches the village children. That is why the children of the village speak English, just as they do in Lima or Cajamarca.

"Goo-by, gringo," the children shout.

"El habla perfecto," the gringo says, in his bad Spanish.

"Perfecto," the mechanic announces to the assembled multitudes. He points to the young man in the cardigan. "Perfecto."

The young man squares his shoulders, as if a great weight has been lifted from them. He smiles broadly, but there are tears in his eyes. "Sank ju berry mush," he says, his voice thick with emotion. He grabs the gringo, squeezing him mightily in a strong Latin embrace. Everyone cheers and laughs. The gringo is rather embarrassed, and he stands facing the 3,768 members of the mechanic's family, smiling in a fixed manner and thumping the English teacher's back. The young man is facing the wall. He is thumping the gringo's back with one hand and wiping the tears from his face with the other.

The steady drizzle outside has turned into a tropical thunderstorm. Water pounds down onto the tin roof with a deafening clatter. Everyone is shouting now, and there is much *jugo de caña*, fermented sugar cane juice, to be consumed before dinner. It is sweet, rather like weak orangeade, this *jugo*, with just the vaguest yeasty hint of alcohol. Everyone drinks quite a lot if it, and the noise works its way up to jackhammer levels.

Dinner is served. Women and children, as is the custom, sit on the floor and watch the men eat. The gringo is seated next to the mechanic's brother, so that they may speak English together. No one is listening to them now; so the two converse in a kind of Spanglish.

The mechanic's brother did indeed study in Lima, and he did have his teaching degree, but he had never studied English there or anywhere else. There had been five applicants for the job he now held—a prestigious position—and he had lied about the English because it set him apart from the other men. He was really trying to learn from books, and he taught the children to read, not speak. No one who spoke English had ever stopped in his village, and when he first met the gringo, he had been so frightened that he had said "gooby," though he knew perfectly well that the proper greeting was "jello."

Dinner consists of a boiled, stringy, tasteless substance that turns out to be yucca root, and a porklike substance in yellow gravy poured over rice. The meat is *cuy*, "guinea pig," a source of Peruvian protein since the time of the Incas.

The mechanic sees to it that the gringo's cup of jugo is never empty, and toward the end of the meal, he finds himself singing Paul Simon's version of *El Condor Pasa*. The brother translates the English words for all 4,239 members of the family, clearly winging it, and there is much laughter and applause. Later there is some pogo-type dancing to rhythmic clapping, and after the rain lets up, the men step outside to be near the huge vat of jugo.

The toasts range from the gringo's "Here's mud in your eye," to "Salud," to those of a more ribald nature. The gringo is particularly enchanted with one that translates: "To fifty women and one hundred breasts." The last thing the gringo remembers, he is shouting loudly, and in English, "Saint Fermín is the best goddamn saint there ever was, and anyone who says different can kiss my ass."

He wakes up on a wooden pallet with a tin roof over it. He is wrapped in several warm Peruvian blankets. It is late—the sun has been up for several hours—and there are coffee beans drying all around him. The mechanic is there with a hot cup of coffee, heavily laced with sugar. The gringo considers his performance the previous evening and wonders why the mechanic seems to be treating him with respect, even awe.

The gringo has a great deal of difficulty achieving coherence and feels as though he is trying to swim his way up from the bottom of a vat of thick custard. The mechanic is speaking rapidly, and though the gringo can't make out all the words, the gist of it seems to be apology of the most abject sort. The two men are walking toward the garage, and the mechanic says the gringo should have told him about the work—the mechanic whispers in a conspiratorial manner, though there is no one in sight—the secret work, the very secret work he is doing for the government of Peru.

The gringo can only mutter that he doesn't understand, and the mechanic smiles and says he understands why one doesn't understand. After all, the work is secret, and for the government. There was too much jugo last night, the mechanic says, and the gringo told this secret thing to his brother, who spoke English so perfecto.

And there is the car, sitting beside the rutted dirt road, the skid plate newly bolted to the frame. It has been cleaned inside and out.

The mechanic explains that his brother woke him early and told him it was *muy importante* that the gringo leave the village *ahorita y no más*, this very day.

The gringo pays his bill and drives on toward Brazil, offering up a little prayer of thanks to San Fermín, who, he supposes, must be the patron saint of stranded gringos and unilingual Peruvian English teachers.

The Lost World

To understand what happened, you have to see it the way the soldiers did.

It was near midnight, and the swollen jungle river called Río Cuyuní lay leaden under a full moon. At the southern end of the bridge spanning the Cuyuní, the Venezuelan National Guard had established a checkpoint. Earlier that week, a kidnapped American businessman named William Niehous had been rescued from a nearby jungle campsite, but in the confusion, his kidnappers, members of a Marxist group calling itself the Argimiro Gabaldón Revolutionary Command, had all eluded capture. So there were still guerrillas out there in the dense Venezuelan jungle, and the troops manning the Guardia checkpoint were acutely aware of it.

What they saw on the night of the full moon was undeniably ominous. Two Land Cruisers pulled up side by side on the bridge, bright lights glaring. Five men, shadowy figures behind headlights, clambered out onto the bridge. The soldiers leveled their weapons and trained a spotlight on the cars.

At that, the newcomers climbed back into their Land Cruisers and rolled slowly to the checkpoint. The soldiers kept their automatic weapons trained on the occupants. One of the drivers, a big American with a shaggy brown beard, opened his door and started to get out again. As he did so, he lurched awkwardly toward one of the soldiers. The Guardsman jammed the muzzle of his rifle squarely into the American's stomach.

The gringo was sweating in the humid heat, and he began babbling in incoherent Spanish. He had not meant to attack the soldier; he had only lost his footing. While he mumbled on, the other four men stepped from the cars, their hands in the air.

Two of the men, Pedro Benet and Luis Carnicero, were employees of Venezuela's Ministry of Youth, a government agency in Caracas that sometimes concerns itself with the exploration of remote areas of the country. Trying his best to keep the conversation light and fast, Pedro Benet began to explain the situation, and as he spoke, the soldiers gradually lowered their rifles. The three gringos he was shepherding, Pedro told the soldiers, were all obsessed with a book written many years ago by an Englishman. A boys' book it was, called *The Lost World*, and it was full of improbable adventures and dinosaurs. The dinosaurs in the book lived on top of Mount Roraima, and the gringos had put an expedition together in order to climb that mountain. First, though, they wanted to explore the plateau, see Angel Falls, swim in the rivers. . . .

One of the soldiers interrupted Pedro.

"They want to climb Mount Roraima?" he asked.

"Yes, yes."

"In the rainy season?"

"Yes, yes."

"Wouldn't it be more clever," the soldier asked, "for them to climb it in the dry season?"

"Yes, clearly, but that is just the point," Pedro said. "No one has ever climbed the mountain in the rainy season. The gringos want to be the first. They want to see all the waterfalls and things no one has ever seen before up there."

"They want to climb that mountain in the rainy season because of a book about dinosaurs?" the soldier asked in a level voice. Then he checked the gringos' passports very carefully.

What the passports showed was that the tall gringo laden down with cameras was a photographer named Nick Nichols. The mustachioed one was a geologist called Mark Stock. As for the big one with the beard, he was a writer named Tim Cahill.

"They thought we wanted to blow up the bridge," Pedro said later. "They say to me that in one-half more minute, they shoot us."

"They almost shot us," I said, incredulous.

"When you slipped, the soldier thought you were fighting with him. He said he was going to pull on the trigger."

"They almost shot us," I said again.

It was a bad twenty-four hours for guns.

Not far from the Guardia checkpoint, there is an unmarked road that leads to the infamous El Dorado prison. This jungle work farm, which figures in the works of Henri Charrière, who called himself Papillon, was once a symbol of inhumane treatment. It was a hellhole where prisoners suffered all the maladies of the lowland jungle, where the mind became warped in the rain and the heat, where the soul rotted inside a man. It has been closed for well over a decade now.

Though the ruins of the prison are off limits to civilians—and especially to foreigners—the soldiers said we could camp there for the night because we had letters from the Ministry of Youth requesting cooperation from the military. As we entered the prison, we passed a low fence flanked by rickety wooden guard towers standing ghostly in the moonlight. There was a clearing in front of what appeared to be the administration building, and there we set up our tents.

It was hot: so hot that the minor exertion of pitching a tent drenched a man in sweat. I lay there for some time in my underwear, a pair of black competition swimming trunks that are handy for traveling because they dry quickly and can be washed every day. Presently, a light rain began to fall, and I stepped out of the tent, hoping to cool off. Nick and Luis joined me, and we began walking down the swampy road, deeper into the ruins of the deserted prison.

To our left was a high, whitewashed cement wall, and at one corner there was a circular guard tower. We found a doorway, flicked on our flashlights, and started climbing a spiral cement stairway to the top. About halfway up those dark, wet stairs, we came across a lone vampire bat hanging from the ceiling. It was about three inches long and weighed perhaps an ounce.

Vampires like to feed on the blood of sleeping mammals. The bite itself is all but painless, and few human victims are awakened by it. The bat licks up a small portion of the blood and departs. But there is, in the bite, an anticoagulant, so the victim bleeds merrily on long after the bat is gone.

Vampires tend to strike humans on the toes, elbows, and the tip of the nose. This last can be a ghastly experience: imagine looking into the mirror in the morning and finding your face caked with dried blood.

We ducked under the bat and climbed to the circular observation deck. Moonlight shone silver on the overgrown prison yard below. When we came back down from the tower, the bat was gone, but off in the distant jungle, there was a disturbing sound amid the usual barks and shrieks and whistles of the night. It was the revving engine of a car or a truck.

Long before we saw the headlights, I had thought it out. Since it was illegal for civilians to come to the prison, our visitors were either guerrillas or soldiers. And what would either guerrillas or soldiers think about a man walking around in these ruins clad, as I was, in what must appear to be black silk panties? Just then the headlights caught us, and I raised my hands over my head. My major emotion, I was startled to find, was not fear but a terrible sense of embarrassment.

The car came to a skidding stop inches from where we stood. It was a Land Cruiser, like the ones we were driving. The door burst open, and out stepped Pedro, laughing. Was it not a funny thing, Pedro asked, to have a car come screeching up on one so? Had we been very frightened? It was funny to see us all with our hands in the air. Were we not laughing now?

Yes, we told Pedro, ho-ho, it was to laugh, such a trick of humor. And, ha-ha, perhaps now it was time to play a trick on Pedro. We would, ho-ho, just stake him down on those slimy stairs in the tower and, ha-ha, let the goddamn vampires bleed him for a week or two.

I am frightened by the jungle. I am frightened by the sickly sweet odors, by the moist darkness, by the dank fecundity. I am frightened by the chaos: green things lash about in slow motion, choke off lesser plants, rise toward the sun like those subconscious horrors that sometimes bubble up into the conscious mind.

I have been in the jungle many times over the past few years. I was in Guyana, at Jonestown, a week after that danse macabre of suicide and murder choreographed by Jim Jones. There were soldiers there, too, and they poked at the reporters with their rifles as we moved through the debris. We found letters from the residents in the home of Jim Jones. In them, people admitted to aberrant sexual desires, to visceral and murderous hatreds.

Now, standing in the early-morning light by the administration building of El Dorado, I found myself sorting through records of infractions committed by inmates while in prison. This one made for himself the "blouse of a woman," another had committed "open carnal acts," another had pushed a sharpened board through the body of his cellmate.

A short walk from the main buildings, past the row of tiny solitary-confinement cells, I came upon a statue of Simón Bolívar, the great liberator of much of South America. An inscription at the base of the statue read "El Padre de la Patria" and was dated September 24, 1956. In twenty-three years, the statue had become a grotesque and ghastly thing, covered with a beige claylike substance that had begun to rot away, revealing a coarse, dark stone underneath. The convex orbs of the eyes, especially, had suffered this rot, and they stared blindly out toward the empty prison. Great dark gouts, like ebony tears, ran from the eyes.

Later, while breaking camp, Pedro and Luis told us about the gun. In one room of a remote building, they had found a drawer containing a 9-mm pistol. They had never thought of taking the gun. To be caught with such a weapon in this part of Venezuela is like admitting to being a guerrilla. Pedro and Luis said that they wished they had never even seen the damn thing.

Still, Mark Stock was curious. Had there been only one gun, or more? Was it in working order or was it junk, abandoned when the prison was closed? Pedro said he didn't know. Mark got directions and went off to look by himself. He came back on the run.

The room was there, just as Pedro and Luis had described it. It was a wet morning, and there was a cement floor. A set of bare footprints led across the floor to the drawer. The gun was missing.

All around were the sounds of birds and insects. Off on the river, two waterfowl squabbled, sounding like children at play. Someone was watching us from the darkness of the jungle— someone with no shoes and a 9-mm pistol.

We were in the cars in an instant, and we splashed through the swamp at top speed. I never knew what to make of the incident. It was just one of those dark and inexplicable things that happen in the jungle.

South of El Dorado, the red clay road rises out of lowland jungles, finally emerging onto the vast plateau known as el Mundo Perdido, the Lost World. The plateau, sometimes called the Guiana Highlands, is about the size of Texas, Louisiana, Arkansas, and Oklahoma combined. It accounts for almost half the area of Venezuela and spreads out into Guyana, Brazil, and Colombia. There are some jungles near the rivers and on the slopes of the mountains, but for the most part, the Lost World we saw is a treeless, virtually unpopulated rolling grassland that looks something like the wind-whipped high plains of Wyoming.

Scattered about the plateau are dozens of foreboding, flat-topped mountains whose vertical walls seem to rise directly out of the grassland. These mountains, called *tepuis* by local Indians, rise as high as nine thousand feet. Geologists say the great mesalike formations are composed of sedimentary rock, sandstone laid down 2 billion years ago. About 70 million years ago, a series of uplifts cracked the sandstone monoliths vertically, giving the tepuis their strange, blocklike appearance.

Unexplored until shortly before the turn of the century, this is the area that inspired Sir Arthur Conan Doyle to write *The Lost World*—and his fantasy, in turn, was so compelling that it gave the area its name. It appears that Conan Doyle based his book specifically on reports he had read about Mount Roraima, a nine-thousand-foot-high tepui whose summit covers over twenty-five square miles. Roraima lies where the borders of Venezuela, Guyana, and Brazil come together. It has been climbed many times over the years, and though no dinosaurs have been found, there are strange marshes, stunted forests, and rivers that flow over beds of milky-white quartzite crystals.

Inevitably, the strange landscape of the Lost World had shaped some strange human beings. We expected to meet and hear tales of bush pilots and explorers, diamond miners, outlaws, and madmen. We also expected to get more than a little wet. Why did we want to do all this? The urge to climb Mount Roraima in the rainy season is simply inexplicable without reference to psychiatric literature—and the tales of adventure one reads in childhood. Some people have shivered through entire winters in Antarctica or sailed through menacing seas for the same reasons. The urge, I think now, has something to do with the desire to see just how truly rotten life can be.

The rainy season in the highlands is biblical in proportion. Great warm drops the size of half-dollars begin to fall in the river valleys. Then the sky rips open and solid sheets of water tear into the earth. The rivers rise hourly. Huge jungle trees, like half-submerged barges, float down toward the sea.

On the mountaintops, the rain falls cold, driven by howling winds. There, marshes are formed, and they puddle into rivulets that flow into big, strong-running rivers. These high, cold waters seek the warmth of the Orinoco, Venezuela's great lowland river. They snake on through the broken, alien landscapes of the mountains, then erupt over the lip of some high vertical wall, falling one, two, three thousand feet. The most famous of these waterfalls, the highest waterfall in the world, Angel Falls, drops from a Lost World mountain called Auyán-tepui.

The story of the discovery of the falls has been told so many times, so many ways, that it qualifies as modern legend. Back in the early 1920s, the American bush pilot Jimmy Angel was sitting in a Panama City bar when an excited man approached him with tales of "rivers of gold" located . . . well, the man knew where they were located. Angel flew him south without instruments, and the man directed him with jerks of the thumb. They landed atop one of the table mountains, near a river, and from that river, in less than a week, the two men took more than sixty pounds of gold.

Angel devoted much of the rest of his life to a vain effort to find the river of gold again. On one of his sorties, in 1935, he flew his light plane up the Carrao River, which skirts the huge 8,000-foot-high, 250-square-mile mass of Auyán-tepui. Turning south, he followed the Churún River in a wide, deep canyon. When he was halfway to the head of the canyon, on the west side, Angel saw the immense free-falling cataract that bears his name.

Two years later, Angel added to his legend when he put his plane down on top of Auyán-tepui, near the river that feeds Angel Falls. As he was landing, the plane hit a soft spot, and its prop was buried in the mud. Angel walked eleven days through uncharted territory before he reached safety.

In 1949, Ruth Robertson, a remarkable woman who worked for the *Daily Journal*, the English-language newspaper of Caracas, organized an expedition to the base of the falls. It was a long and hazardous journey in those days, but when her group finally arrived, and when the surveyors had completed their work, there was no longer any question: at 3,212 feet, Angel Falls was the highest in the world.

These days, only thirty years later, a person with four or five hundred dollars can be boated to the falls in relative comfort. The trip takes anywhere from three to seven days, depending on the depth of the river and the number of shallows the boat has to be pulled over. The starting point is Canaima, a jungle resort on the Carrao River. The forest around Canaima more closely resembles the tropical paradise of legend than it does the Heart of Darkness. There, the Carrao roars over two impressive falls and pools up into a spectacular lagoon large enough for sailing or water-skiing. Pinkish white sand beaches fringe the lagoon, and the air is heavy with the scent of tropical flowers.

We chose to make the trip to the falls with "Jungle Rudy" Truffino, a famous guide who has been running such trips for twenty-five of his fifty-one years. Like the other guides, Rudy uses long dugout canoes equipped with forty-horsepower Johnson motors.

The first thing one notices out on the river is the color of the water. The Carrao and the Churún are not leaden, like the Orinoco or the Cuyuní. In the shallow spots, the water is the color of strong tea or good bourbon. In the deep pools and lagoons, it is silvery black, like the polished barrel of an expensive rifle. For some reason, those aquatic South American killers, piranhas, cannot abide these dark waters. Where the rivers are brown or black, it is generally safe to swim.

Jungle Rudy's Angel Falls camp was a house he had built of

river rocks and cement on the banks of the Churún. It was about an hour's walk through the jungle to the base of the falls. We caught a few hours of sleep and rose at four the morning after our arrival. Thunder rumbled ceaselessly down the canyon, and lightning flashes froze us in cold, white, stroboscopic bursts as we dressed for the walk. With our miner's headlamps glaring, we crossed the Churún and began trudging sleepily up the steep trail to the base of the falls. The jungle vines plucked at us like a small, insistent child, but we arrived at a lookout over the base just before sunrise.

The canyon wall faced due east. Miraculously, the day dawned blue and clear. The sun on the wall was a brilliant pink and sandy rose. The water fell like molten silver, shining in the sun, stark against the luminescent red rock.

About halfway down the wall, the waters separated into a fine mist; the mist was carried by the wind, and as the sun rose higher, rainbows danced at the mossy base of Angel Falls. There were two, three, sometimes four rainbows, and they fell with the mist and shifted in the morning breeze like flags in the wind. There was no sound, no roar of water in the mist at the base. It was eerily silent among the rainbows.

Later, clouds formed at the precipice and dropped near where the falls became mist. The clouds were the same color as the water. It seemed as if they had suffered some terrible wound, as if they were being drained of their life-forces. I saw why the Indians call this falls "the water that comes from the clouds."

When the clouds parted, we dozed for a while, then found the first pool under the falls and swam for an hour before the inevitable rains. The sun was hot; the waters were deep and golden brown. I felt sanctified—overwhelmed by the spectacle and giddy with awe. It was as if I were splashing about in a pool of the finest bourbon, as if I had drunk deeply of the pool.

In the bar at Canaima, the oldtimers speak of the hermit Alejandro. He had lived longer in the area than anyone else, Indian or white. Once he had been a famous explorer, and he had found diamonds on the mountain as well. He was old now, they said, and his wife and child had left him. He lived alone in the jungle, and on those rare occasions when he came down to Canaima, he spoke only of philosophy and science. He no longer mentioned the strange, ancient beasts he had seen on Auyán-tepui.

We chartered a boat to the hermit's place. He lived in a canyon shaped like a drunken horseshoe cut out of the awesome bulk of Auyán-tepui. There were twenty separate waterfalls pouring from the canyon rim; one erupted from an oblong hole halfway down the pink canyon wall.

The hermit's house looked like any local Indian home. It was constructed of jungle-cut poles and covered over with a thatched roof. In the clearing surrounding the house was a garden: the hermit grew mangoes, lemons, cucumbers, sugarcane, bananas, grapefruit, and oranges.

The hermit met us at the door. He had white, spiky hair, a grizzled beard, and the thoughtful, somewhat troubled face of a man with work to be done, a deadline to be met. He was naked but for a threadbare green blanket fastened around his waist with a leather belt, and a pair of cracked leather boots he wore without laces. His name was Alexander Laime, pronounced *limey*. He had been born in Latvia sixty-eight years ago, and he had the broad, muscular body of a man half his age.

He shook hands, invited us in, accepted our gifts of food and beer, then told us it was fine with him if we camped in his garden for a few days. He spoke good English, with just the trace of a central European accent. When we arrived, he was sitting at a homemade desk on a tree-stump chair. The book he was reading was about the structure of the cell. He wanted to learn about cells, he said, to better understand embryology, which he was studying because he felt that somewhere along the evolutionary line, mankind had lost track of the proper meaning of life.

We nodded uncertainly.

For nineteen years, Laime had lived alone in the jungle, nineteen years alone with his thoughts. On his desk there were three smooth stones from the river. On these rocks, he had drawn sternly smiling faces that gazed at him as he read.

Also on the desk, near the rocks, was a cocoon. Laime said he always had one in the house. It thrilled him when the ugly little thing split, when the butterfly shrugged off its drab prison.

"There are some things I have to clear up in my mind," Laime said, about five minutes after we met him. These things had to do with meaning. There was, he felt, some truer meaning lost in this life. "Thinking," he said, "is the same thing as dreaming." He was neither lecturing nor trying to convince us of anything. He was simply trying to puzzle it out, like a hound on an unfamiliar scent. "If you could only find the way," he said, "I think you could awake from thinking the way you awake from dreaming." He had done this himself, he said. He had awakened from thinking and moved into a crystalline cerebral state, devoid of the fogs of reality. It happened infrequently, this sudden clarity, and it was important not to question it, otherwise one sank back into the dream of thinking. What he saw, Laime said, when the dream of thinking dropped away, were visions very like those described by the saints or by people who had been pronounced dead and then were brought rudely back to life on the operating table.

Laime had left his native Latvia on August 2, 1939, for a short visit to Holland. When the war broke out, he was unable to return. His travels took him to South America, where he got a job as a surveyor for a large oil company. The work took him to remote areas of the jungle. Soon, he was spending almost as much time in the bush as he was in Caracas. In 1949, he moved to Canaima. The resort then consisted of two tents on the beach of the big lagoon.

Laime got a suitcase down from the shelf. It was crammed with old newspaper clippings. Most of the clippings concerned Laime's extraordinary explorations; most had pictures of him. He was beardless in the photos and generally dressed in a suit and tie. The face was younger, but the eyes were the same: deep, thoughtful, troubled.

In 1949, Laime led the Ruth Robertson expedition to the base of Angel Falls. He is the first man known to have stood among those misty rainbows. (The local Indians didn't go into the deep jungles surrounding Auyán-tepui: farming and hunting are better in those spots where the grasslands meet the jungle.)

In 1952, Laime led a second expedition to the base of the falls. In 1955, he cut a trail to the top of the falls. Once again, he had reached a spot where no man had ever stood. That was also the year he led an expedition to the top of Auyán-tepui, the year he located the remains of Jimmy Angel's airplane, and the year he discovered diamonds.

Diamond mining was then and is today a hazardous business.

Even if you hit the Big Strike alone, you're going to have to sell your diamonds to a registered buyer. It is in the buyer's interest to get more men to the dig so that diamonds will become more plentiful and the price will go down. Quite often, an Indian is hired to track you back to the site of the dig. Claim jumping is common.

Laime remembered working one dig when he heard noises in the bush. It was an old drinking pal of his from Canaima, Anatoly the Russian, and five hired men, all Italians. Each of the six men carried a gun. Laime grabbed his rifle.

"Now this is our claim," Anatoly said.

"No," Laime said, "it's my claim."

"What you say is true," Anatoly said, "but you see, among us we have six rifles."

Laime thought about this. He stood near cover. The others stood together in a group, in the center of the clearing.

"I have six bullets," Laime pointed out.

The five Italians looked at one another, then at Laime. They had no wish to die for the Russian. Exit the five Italians. Exit Anatoly.

Laime sorted through the papers in the suitcase, looking for a diamond claim to show me. I saw a number of snapshots in among the clippings. Several of them were of a handsome older woman and a smiling young man. In one, they were sitting in what appeared to be an elegant restaurant, sipping wine from crystal glasses.

"Who are they?" I asked.

"Oh . . . well, that's my wife and my son," Laime said, turning his head away a bit. "They applied to go to the States, you know. In 1960, they were approved. It was either go then or wait many more years. I said go. I had to stay. I hadn't finished my thinking." There was, I felt, something more to the story, probably something painful.

"You stayed," I said.

"Yes. Well, you see, I cannot think in the States. Even in Caracas I am lost. I . . ." Laime sorted through his papers nervously, anxious to change the subject.

"Here," he said, handing me a sheet of paper. It was a drawing that would have delighted Conan Doyle himself. It showed a black, vaguely prehistoric-looking beast, an animal Laime said he had seen in 1955, on the same trip during which he had discovered Jimmy

Angel's plane. Laime said he had been walking in the river itself. Quite a bit ahead of him, he had seen some strange, dark shapes sunning on some rocks in a deep pool. They looked like seals. Laime moved closer. They were not seals. They had elongated necks and ancient, reptilian faces. Each had four flippers; two in front, two in back. When the things saw him, they slithered off the rocks and dropped sleekly into the water. There had been three of them, and each had been about three feet long.

Laime went to his bookshelf, pulled out a volume on prehistoric animals, and showed us an artist's rendering of a ten-foot-long marine reptile called *Plesiosaurus*. It looked vaguely seallike, with an elongated neck and four flippers. *Plesiosaurus* died out 60 million years ago, in the early Cenozoic. Laime had underlined that.

The second study he showed us—which, like the first, has been discredited by later scholarship— was a pamphlet about the geological history of the Guiana Highlands. Millions upon millions of years ago, the report said, an eastward-lying continent had laid great masses of sediment on the ocean floor. The report said that the jolting uplifts of 70 million years ago had lifted much of the highlands out of the sea.

Laime had spent a lot of time thinking about what he had read: with so many thousands of square miles boiling up out of the sea, certainly some marine animals must have been lifted up along with land. That was 70 million years ago. The great dinosaur die-out had happened 60 million years ago. Laime thought that in 10 million years, *Plesiosaurus* might have evolved into a smaller, freshwater animal.

He had gone back to the spot many times, looking for the animals. They were like him, he said. They lived alone on the mountain. "Maybe now they have all died out," he said. "Maybe I saw the last of them." He walked to the door and stared numbly out toward the mountain. When he came back into the house, there was a shimmering glaze in his eyes.

"You know what the word *canaima* means?" he asked. "It is an Indian word for a spirit, an evil spirit or a bad omen. You see, Charlie Baughan, the American pilot, he saw this place many years ago and wanted to make a tourist camp. He didn't understand the language, but the Indians were always talking about canaima, canaima. He liked the word, and that is what he called the place.

"The Indians hate the idea of death, you see. It makes nothing of a person's life. Whenever anyone dies, someone else always says they saw a canaima the day before: an albino parrot, a misshapen fish. Much better that someone should die from supernatural causes, no? If death is magical, then life is more important, you see."

Laime didn't talk about his own death. He fingered the gray cocoon on his desk and said, "I am awake all night, while I dream, you see. While I dream, I am conscious. But it seems as if I just close my eyes, and it is morning." He looked at me, then turned to the smiling river rocks on his desk and shrugged in an embarrassed fashion. "On the calendar, I see the years have gone by. Twenty years. But I don't feel it. I go to a place inside." He tapped the back of his skull. "I see cities and forests, and all the colors are bright. These places are all new to me."

He looked down at the cocoon in his fingers. "I see in the mirror that I am growing old. But it is like a dream and I don't feel it. I feel as if I am living out of time."

He held the cocoon up to the sun and stared at it for a long time, trying to see the winged creature within.

The red road south from El Dorado was pitted with potholes filled with what appeared to be muddy tomato soup. It was raining. It was always raining. Sometimes the Land Cruisers seemed like submarines at the bottom of a turbulent gray sea. On Roraima, so we had been told, it rains four hundred days a year.

We turned left at the village of San Francisco, then clattered over fifteen miles of grassland until we came to a river that defeated the Land Cruisers. We collected our gear and made off on foot for Peraitepuy, the last village before the mountain.

Peraitepuy consisted of about twenty thatch-roofed huts. People watched us curiously from doorways, then ducked inside when we approached. They smiled but would not let us get within twenty feet of them. However, when the sky burst open and the steady drizzle became a torrent, a nervous young man approached and asked us, please, to take refuge in the village schoolhouse. We thanked him and asked him if he could find Feliciano, the guide. Yes, the man told us. Feliciano would come soon.

The schoolhouse had a tin roof, and the rattle of rain upon it was deafening. Just before dark, as lightning flashed and thunder rumbled over the ridge, Feliciano entered the schoolhouse. Like most of the local Indians, he was short, barely over five feet tall, but he was broad in the chest and shoulders, a powerful-looking man. For a fellow named Feliciano (the Happy One), he didn't smile much.

We could, he said, reach the top of Roraima in two days of hard walking. But that was in the dry season. He didn't think it was possible to go in the rainy season. We would have to ford the Kukenam River, which was very wide, very fast, very dangerous. The top of Roraima was all marsh and rain, all fog and wind and thunder and lightning. The only person Feliciano had ever heard about who went to the top in the rainy season was a solitary hiker from Caracas who had supposedly died in the frigid rains there.

There followed a long discussion, shouted over the roar of rain on the roof, and in the end, Feliciano agreed to take us as far as the Kukenam.

The dawn was rosy and clear. We could see the bulk of Roraima in the distance. Rising next to it was the tepui called Kukenam, and north of that were two more of the immense tabletop mountains. They were more than twenty-five miles away, but they loomed over the village and seemed close enough to reach out and touch.

Late that afternoon, we reached the Kukenam River. It had been raining steadily for hours; one of those constant, drenching downpours; a rain that made one feel as if it would be like this until the end of time, gray and cold and pounding away until it turned the brain to jellied pus.

When Feliciano saw we meant to cross the river with or without him, he began muttering mysteriously, then followed us across.

The Kukenam was about fifty yards wide and waist-deep on me. Crossing a fast-flowing river with a sixty-pound pack on one's back is a hazardous undertaking. The river bottom consisted of smooth, slippery stones, and they turned under our boots, so that in midstream we found ourselves rocking back and forth with each step, like inept tightrope walkers. The idea of falling into those swirling waters and being swept downstream into the rocks and rapids was not a happy one.

When we were all safely on the Roraima side of the Kukenam, Feliciano smiled for the first and only time.

Roraima rose above us. There was a lower slope to the mountain, and it was covered over with a dense rain forest. A finger of the forest crawled up the sheer rock where the walls became vertical, then it crept along a rising ledge. The trail had been cut through that part of the jungle.

The first pitch was steep and so slick with running water and minor mudslides that it was a good idea to take it on all fours. This jungle was different and unutterably worse than the lowlands around El Dorado. There, the trees were high and straight, and the canopy they provided hid the sun and kept the jungle floor somewhat free of foliage. But this sidehill rain forest was a choking vegetable metropolis. The competition was fierce, deadly. The soil was thin, and roots could take no firm grip in it, so trees tottered and leaned, one against the other. Vines, like tentacles, lashed out and wrapped themselves around this branch or that. Parasitic flowers erupted everywhere. Branches, vines, and strange bits of bushy foliage twisted and snaked about through the tortured, thorny gloom, looking for a place in which to steal the sun. Each of these twisted, growing things longed for the death of its nearest neighbor.

We pushed on, slipping in the mud or on the mossy rocks, grabbing anything to keep from falling: grabbing long white vines the color of flesh and slick with some sort of slimy mucus, grabbing branches the size of a fullback's thigh, branches that crumbled in the hand and stank, morguelike, of rot and decay.

The jungle tangled our feet and grabbed at our legs. It slapped at our faces with thorny vines. It held us back, tugging at our packs like a boorish, drunken host who won't let you leave his party. The jungle, it seemed, was jealous of the mountain and would not allow us to climb it.

By the time the trail, such as it was, rose above the tree line, I was exhausted, deadened with fatigue. We passed behind a waterfall, then began climbing a boulder fall that seemed to have come from the summit. Here and there, we could see a few dead leaves, carried up to the rocks by the wind. The leaves had not rotted or withered. They were exactly as they had been in life, except that they had turned glistening black in the rain. They were the same color as the rocks.

At nine thousand feet, we came over the lip of the summit. We were in the clouds, and the prevailing weather condition might best be described as howling mist. This was Conan Doyle's Lost World: alien acres of black, tortured rock. There were no dinosaurs and no place in which one might comfortably sleep. We found no spot on top of the mountain where it would have been possible to pitch a tent. What wasn't rock was marsh. The mountain, it seemed, was a reluctant host, and it resented our presence.

An overhang at the bottom of a small cliff was the only place we could find to camp. It was cramped and dank. We curled up in our bags as darkness took hold of the mountain. The wind shrieked, and lightning cracked among the rocks.

Mornings were particularly unpleasant atop Roraima. Everything was wet and gritty. Wool socks were wet and gritty. Wool shirts were wet and gritty. All rain gear was wet and gritty. Once dressed, one simply sloshed out to the marshes.

The top was not perfectly flat. There was a central valley below the cliff, and there, water stood in rocky pools or flowed down to meet a river. In the river and the pools, I found hundreds of milky quartzite crystals. One explorer had called Roraima the Crystal Mountain.

We had reached our goal, but I found it difficult to think anything at all. The constant torrential rains affected the spirit, made one feel empty and soulless and instantly stupid. When I found myself wondering whether it would be possible to die by lying on my back with my mouth open, I knew I had to get out of the rain. I sat for an hour in a small canyon under an overhanging rock.

The canyon floor was sixty yards long, forty wide. The walls on either side rose thirty to sixty feet. Water dripped down the walls, forming a clear, shallow central pond surrounded by tufts of green-gold grass. Near one end of the pool were three stunted trees.

There was a serene beauty to the pond; it looked like a formal garden. The canyon walls, however, were eerie and vaguely menacing. Wind, rain, and time had carved stone balconies, pillars, and gargoyle shapes. There was a cavernlike quality to the canyon, and the mind does not allow such shapes to go uninterpreted. Some of the rocks looked almost simian: I could see in them the faces of screaming monkeys. Other rocks had a Neanderthal cast to them: the faces formed in the mind's eye were brutish things with heavy ledges over the eyes. There were pig faces and twisted dog faces, all howling in some sort of timeless pain.

Taken as a whole, the images seemed at once mystical, demented, and blasphemous. It was a simple thing to see the canyon as a ruin, the remnants of some ancient, inhuman culture. The altars and balconies and pillars, the strange stone faces grimacing down on the gardens and the pool, all these summoned up images of mindless gods and cruel rituals, of shrieks and curses echoing off the canyon walls, of pale blood flowing with the waters.

Suddenly, impossibly, the mists cleared. The sky above was deep blue, and warm afternoon sun poured down, turning the pond the color of honey and straw. I stripped off my soggy clothes and stood naked under the unfamiliar sun. There was no wind. It was silent in the canyon but for the constant flow of water. Water ran in rivulets down the canyon walls, and water over the rock has the sound of muffled voices. It was as if hidden beings in the balconies were conversing with one another across the gardens below, speaking in some alien, liquid language.

I was warm and dry for the first time in days. Now it seemed to me that the smooth, rounded, dripping rocks, the puddled depressions, the archways and spires, all had overtly sexual connotations. Rivulets splashed down the broken, rocky walls, sounding like laughter, and they murmured sweetly through the grasses to the pond. The waters of the pond emptied through a great V-shaped depression into a semicircular stone trough leading down to the crystal river below. There, at that hard notch, the water gurgled deeply. All these waters—waters from everywhere atop Roraima— would meet at the precipice of the mountain. There, with a terrible roar of release, they'd fall forever into the green world far below.

I have two newspaper clippings on my desk. One, from the back pages of a Caracas daily, features a picture of Pedro and Luis. It says that despite many hazards, they made what is believed to be the first rainy-season ascent of Roraima. Nick, Mark, and I are mentioned in passing. The impression one gets is that we just sort of tagged along with Pedro and Luis. Still, the article makes us all sound like heroes.

The second clipping concerns a plane crash in the jungle. Every time I look at it, it gives me the creeps.

We had driven south from Roraima to Santa Elena, a town near the border between Venezuela and Guyana. In a bar at the Fronteras Hotel, I met Floyd Park, a big, middle-aged diamond and gold buyer, formerly from Texas. Floyd had spent a lot of good years in the bush, and he had seen some pretty strange things. "They got snakes out there, anacondas, forty feet long and as big around as a fifty-gallon oil drum. They eat deer. You see 'em sunning on a riverbank with the horns sticking out of their mouths. When the deer is pretty much digested, they spit the horns out."

We had a few more beers, and Floyd began talking about a mining camp he knew. It had gotten big enough to put in an airstrip, and one of the first planes down contained three West Indian prostitutes. Instantly, it seemed half the camp was suffering from venereal disease.

Floyd was flying in supplies at the time, and one of the storekeepers asked him to bring in one hundred shots of penicillin. The shots were sold for about five dollars apiece. Another storekeeper, who knew a good thing when he saw it, asked Floyd to fly in five hundred shots and "one of those things doctors have to put in their ears."

"You mean a stethoscope?"

"Yeah, that's it, a stethoscope."

With the stethoscope, Floyd explained, the man was able to sell his shots for ten dollars apiece. He looked more professional.

An officer in a neatly pressed uniform approached the table. He wore a mustache that looked very good on him, and he had the dashing air of a military pilot. "I understand you have climbed Roraima," he said. "I, too, am interested in the mountain." His name was José Wilson. He was, indeed, a pilot and a major in the Venezuelan National Guard. It would be his pleasure, he said, to take us on a flight over Roraima so we could see where we had been from the air. He could arrange it for Saturday. Since it was Wednesday, that meant we'd have to stay in Santa Elena more days than we had planned, but the flight seemed worth it. I thanked Major Wilson and told him we'd see him Saturday morning.

"I didn't get to tell you about Old Sammy, the ugliest man in the world," Floyd said. "He was in that camp where they all had the clap. Anyway, they had caught him stealing diamonds and cut up his face with machetes. Cut him real good."

"Jesus."

"Sammy would have died, but some Brazilians came along and sewed up his face with bag needles."

"Bag needles?"

"Needles and thread for burlap sacks. That's all they had. Sammy was a mess, and even after he healed up, he couldn't seem to work at much. Well, Sammy was thinking about buying a bottle of rum and noticed all the empty bottles in back of the store. There was still some penicillin in the bottom of them, so he started trying to collect enough to make a couple of shots he could sell. Then he got greedy. He filled the syringes halfway with penicillin and halfway with dirty river water. That's the way he sold them."

I waited, sipped my beer, and finally said, "And that's all?"

"That's what happened."

"What's the punch line? What happened to Sammy?"

"No one knows. It's just something that happened. There are no punch lines in the jungle."

Saturday, we went down to the National Guard headquarters and asked for Major Wilson. They said he was supposed to be flying down from up north, but his plane was late—twelve hours late. No one wanted to say it, but it seemed certain that Major Wilson had gone down.

On the way north from Santa Elena, we stopped at the big army base of Luepa to inquire about Major Wilson. The soldiers at the gate wouldn't answer our questions, but they did take us to the officers' club. Above the bar was a large motto: *La selva es nuestra alidad* ("The jungle is our ally"). It was one of those sentences you know is untrue on the face of it, sentences like "The policeman is your friend" or "The dentist won't hurt you." A tired-looking officer listened to our story, then bought us a drink. Major Wilson, he told us, had definitely crashed.

By the time we got to Caracas, it was front-page news. The report from Venezuela said that a mail plane had gone down "on the border." The report from Georgetown, Guyana, was much more specific. The plane had crashed near an airfield called Johnson's Ridge, well within Guyanese territory. The report said the pilot had lost his way, that he had become confused by the lights at Johnson's

Ridge. Several soldiers aboard the plane had been killed. And Major Wilson, who loved Roraima and Venezuela, was gravely injured. In another twelve hours, we would have flown with him over the mountain, but he had gone down in Guyana, at Johnson's Ridge.

I knew that airfield. There was an army base at the field. I had landed there on my way to Jonestown, some fifteen miles away.

I had a sudden vision of all those wasted lives, all those bodies bloating in the heat and the rain at Jonestown. The thought of more bodies lying out in that stinking jungle choked me, brought a taste of bile into my throat. *La selva es nuestra alidad.* The jungle is your friend. The jungle won't hurt you.

There are no punch lines in the jungle.

The Underwater Zombie

A zombie walks around all day in a rotten mood. Walking death does that to a guy. It's worse than bursitis. Most people don't enjoy the company of zombies. How many times have you heard some bigot say, "I'm not going to any restaurant that serves zombies," or "Marge, let's not go to Cleveland. The place is full of zombies." Zombies resent this sort of prejudice, and that's why they go around ripping up people like confetti.

These days, a new, bitter chapter is being written in the zombie saga. The walking dead, it appears, have taken to the sea. Probably not one diver in ten thousand knows what to do when confronted by an underwater zombie. Of course, these dead denizens of the deep are pretty rare, but a little preparation never hurt anyone. Expect them to walk on the bottom. They come strolling out of the deep, and they like to hold snorkelers down, and rip the regulators out of divers' mouths. They are extremely strong, impervious to pain, and no fun at parties.

I learned about the dread underwater zombie from a woman who lives in Cozumel and sometimes works as a shark handler for underwater films made in those waters. *"The Zombie* is a very successful Mexican horror film," she said. "In *The Zombie II*, he hangs out underwater a lot, and he mostly goes for girls who dive topless."

"I've never seen any woman dive topless around here," I pointed out.

"That's an instance where *The Zombie II* may not be entirely true to life. Anyway, they had this starlet who was diving topless, and the zombie came walking up."

"He wasn't a *real* zombie?"

"No, he was an actor playing a zombie. His shoes weighed fifteen pounds apiece, and they kept him down. He walked real slow. Just like a zombie. He'd take a breath, you know, buddy-breath with a support diver, then walk four or five steps with the camera rolling. Then they'd cut, and he'd take a few more breaths.

"All the local captains were in the water, watching this scene with the topless girl. Some of them, I know for a fact, hadn't been in the water for years."

"They were pretty curious about underwater zombies, I bet."

"No doubt. As it turns out, the thing to do with a zombie underwater is to hold up a piece of coral. Apparently they hate that. It's like vampires and crosses, I guess. Anyway, the girl held up the coral and zombie put his hands in front of his face and went 'arrggh' underwater and trudged back to the support diver. The girl surfaced, and every one of the gallant Mexican captains managed to give her a hand before she could get into her robe.

"That was the end of that scene. Now they were ready to film the grand finale to the movie: a fight between the underwater zombie and a shark. We had this nurse shark, six or seven feet long. We had six handlers: three of us holding the shark on one side, just out of camera range, and three waiting on the other side. The guy playing the zombie was in the middle, in front of the camera.

"My team pushed the shark over to the other team. They'd grab it, turn it around and push it back. I mean, this was a docile shark, and it just sort of drifted by the zombie guy. But they could cut the film so that it'd look like, you know, a series of darting attacks, what with the zombie waving his arms and everything."

"Can an underwater zombie take a shark?" I asked.

"No way. First the shark took off one of the zombie's arms. It was a fake arm, of course, and we had a pretty hard time getting the shark to take it. Then all this fake blood came out of the place where the arm used to be, and the zombie thrashed around for a while until the shark came along and dragged the zombie out to sea. The guy playing the zombie didn't much care for that last scene.

"You have to imagine it. He's got all this makeup on his face, and no mask, so he can hardly see. He's got a wire-cage deal hanging off his shoulder, and his real arm strapped to his body inside heavy clothes. He's wearing thirty pounds' worth of boots. And he's got one breath. The shark was supposed to bite the wire cage, and drag him away. We were supposed to catch the shark and get the regulator into the zombie's mouth.

"Well, the zombie wanted to talk to the director before this scene. They talked for quite a bit, and if I was the zombie, I would have asked for a hell of a lot more money for that scene. They talked for quite some time."

I could see the situation in my mind's eye. Half a dozen boats bobbing in the mild swell, blue sky, the sun blazing away, and here's a guy with a horribly distorted, rubber-looking face and one arm, arguing with some guy who's got a gold medallion hanging from his neck.

"The zombie must have gotten some assurances—probably he got some money—but anyway, he got back into the water and lumbered over to his spot. The shark took him. We got the shark and saved the zombie."

The lady shark handler and I had another drink. I had learned three almost important things. One: underwater zombies can be repelled with coral. Two: those who play underwater zombies in movies are pretty gutsy. Three: *The Zombie II* is another in a long series of Mexican horror films that I am going to force myself to miss.

Cahill Among the Ruins in Peru

⟡

In the northeastern section of Peru there is a state called Amazonas, and the capital city of six thousand is Chachapoyas. Three blocks off the Plaza de Armas, down the narrow streets between clean pastel houses, there is a high wooden door that leads into a courtyard, and just off that courtyard, under his second-story apartment, Carlos Gates, the supervisor of Archaeological Monuments for Amazonas, keeps an office. For Chachapoyas, it is a luxurious affair. The floor is poured concrete, not dirt, for one thing, and for another, there is an electric light. On the walls there are various certificates and diplomas, along with the obligatory framed painting of Christ showing the Sacred Heart glowing in His chest.

A man in his middle years, Gates, like most of the people of Chachapoyas, is short, no more than five feet two inches, and very broad in the shoulders and chest. Despite his exuberant gestures, Carlos exuded grace and dignity. He smiled often, in a kindly fashion, and gave us no help at all.

"It is very difficult for you to explore here," he said in Spanish. "You must have a permit to dig."

Laszlo Berty, who spoke the best Spanish, said, "But we do not wish to dig. Only explore." The other two members of the expedition—Tom Jackson and I—nodded our assent.

"To explore, you must have a permit. You must have a permit to go into certain areas," Gates said. He suggested we visit the known ruins: Kuélap, Congona, and others.

Laszlo explained that we would certainly want to see those ruins, for we had read of them and we understood that they were beautiful. Still, our research indicated that there were other, unexplored ruins in Amazonas, and our goal was to find some of them. Señor Gates knew more of these ruins than any man alive. Could he not give us help on our expedition?

Gates stared at his desk top in what appeared to be great sorrow. Sometimes, he said, it is not good when new ruins are discovered. Men come searching for the gold and they destroy what is left of the ruins. *Huacos*—prehistoric objects—are removed and sold to wealthy collectors, and the work of scientists is made difficult.

Laszlo explained that he intended to run commercial trips down the rivers of Amazonas and that he wanted to find ruins near the rivers where he could take his clients. Tom Jackson worked for the South American Explorers' Club and he would note our discoveries, in a scientific fashion, in that club's journal. I intended to publish the results of our expedition in an American magazine. We would not dig and we were not *huaqueros*, not grave robbers.

Gates apologized profusely. He did not mean to suggest that we were huaqueros—never. It is the men who come later, like vultures, who defile the ruins. He was referring to those men and not to us.

There was silence. We were getting nowhere. Finally Laszlo said, "It is true that we are not professors of anthropology or professors of archaeology. We are adventurers. But adventurers with an object." He fixed Gates with his most sincere stare. "In the life of a man," he said with great dignity, "it is important for adventure. What else is in life?"

I am incapable of uttering a statement like that. It would wither and die on my tongue like a snake in the sun. But it was Laszlo's genius, when dealing with Peruvians, to say the right thing at the right time. Carlos nodded sagaciously as if he agreed that, yes, it is adventure and adventure alone that is important in the life of a man.

Laszlo knew enough not to push any further at this point. We would visit Kuélap, he said, and the others. When we returned to Chachapoyas, perhaps Señor Gates would be able to help us then.

Yes, Carlos said, if he could find the time, perhaps.

There is, in northern Peru, a unique area known as the *montaña* located just east of the Andes and west of the awesome forests of the Amazon basin. It is a wet, mountainous, transitional surface between the mightiest mountains of the Americas and the largest jungle in the world.

The montaña is close to the equator; and, along rivers such as the Utcubamba, people grow tropical fruits and rice and sugar cane. But the vegetation of the surrounding mountains seems strangely inverted to those familiar with ranges in the temperate region. The lower slopes are poor and sandy—a cactus and mesquite environment similar to what we call high chaparral. Above the cactus the land becomes fertile—it is much like the American Midwest—and here people raise livestock and grow corn and potatoes and melons on small terraced farms called *chacras*. Above the chacras, one comes upon the strangest inversion. The terraced fields rise into thick, choking jungles. It is as if the tropical forests of the Amazon basin had made one last effort to claim the entire continent. These mountaintop jungles of the montaña are known as the *ceja de selva*, the eyebrow of the jungle.

From the highest points on the ridgetops, it is possible to watch clouds form, wispily, in the great river basins four thousand and five thousand feet below. They rise to the ridge, thicken into great roiling banks, drop a hard cold rain, and fall again into the valleys.

The ceja, then, is a jungle formed of clouds—a cloud forest—and one thousand years ago there was an Indian people, the Chachapoyas, who lived among the clouds, in fortresses constructed high on jungle ridgetops. It is thought that they chose the cloud forests for their cities for obvious defensive purposes, and also to avoid the malaria and other tropical diseases endemic to the river valleys.

Conquered by the Incas in 1480—who were, in turn, conquered by the Spanish in the 1530s—the Chachapoyan empire fell into obscurity and ruin. The great fortresses, the graceful stone cities, the grand plazas of the Chachapoyas were abandoned, left to the jungles. Many are known to archaeologists, but they are little studied. Other cities and fortresses—dozens of them, perhaps hundreds—lie undiscovered, undisturbed in a millennium, in seldom-visited frontier country the Peruvians describe as *silvestre* and *salvaje*, wild and savage.

During the month of July, *Outside* magazine launched an expedition into the montāna of northeastern Peru. Our objective was to locate undiscovered jungle ruins of the people of the clouds.

The expedition was the brainchild of Laszlo Berty, thirty, of Erie, Pennsylvania, the owner of Amazon Expeditions, a fledgling Peruvian river-running operation. Berty had been both a computer systems analyst and a Marine, and he managed to combine the fine attributes of both these professions into one remarkable personality.

Puns and jokes were lost on Laszlo. The English language is best suited for issuing orders so that one may achieve specifically stated goals.

"Don't do that," Laszlo would say.

"What?"

"Put that cup on the filthy ground."

Laszlo had outfitted the expedition—tent, sleeping bags, stove, cooking equipment—and it was important to him that these things be kept spotless. He didn't like me putting the sleeping bag I was using—his bag—on the filthy ground. He didn't like Peruvians to drink out of his canteen because you can never tell what strange diseases they might have. Driving along the broiling river basins, we were frequently obliged to bake in the car with the windows up because Laszlo is *allergic to dust*.

In the little cafes, Laszlo ordered the waiters to stop wiping his bottle of Amazonas Kola with their towels. The towels were invariably *sucio*, filthy. My hands were usually sucio, Tom Jackson's hands were sucio, even Laszlo's hands were sucio at times, a condition which disturbed him greatly. He'd examine his fingers and mutter, "Filthy, filthy."

It is fair to say there was tension between Laszlo and me. By the morning of the third day—no later—we had come to an unspoken agreement. At odd intervals I'd simply explode. Laszlo would regard me with injured dignity and apprehension—you can never tell what a crazy person will do—and I'd shout in his face for five or ten minutes at a crack, walk off stiff-legged and steaming, think of something else and charge back to stand inches from him, waving my arms and pointing. After one of these berserk tirades, Laszlo and I would be very polite to each other for, oh, two or three days. Then the cycle would start over.

Tom Jackson, twenty-five, the third member of the expedition, watched these outbreaks in noncommittal silence. He was a slight, handsome fellow, and a missing tooth in the front of his mouth gave him a boyish, Huck Finn look. Tom had accompanied Laszlo on a previous river trip, and I assumed that he had sided with Laszlo during that first high-volume confrontation. I was wrong.

"Naw," he told me privately, "I was hoping you'd punch his lights out."

Jackson swallowed what I interpreted as a lot of abuse from Laszlo: orders issued in bored disgust, as if Tom were some witless incompetent. Because *Outside* had funded the expedition and Laszlo had organized and outfitted it, Tom attempted to remain neutral regarding the basic unsettled question of who was to lead the party. It took him a week to break. When he finally did, he erupted, burning Laszlo with a number of acid and intolerable comments. After some time I was invited to arbitrate. Who would continue with me, who should return to Lima?

Wrong approach, I said. Stupid. Together we were a complete entity. Apart our chances of success were minimal. We were all pretty fair woodsmen, but Laszlo had a knack for getting information out of Peruvians. Tom was the most accomplished climber, the hardest working, the most adept at fixing mechanical things. I was the strongest swimmer—we would have to get our equipment across a number of rivers at the rapids—and I had done more reading on the area, more recently. Decisions, I suggested, should be a three-way affair.

In the end, my position prevailed. Still, we spent the next few weeks gnawing on one another's nerves like rats on a rope. Laszlo had to put up with incredible stupidity on my part, and at times Jackson was even dumber. Once we found ourselves halfway up a mountain just as the sun set. We were on a grassy flat and we could see several two-story wattle-and-daub huts: two feet of mud and clay packed onto a frame of branches and thin tree trunks. The huts were empty.

We had drunk all our water on the climb. We were exhausted and sweated out and my tongue was stuck to the roof of my mouth. I suggested that our first order of business should be to find water.

Laszlo could hardly believe I had said such a thing. "There's no water up here," he said. It should have been self-evident. "That's why there's no people here. They only come up in the wet season." He paused to let this sink in. "When there's water."

Still, you can't talk good sense to cretins. Tom and I decided that since there was new corn and wheat in the chacras, and since we could see horses in a pen, and since there had been a fiesta in the town below, that the people who lived in the huts were at the fiesta, that there had to be water for the crops and livestock, and that we would look for that water. Laszlo, who knew the search was fruitless, lay on his back in the grass, wisely conserving energy.

At dusk Tom found a small pool, about two feet in diameter, behind a stand of trees. Later, after dinner and over coffee, I expressed the opinion that Tom had saved our ass, finding the water.

Laszlo sighed heavily. "Of course you found water," he explained. "Water runs down the side of a hill. You guys walked across the side of the hill. *Anybody* could have found water."

This was the kind of irritating idiocy Laszlo had to put up with *every single day.*

Shortly after our second visit to Carlos Gates, we drove south from the city of Chachapoyas to Tingo, where we started the long walk to Kuélap. That fortress, discovered by Juan Crisóstomo Nieto in 1843, was the keystone of known Chachapoyan culture. It is simply massive—the largest pre-Inca construct in Peru—and the fort is set like a ship upon high, crumbly cliff walls. The battlements rise some sixty feet above the cliffs and stretch for nearly half a mile. One stands before the main gate feeling dwarfed and impotent.

Kuélap had been cleared in spots, but for the most part it belonged to the jungle. It was an easy matter to become lost *inside*, and wander about, stumbling into typical Chachapoyan circular habitations. These are round stone buildings, usually open at some point to form a door, and constructed out of what appears to be local limestone. They are five, ten, fifteen, sometimes twenty feet high. In all probability, the circular habitations (or "circle habs," as we soon began to call them) had been covered with the same kind of thatched roof we had seen on the huts below. They were now, of course, open to the sky, and countless generations of jungle plants had grown in their interiors—grown and died and provided the loam for other plants so that most of the constructs were filled with soil. Flowers and trees and thorns grew where the roofs had been.

There were more battlements, rising in concentric circles behind the main walls, and everything there built by the hand of man, even the outer walls, was curvilinear. Small trails wound among the circle habs and underground chambers and mossy walls. Off the trails, the jungle was so thick it took a good fifteen minutes of machete work to move a hundred yards.

The vegetation was thick and rank and thorny. To walk it was necessary to clear an area from head to thigh. It was impossible to see more than three feet ahead, and the odor was intense. Everywhere there was the smell of faded lilacs, a sickly sweet odor, that combined with something thick and dead and skunklike.

We camped for a night atop a tower situated at the highest point in the fort. Twenty-seven feet high with crumbling steps to the top, it had been cleared, and there was a grassy spot for our tent. We could see forever, in every direction.

As the sun set, we listened to the jungle. At twilight there was a last frantic avian burst: green parrots shrieked over the constant chatter of smaller birds and occasionally we heard a series of strange, high-pitched whoops. As darkness fell, the birds gave way to crickets and the odd frog, croaking deep and resonant, like the sound of two rocks striking together underwater. Fireflies flashed in the jungle and, this night, there was a full moon; the tops of the trees shown silver in its light. Occasionally, there was a deep-throated wail, probably a monkey, followed by about half a dozen barks or grunts.

I slept the sleep of a Chacha warrior, secure in this fort at the center of the universe.

Virtually nothing is known of the Chachapoyan people (also called Chachas) before the Incas. We have some information—about a page and a half—in a book written by Garcilaso de la Vega. Born in 1539, Garcilaso was in a unique position to record the events of the conquest of Peru by the Spanish; his mother was the granddaughter of the Inca Túpac Yupanqui, his father was a conquistador with Pizarro. Combining his own memories of the conquest and interviews with Inca court historians—the Indians had no written language, but their historians memorized a set chronology, using colored ropes in which various knots had been tied as mnemonic devices—Garcilaso wrote his massive Royal Commentaries of the Incas.

The Chacha women, he tells us, were considered especially beautiful and the men fierce fighters. They worshiped the serpent and they lived in a hard, mountainous land where travelers were routinely required to raise and lower themselves by rope. In the late 1470s, the eleventh Inca, Túpac Yupanqui, moved north from the Inca capital of Cuzco on a march of imperial conquest. In 1480, his armies conquered the Chachapoyas and subdued seven major cities. Garcilaso places these cities in a rough geographical context: one can be found on the other side of a certain snowy pass, another located atop a sloping hill so many leagues long.

In the mid-1960s, an American explorer, Gene Savoy—inspired by the exploits of Hiram Bingham, who discovered Machu Picchu in 1911—launched a series of expeditions into the montaña in search of the cities mentioned by Garcilaso. A University of Portland dropout and former newspaperman, Savoy was not a professional scientist. "I taught myself what I know about archaeology, anthropology and history from reading, study and practical field experience," Savoy states in his book, *Antisuyo*. (The name refers to that quarter of the Inca empire east of the Andes.) In his last expedition, Savoy may have discovered as many as six of the seven cities mentioned by Garcilaso.

In his travels, Savoy hoped to examine a theory first propounded by Dr. Julio C. Tello, one of the fathers of Peruvian archaeology. Having discovered one of the the first full-blown Peruvian cultures—the Chavín, dated about 900 to 400 B.C.—Tello postulated that the forerunners of the Chavín may have originated in the jungle.

More accepted theories say that culture there first evolved among less sophisticated local peoples or that it was imported by Central American or Mexican peoples who migrated to northern Peru. The idea that culture in Peru might have originated in the montaña or jungle is not taken seriously by most archaeologists. The jungles of both regions, it is thought, could not have supported a high culture.

But what if a major migration had taken place along long-forgotten jungle trails? If so, it was possible that the remains of a culture earlier than the Chavín existed, undiscovered, somewhere in the tropical rain forest.

Savoy's expeditions in Amazonas did not prove, conclusively, that ancient man in Peru rose up out of the jungle. However, the dozens of cities, the hundreds of curvilinear Chachapoyan ruins Savoy found, did prove, he wrote in *Antisuyo*, that the mountaintop jungles of the ceja de selva "could support a vigorous civilization whose monumental remains are as imposing if not superior to anything found on the coast or sierra." Potsherds taken from Savoy's finds were carbon-dated and found to be between 800 and 1400 A.D. All were from superficial grave sites, and test pits undoubtedly would have yielded older specimens.

Throughout *Antisuyo* one senses an obsessiveness: "Where did the Chachapoyas originate and who were their forerunners . . . from an explorer's point of view, the work has only just begun—with three million square miles of tropical forest still to be archaeologically explored, one hardly knows where to begin. I believe that tropical Amazonas holds the vestige of ancient cultures of which we know nothing—perhaps a civilization of far greater magnitude than we suspect (the size of the Chachapoyan ruins, which surpass those of Cuzco, hint at such a possibility)." Unstated in *Antisuyo* is a glittering vision: the great mother metropolis with its massive towers and battlements and plazas, out there—somewhere—in Amazonia. The cradle of the continent's civilization. The final discovery.

When Pizarro landed in 1532, Peru was bleeding in the aftermath of a brutal civil war. Following the death of the Inca Huayna Cápac in 1525, Atahuallpa, the Inca's son by a concubine, launched a war against Huáscar, the legitimate heir. Huáscar's forces were defeated, he was imprisoned, and Atahuallpa assumed the throne.

Pizarro and less than two hundred men crossed the mountains and established themselves in the great Inca plaza at Cajamarca. Atahuallpa and an unarmed retinue of thousands entered the plaza in good faith to meet the strange white men. There, Pizarro's chaplain approached the Inca and informed him that a certain God the Father, who was actually a Trinity, had created the world and all the people in it. But, because people had sinned, God the Father had to send His Son, part of the Trinity, to earth, where He was crucified. Before that happened, the chaplain explained, the Son, whose name was Jesus Christ, had conferred His power upon an Apostle, Peter, and Peter had passed that power on, successively, to other men, called Popes, and one of these last Popes had commissioned Charles the Fifth of Spain to conquer and convert the Inca and his people. Atahuallpa's only hope of salvation, the chaplain concluded, was to swear allegiance to Jesus Christ and to acknowledge himself a tributary of Charles the Fifth.

Atahuallpa then informed the chaplain that he, the Inca, was the greatest prince on earth and that he would be the tributary of no man. This Pope, he said, must be crazy to talk of giving away countries that didn't belong to him. As for Jesus Christ Who had died, the Inca was sorry, but—and here he pointed to the sun—"my God still lives in the heavens and looks down on his children."

The conquistadores lay in wait, hiding in the massive buildings that surrounded the square. When the chaplain returned with the Inca's reply, Pizarro, his foot soldiers, and cavalry erupted into the plaza. Muskets and cannons firing, they slaughtered between two thousand and ten thousand unarmed Indians that day and took the Inca prisoner.

Atahuallpa, in captivity, spoke often with the Spanish, and he understood soon enough—all talk of Popes and Trinities notwithstanding—that it was the love of gold which brought the white men to his country. He offered Pizarro enough gold to fill a room measuring seventeen by twenty-two feet to a height of nine feet.

It would be a simple matter, Atahuallpa told his captors, for the interiors of the temples at Cuzco were literally plated with gold and all ornaments and utensils used in religious ceremonies were fashioned of gold or silver. There were immense silver vases and statues, and silver reservoirs to hold water. Even the pipes which carried water into the sacred buildings were made of silver. In the temples and royal palaces there were gardens of gold and silver: sculpture representing corn, potatoes, and other crops grew from a glittering soil of gold dust.

Before the king's ransom had been completely paid, Huáscar

was murdered in his prison cell. Pizarro said Atahuallpa had issued the order, and a swift trial was followed by a swifter execution. Pizarro had seen that the Inca empire was an absolute theocracy and that without the Inca—especially in the wake of a bloody civil war—the Indians would fall into disorganization and despair.

The gold and jewels that the Spaniards took out of Peru in the following years is estimated at over $11 billion. And yet, after the conquest, the Incas themselves told the Spaniards that they had seen only a small fraction of the actual wealth of the empire. During the time of the ransom, most of the gold—tears of the sun, the Incas called it—had been hidden in the jungles or thrown into the lakes. (One treasure, mentioned in some chronicles, is a massive chain of gold, *seven hundred feet long*, fashioned in celebration of Huáscar's birth.) Many historians and treasure hunters believe that the gold of the Incas was smuggled over the Andes, into the eastern land that was called Antisuyo.

The day after our night on Kuélap, we drove south along the Utcubamba River to the town of Leimebamba. This area must have been important to the cloud people, judging by the number of ruins to be found there. Leimebamba itself consists of a paved square and about half a dozen rock-strewn mean streets where black wiry-haired pigs doze in the sun and goats root among the rocks, and the old white-haired Indian women in black robes sit cross-legged in the dust, spinning wool.

We sat at a rickety table in the Bar El Caribe, a dank, dirt-floored restaurant just off the square, and studied our maps and diagrams. The owner, a sly, hatchet-faced man with a severe crewcut, lurked about—a pace or two away—staring over our shoulders.

"You have come for the gold," he informed us. "You have a metal detector."

Laszlo told him that we were only tourists, not interested in gold, and that metal detectors are too heavy to carry up mountains in a backpack.

The man would not be taken for a fool. "There are portable metal detectors," he said.

As was usual in Amazonas, where gringos are seldom seen, we

were surrounded by friendly people who simply stared for minutes on end before opening up with questions.

"You search for gold?"

"No."

"You are huaqueros?"

"No."

"Why have you drawn your own maps then?"

Leimebamba was rife with rumors about Gene Savoy: he had come into the area with experts, had followed the old Inca road, and had found a body of water which he called the Lake of the Condors. There he sent a scuba diver down, and when the diver came up he and Savoy had a fight about the gold. People believe that the treasure of the Incas is buried in the ruins; that it is gleaming there, beneath the waters of the Lake of the Condors.

Savoy, so the rumor goes, returned to Leimebamba alone. Later he was seen, it is said, crossing the mountains on the trail to Balsas, which is on the Marañón River. With him were two heavily laden mules. No one who tells the story doubts that those mules carried gold. Here the details get a little fuzzy. At Balsas, Savoy was arrested, or perhaps only detained. Some say he was deported as a huaquero. Others say he escaped to Ecuador.

The owner interrupted to show us a prize possession. It was a cassette tape recorder and he stroked it as if it were a favorite pet, then slipped a tape into its mouth. It was American music, country and western, and the song we heard was about a bunch of cowboys who find a fortune in gold and end up killing each other.

There are, in Amazonas, several stories of people who have entered or violated ruins and these people invariably have sickened and died, victims, it is said, of *el abuelo*—the grandfather—an unpleasant transference in which all the diseases of the gathered dead enter and infest the interloper's body.

The first person we met who actually showed fear approaching the ruins was one Manuel Anunsación Hidalgo Garcia, nineteen, but he was very cagey about it. After guiding us along an easy trail from Leimebamba to a high meadow near the mountain ruins of Congona, he simply pointed into a wall of thorny brush and left us to machete our way the remaining quarter-mile.

The odor was sharper than at Kuélap, more like licorice or anise, though still pervaded by that melancholy smell of faded lilacs. Congona was thick with a massive-trunked tree that adapts itself to the jungle canopy by sending out thick branches in grand horizontal thrusts. These branches were hung with green streamers and moss, and wherever a branch found the sun, there were large, sharp-petaled red flowers.

The first circular habitations we saw were unimpressive, but as we moved higher, they became larger and more ornate. In places, the branches of these massive trees had burst through the walls of the ruins. At the summit, we found a grassy meadow fronting a magnificent double tower with a winding stairway to the top.

Where Kuélap had been awesome, Congona was a marvel of symmetry and grace. There was an ineffable beauty to it, even in ruin. Huge yellow flowers grew around the rim of the central towers and green creepers fell along the mossy walls. There was no apparent military value in the towers and they suggested nothing so much as a place of worship, a cathedral in the jungle.

After we established camp at the top of the towers, I hacked my way, alone, through vines and creepers, the odor of licorice thick in the dying twilight. The inside of one of the less ornate circle habs I found had been cleared, and the work had been done, at a guess, two or three years previously. Moving into the ruin, I saw something wrong and bad, something that seemed palpably evil, and I felt, for a chill moment, the Thing that had caused Manuel Anunsación Hidalgo Garcia to leave us at the lip of the jungle.

There, dead center in the floor of the ruin, I saw a grave-shaped hole, five feet deep, three wide, four long. The sides of the hole were covered with thick green moss. Huaqueros—grave robbers—had been to Congona.

A few feet above the hole, four or five flat black insects, like wasps or hornets, hovered in formation. It was a simple matter, in the near darkness, to let oneself go, to feel a dread like paralysis taking hold of the arms and legs. I could imagine the golden priests atop the central towers and the people of the clouds strolling among the most graceful achievements of their culture. Momentarily, in that mood and in the presence of a defilement, I tried to believe that we were wrong to be there, that these ruins were best left to time and the jungle.

In the morning, that shivery sense of blasphemy seemed a conceit, a romance. Early that afternoon we returned to Leimebamba, walking three abreast and filling the narrow streets. There were scratches on our arms and faces and our machetes swung by our sides. We were giants, taller and heavier than the biggest men in town. The old women gathered up the children and shooed them indoors as we passed. We had come from Congona, and something in the eyes of the people begged us to swagger. We were brave men, foolish men. Soldiers of fortune. Huaqueros.

When the owner of the Bar El Caribe delivered our drinks and asked if we had found gold, we smiled and gave noncommittal answers.

There is no such thing as a good map of Amazonas, and we have Ecuador to thank for that. In July of 1941, that country, claiming the land from its border south to the Marañón River, launched an undeclared war against Peru. At the battle of Zarumilla, Peruvian forces won a stunning victory and Peru retained control of 120,000 square miles of land. There are Ecuadorians who object to this state of affairs and, in the hinterlands of Amazonas, one still hears of sporadic border clashes.

Good, detailed contour maps of the state, then, have a military significance and they are impossible to obtain. Additionally, the Guardia Civil, a national police force, maintains control points along the only road into the jungle; there foreigners must show their passports and explain what they are doing in that area of Peru.

Hotels are required to obtain the same information, as is the PIP (pronounced "peep"), the Peruvian Investigative Police, an FBI analog. Officers of the PIP—we called them pipsqueaks—wear plain clothes and strut around looking significant. My favorite was the chief—El Jefe—of the Chachapoyas division. One night at the Bar Chacha, four pipsqueaks surrounded our table and told us there was some problem with our papers and that we must go with them to headquarters. We were shown into a large room where El Jefe, a fat man of middle years, pretended not to notice us. His flowing black hair gleamed under the electric light and smelled strongly of rose water. He wore blue-tinted aviator glasses, an iridescent blue raincoat, and a blue-and-white polka-dot ascot. On one side of his desk there was a neat pile of official documents without stamps. On the other side was a smaller pile of official documents that had been stamped. In the middle of the desk, just behind the nameplate that read "Miguel Zamora," there were half a dozen different stamps. Miguel took his time with a couple of documents, looked up with an oleaginous smile, and asked, "What can I do for you gentlemen?"

"Can you walk like a duck?" is the only appropriate response to that question; but, of course, we didn't say that. There were many things we didn't say to police officers during our stay.

Carlos Gates, the supervisor of archaeological monuments, was actually beginning to like us. We were well read, well prepared, and we were persistent. Between trips to the known ruins we visited him a total of four times, and missed him on three other passes. Finally, Señor Gates stopped talking about permits and broke out the gin in the middle of one of our visits. We were getting somewhere.

Because our Spanish was not the best, Gates spoke slowly and distinctly, and tended to shout a bit, as if we were also hard of hearing. He helped us out with gestures and expressions. If something was large or interesting or beautiful, Carlos would widen his eyes as if awestruck. If something was difficult or dangerous, he would snap into a serious expression and pretend to brush lint off his shirt front with his right hand.

Yes, Gates said, he was the man mentioned in Savoy's book, and no, he didn't believe for a moment the rumors we had heard in Leimebamba. People in Amazonas, he said, are jealous of their history and they delight in its mystery. He knew Savoy wasn't a huaquero because he had worked with him, had helped the American plan his expeditions.

And now he was willing to help us. We knew, of course, that most of the known Chacha ruins were located on high forested peaks near the Utcubamba River. This was clear. Many of the ruins were fortified cities: a fortress at the highest point surrounded by circle habs. There were a dozen or more of these in the Utcubamba basin and the main doors of the forts always faced Kuélap. Gates drew a simplified sketch.

The known ruins lay in a rough semicircle, east of Kuélap. The area west of Kuélap had yet to be explored. Gates drew a second diagram.

On this diagram Gates indicated that there would be ruins in the area west of Kuélap. It was his theory that the Chachas would have had cities or fortresses there for reasons of defense and symmetry. If we were willing to share our findings with him, Carlos said, he would introduce us to Don Gregorio Tuesta, a landowner in the area, who could find us a guide who knew the trails there.

We looked at our map. There were no trails marked in the area, and only one pueblo. "What's the land like there?" Laszlo asked.

Carlos said he'd never been there, but from what he'd heard, it was (here Señor Gates popped his eyes for us), but also (he brushed lint off his shirt).

One cool, misty morning I found myself just outside of a seven-hut pueblo called Choctamal, a four-hour walk west of Kuélap. Not far away, on a heavily forested ridge, there was a fortress known as Llaucan, the last known Chacha ruin west of the Utcubamba. This day we were to push on: climb the mountains separating the Utcubamba River basin from the Marañón River basin. There would be, we fervently hoped, unknown ruins ahead. In a sense, it was the start of our expedition.

I was squatting in the bushes with the last of the confetti they call toilet paper in Peru. The local pigs had just demonstrated to me, in the most concrete manner, that they would eat *anything*. Not only that, but they seemed to prefer it directly from the horse's mouth, as it were. For this reason, I was clutching a long sturdy stick, the better to crack the porcine bastards as they made their move. So they milled about, just out of range, squealing and grunting and fixing me in their beady little hungry pink eyes. Not an auspicious start for an expedition of discovery.

Don Gregorio Tuesta, fifty-five, the man whom we had met through Carlos Gates, was big, five feet ten inches and 175 pounds—a giant of a man for Amazonas. He had eleven children, was a rich man, and walked a lot like John Wayne, only faster. Carlos Cruz, twenty-two, a local potato farmer and hunter, tended the mule carrying our supplies. Carlos was a little over five feet tall, dark of skin, and poor. He and Tuesta chewed coca leaves together in a friendly fashion.

"You need coca to make you strong to climb to the ruins," Tuesta said. Strictly in the interests of good journalism, I chewed about a pound of primo coca. Taken along with a taste of quicklime, called *cal*, it tended to depress the appetite, deaden the tongue, and overcome fatigue. The rush was minor and somewhat disappointing: about what you'd expect from a chocolate bar eaten late in the afternoon of a particularly hectic day.

"What's the trail like ahead?" we'd ask Tuesta.

"*Muy fácil*," very easy, he would lie. We came to calibrate the difficulty ahead by a system I called the coefficient of coca. If Carlos and the Don plunged on with only a single mouthful, it would be a bearable climb; three or more mouthfuls meant we were in for hell on a hill.

At ten thousand feet we came on some small circle habs. There were three of them, in very poor condition. It was not an impressive set of ruins, but it was unknown to scientists and explorers.

It was there, at our first discovery, that I was treated to an example of Carlos's humor. In a steep clearing, the loose forest loam turned muddy and I slid a fast dozen yards down the slope on my back. Dirt poured into my pants, and, when I finally managed to turn over and pull myself to a halt by grabbing handfuls of ground cover, I saw Carlos laughing like a lunatic at a parade.

"Don Timoteo," he said, "*ichunga*."

Ichunga, I found to my discomfort some moments later, is a small prickery plant that imparts a painful chemical sting that lasts for half an hour. The palms of my hands were on fire and the dirt in my pants was full of ichunga. Carlos could hardly stand it. He kept muttering "Don Timoteo" and chuckling to himself for minutes at a stretch. I was convinced that he had the brain of a hamster.

An hour above the first circle habs, we explored a sparse, almost dry jungle where we came upon a series of high, natural rock walls. Where these walls met the forest floor there were a number of overhangs, some of which contained small caves. In a rock pile under one of the overhangs, Don Gregorio spotted a human jawbone. Tom crawled back into a cave and came out with three complete skulls, two of which were bleached pure white and one was a pale muddy brown.

We found nearly a dozen skulls in all. The beige pottery fragments scattered among the skulls had a red line around the inside lip, just above a contiguous series of broad red spirals. The fragments were similar in size, shape, color, and design to a bowl I had seen in Lima at the National Museum of Anthropology and

Archaeology. That bowl had been taken from Kuélap and was dated at 1000 A.D.

These bones had lain in place perhaps a thousand years or more. They were not, as I had expected, brittle, but were, instead, very flexible. Perhaps it was the dampness or the acid in the soil, but you could squeeze these skulls at the temple and they would give several inches. Then, slowly, they would settle back into shape. The urge was strong to squeeze each skull.

A heavy cloud rolled up from the Río Tingo below and cast everything in a pale, leaden light so that the dry moss on the trees hung gray and lifeless. What had earlier been a slight breeze became a chill wind and, at odd intervals, we heard the caw of an unseen bird. It was a harsh, mechanical sound and it contrasted eerily with another animal noise, a soft mournful cooing that seemed to be very near.

Don Gregorio anointed our fingers with a fragrant oil; protection, he said, against the *antimonia*, a supposed disease caused by breathing the dust of archaeological excavations. A person suffering from the antimonia, it is said, will die coughing up the entire volume of his body's blood.

The mountains that form the watershed between the Utcubamba and Marañón rivers rise to 12,000 feet and higher. Above 10,400 feet or so, the jungle gives way to *puna*, cold, wind-whipped grasslands. At night the temperature drops well below freezing and cold stars howl in the sky.

There was a pass, Abra Asomada, behind us, and we were making our way through a region of intermontane passes that seldom dropped below eleven thousand feet. (Don Gregorio had returned to Chachapoyas, and now Carlos led, forging the trail with uncanny skill.) The ground looked like easy walking, but it was treacherous. High green-brown grasses hid impassable marshes and there were sinkholes deep enough to drop a man from the face of the earth.

Coming out of the marshes, we followed a ridge toward a high stone outcropping. Nearing the outcropping, we came upon a round grassy indentation. It was, unmistakably, a circular habitation. The hill above was pockmarked with circle habs, twenty-five to thirty of them scattered like a skirt before the rock above. To the north, over a gentle ridge, there were twenty more.

And the rock outcropping itself: where there were gaps in the natural stone, we saw high limestone walls. It was a fort, and we hurried to climb our way to the top. At 11,720 feet, the highest point in the fort proper, there was a small tower, similar in shape to the one we had seen at Kuélap.

To my knowledge, this miniature Kuélap was the first Chachapoyan fort to be found *above* the cloud forests. Located as it was, on a commanding position over a natural Marañón-to-Utcubamba route, I imagined the fort was Kuélap's defense early warning point. The vision goes like this:

The tower lookout spots suspicious movement from the Marañón side. A staggered series of runners is dispatched to Kuélap. A drum sounds, and those in the circle habs, warriors all, march out to meet the invading army. Repulsed by superior numbers, they retreat to the fort, which they can hold indefinitely. The invaders, anxious to claim richer prizes below, march off toward the Utcubamba.

Where the warriors of Kuélap are lying in ambush.

I don't know why this should be, but finding a fort, a military installation, is more thrilling than coming upon the remains of an ancient but apparently peaceful community. It has an effect on the ego and, I suspect, this is especially true of rank amateurs like myself who enter into expeditions not really convinced there is anything out there to find. We become Explorers, with a capital E, and that gives us the right to call things by any name we choose.

Never mind the handful of local hunters who know of the place and call it something or other in some goddamn foreign language. Just because a sheer accident of birth and geography put them there first, just because we are talking about their country and their ancestors, these arrogant bozos think they have the right to go around slapping names on things willy-nilly. The hell with them, I say.

It's up to us Explorers to name these places. We rush into print, the better to screw our expeditionary friends. It gives us near orgasmic pleasure to consider the other fellow—Laszlo Berty, let's say—reading our report in a mounting fury. We like to think that now—at this very moment—the color is rising in his face, making it all red and mottled, like a slice of raw liver. We chuckle over our typewriters. We are Explorers. We get to name things.

Okay?

Okay.

Henceforth, let the fort above Abra Asomada be known as Fort Big Tim Cahill. This is a good name, and I think it sings.

The passes and the puna formed a natural boundary line, like a river, and I imagined that Fort Cahill would be the last Chacha construct we would find west of the Utcubamba. I was wrong. We swept down out of the cold grasslands onto a forested ridge with three prominent peaks. There were dozens of circle habs on each peak and, inexplicably, there was no evidence of fortification. In case of attack, the people of Three Peaks must have retreated back over the puna—which seemed unlikely because of the distance and the cold—or they massed at some yet-undiscovered fort, another Kuélap perhaps, on the Marañón side.

Dropping from 10,500 feet at Three Peaks to 9,250 feet at a grassy area called Laguna Seca, we chose a steep ridge-running trail. At 9,300 feet, we came upon a score of circle habs just off the trail and, rising with the ridge, we found dozens more. This was one of the wetter jungles we had seen and the walls of the ruins were badly crumbled. In places we would come upon a high, unnaturally round mound of earth. A machete sank two feet into soft loam before striking solid stone. We attempted to clear one of these buried circle habs, but it was painstaking work. Wrist-thick roots had burrowed through the stone, and it was difficult to remove them without damaging the structure.

There were perhaps a hundred circle habs on the ridge, and still we found no evidence of fortification. At one point, we came upon three rectangular buildings, each thirty feet long, sixteen across, separated by alleys six feet wide. Rectangular construction was characteristic of the Incas, and a good guess would be that these had been built sometime in the 1480s, just after Túpac Yupanqui conquered the Chachas.

Following the ridge from about 9,500 feet to 8,300 feet, we found over a hundred more circle habs and about twenty-five rectangles among them.

Below the ridge, the jungle opened into bright green broadleaf plants, and the trees were hung with brilliant red and yellow and green creepers, so that it was rather like walking through a continuous bead curtain. Dozens of large black butterflies with white Rorschach patterns on their wings rested on the broadleafs and darted among the creepers.

On my map of the area, I found one pueblo, Pisuquia, and the trail brought us there early one steamy afternoon. The pueblo consisted of four or five stone and mudpack houses, a few huts, one haggard young man, a suety señora, two bony pigs, a flock of decrepit chickens, and half a dozen of the dirtiest, most sullen children in the universe. There were, the young man told us, ruins on that ridge—he pointed south—and that one—east—and that one—west. Not to mention the two hundred and some ruins we found on the ridge that brought us into Pisuquia.

The people of Pisuquia farmed with wooden plows and lived in dirt-floored huts that crumble in about twenty years. It was boggling to think that a thousand years ago there were not only *more* people living in the area, but that they were certainly more accomplished builders, and probably better potters, jewelers, and farmers than the present locals. The Chachas of prehistoric Peru were, by all objective standards, more civilized than the people of Pisuquia.

Three hours beyond Pisuquia, there is a pueblo called Tribulón, and Carlos directed us to a large house where some of his relatives lived. Half a dozen men sat on a low bench in front of the house and in front of them there was a dented metal can that might once have held kerosene. Occasionally one of the men would rise unsteadily and dip their only cup, a cracked wooden bowl, into the can. He would then shout *"jugo do caña"* and down the pale liquid in a rush that left half the contents streaming down his shirt front. The men had a glazed and sanguine look about the eyes and their lips were green from the coca they chewed.

It was the eve of the feast of the Virgin of Carmen, reason enough to drink, and the men greeted us warmly. We were offered bowls of jugo de caña, which is fermented sugar-cane juice. Tom took a few polite sips, but Laszlo and I downed several bowls. It had a thin, sugar-water taste, rather like super economy orange Kool

Aid, and the alcoholic content seemed small. It tasted good after a long, hot walk and Laszlo and I drank quite a lot of it.

An hour or two after sunset, when things started getting blurry, we were ushered into a dark, smoky, dirt-floored room some eight feet wide and thirty long. We sat with the men at a low table with benches a foot or two off the ground and ate corn soup with what I took to be bits of grilled pork floating on top. There were eight or nine women who didn't eat, but who sat opposite us, on the floor, talking quietly among themselves. In the far corner, one of the women tended a small wood fire and she hurried to pour more soup when the men called for it. The only other light in the room was a small candle set high on a wooden ledge above the women. There were bits of stringy-looking meat hanging out to dry on the underside of the ledge.

Between bowls of jugo de caña and sips of soup, I watched the guinea pigs, called *cuy*, scurrying about in the corners of the room. The small ones made high keening sounds and hid under the women's skirts. Larger ones, snow white and the size of small rabbits, moved across the room in a stately waddle. Cuy have been a source of protein in Peru since prehistory. I glanced up at the meat hanging under the ledge, watched one of the big guinea pigs relieve itself near my foot, and examined the little piece of gray meat on my spoon.

"Más jugo de caña," I said. Every time I drank, I seemed to lose half the bowl down my shirt front. Laszlo was developing the same problem.

Tom noted that Carlos had turned out to be a terrific guide: he knew the jungles and trails as if by instinct. I drank to that. Then I drank a couple of bowls in celebration of Carlos's rotten sense of humor.

Laszlo said that he noticed that "*caramba*" was the strongest word Carlos ever used. Caramba translates to something like "Great Scott." Laszlo said he really liked Carlos and was going to teach him some great American swear words and how they could be used in potent combination. He started with the word "fuckload" to indicate a great amount. Carlos seemed acutely embarrassed by this information.

Sometime later, after more bowls of jugo de caña, I found myself in another room where Tom was playing "Oh! Susanna" on his harmonica and I was dancing with Carlos's brother-in-law, who was sweating profusely and whose lips were green. The thing to do, it seemed, was hop around on one foot or the other, machete flopping by your side, with the right hand raised in a fist high above your head and the left held steady behind the back, like a fencer. Faces swam up out of the crowd and most of them seemed to be laughing hysterically.

About midnight we were allowed to spread our bags out in a room on the second floor. Laszlo held forth for some time about all the things he had to do and about how he was going to get up at 3:00 A.M. in order to accomplish them all. There was no doubt about this. He would be up at three. Absolutely. He could do it. He didn't see how all the Peruvians could have gotten so drunk on jugo de caña since he had drunk more than anybody and didn't feel a thing. I was stricken with sudden unconsciousness just after that last statement.

About 6:30 the next morning, I woke to a very imperfect world. Laszlo was still there and I would have said he was dead except that he was snoring painfully. Though seriously ill, I made one of those superhuman efforts you read about—a young mother lifts an auto off her child, that sort of thing—and worked up a passably bright and alert tone.

"Laszlo, Laszlo," I shouted, alarmed and concerned, "it's after three. You have things to do, places to go, people to meet."

He opened one eye. The lid came up slowly, as if it were operated by several tiny men straining away at some heavy internal crank.

"Shut up," he croaked.

Laszlo lurched to his feet several hours later and, despite the fact that he hadn't been drunk, even though he drank more than anybody, his bladder had failed in the night. He had to hang his bag up to dry. It was absolutely filthy. Sucio. Laszlo would have to sleep in that stained and stale bag for the remainder of the expedition. You can imagine how I felt.

In a remote valley called Santa Rosa there is a town called Pueblo Nuevo, and just above the town there are two wattle-and-daub huts belonging to Marino Tuesta, the brother of Don Gregorio Tuesta. We had a letter of introduction.

Marino took us above his farm to a forest where most things—tree trunks, rocks, the ground itself—were covered with a soft ferny moss called *musco*. Everything felt fuzzy and gentle, even the circle habs we found there. Somewhat below the highest point, we came to a gently sloping area where the sun burst through the jungle canopy in oblique golden pillars, highlighting a high, sharp-cornered wall. Probably Inca. I cleared away the foliage while Tom paced off the wall for his map of the city. This is an inexact process because you must walk on broken ground and over fallen trees, hacking your way through where the jungle is thick.

Twenty-five minutes later I caught sight of Tom. *He was coming the other way.* It had taken him nearly half an hour to pace off the building. It was immense—150 feet by 150 feet—and I saw on Tom's face a glazed and incredulous expression. His map indicated that this, the largest single ruin we had found, was the central plaza of a symmetrical jungle city. The arrangement recalled governmental plazas seen in many modern American cities, and something about that realization set the mind diving into chilly waters. There is, in us all, an idiot pride which argues that our age alone possesses civilization. Standing in the midst of indisputable proof to the contrary can be terrifying, like a sudden premonition of death.

The city of the great plaza had been discovered by Miguel Tuesta, the father of Gregorio and Marino. He called it Pueblo Alto, the high city, and Marino said we were the only other people he knew who had ever seen it. He considered the ruins beautiful and went up there often, to think.

On another day, we walked across the Santa Rosa Valley to explore a mountain visible from Marino's front door. There, in a jungle thick with *bejuco*—moss-covered hanging vines the size of a man's wrist—we came on another city. The grand plaza here was larger than the one at Pueblo Alto—270 feet by 261 feet—and it was apparent that the two cities would be visible to each other when the jungle was cleared. We called this place Pueblo Alto South.

On a rise above the plaza we found three very large, very well-preserved circle habs. One had a bisecting wall inside as well as a number of small niches set at about chest level. In the niches we found five hibernating bats. Carlos plucked them from the niches, threw them in a heap on the ground, and, before we could stop him, stomped them all to death with a satisfied smile. They were, he said, vampire bats, and they preyed on the local livestock.

Within minutes, we were engulfed in a heavy downpour during which I reflected on the *relámpago*. This is a belief, common in Amazonas, that those who venture too close to the ruins will hear the thunder roll before they are incinerated by a bolt of lightning. As it was, we only got a little wet. None of us ever spat up any blood, so the antimonia didn't get us; and we didn't have any problems with el abuelo, unless all those dead Chachas suffered from chronic loose bowels. I like to think that our expedition succeeded and that we escaped retribution because we took nothing from the ruins, because we weren't huaqueros. I'm pretty sure it wasn't because we were pure of heart and lived in harmony with one another.

Back in Lima, we took our notebooks to Dr. Ruth Shady of the National Museum of Anthropology and Archaeology. We told her about the burial site and the fort above Abra Asomada, about the city on Three Peaks, about the hundreds of ruins on Pisuquia's ridge, about Pueblo Alto and Pueblo Alto South. Dr. Shady took a few sketchy notes and excused herself. The new American ambassador to Peru was visiting and she didn't have time to listen to a lot of excited talk and speculation about the Chachapoyans, none of whom had ever paid a cent to visit the museum.

So I am forced to draw my own conclusions. We proved that the Chacha culture existed west of Kuélap and extended, in force, into the Marañón River basin. I think there may be a Kuélap-like fort somewhere near the area we explored. We found no evidence of fortification past Fort Cahill, although the Chachas of the Marañón must have had at least one strong defensive position. I think our findings tend to support Savoy's hypothesis: the jungles of the montaña could and did support a vigorous culture. That culture was probably larger and more far-flung than most archaeologists now believe. It is, then, all the more possible that part of the great migration south from Mexico and Central America took place overland, through the jungles. The mother metropolis could be there still, somewhere in the vast rain forest of the Amazon basin.

In the end, I am pleased with the lack of response from the museum and Dr. Shady. It means that vast areas of our world are going to remain unexplored and unstudied. Mystery is a resource, like coal or gold, and its preservation is a fine thing.

There were many ruins our expedition didn't reach for simple lack of time. There are said to be circular habitations above Pisuquia, and in the mountains surrounding Pueblo Alto and Pueblo Alto South. One valley over from Santa Rosa, people talk of finding perfectly preserved mummies. On a mountain across from Fort Cahill we saw a series of ancient terraces, obviously man-made, and their size suggested impressive ruins to be found there. In a place called Chilchos there are said to be mountaintop fortresses. An ancient pre-Inca road leads out of Chilchos into the jungle. No one knows where it goes.

I keep thinking about that road. It leads out of Chilchos. Into the jungle. And no one knows where it goes.

Down Under

and Thereabouts

The Reception at Bamaga

M any people on Thursday Island had already purchased their television sets. There was no station, no transmitter on the island when I was there in late 1981; that was still a year or two in the future. Nevertheless, dozens of families—the Malays, Japanese, Chinese, Melanesians, and Australians—had blank and useless electronic gods set up in their living rooms. Some spent entire evenings in front of the Sony worship altars they had constructed, praying, apparently, for the blessed advent of *Starsky and Hutch* reruns.

I asked a shopkeeper on the island if the signal, when it began, would reach the mainland and Bamaga.

"You bet," he said.

I absorbed the information with a syrupy and sad sense of regret. This is not to say that I am a man who abhors television. I watch local and national news, *Nova*, movies that feature giant insects, and anything that's on when I can't sleep. When someone catches me watching something so mindless as to be embarrassing, I feign anthropological interest. Last week Howard Cosell told me that *The Battle of the Network Stars* was sport in its purest sense, and I did not rush screaming from the room.

I suppose my objection to bringing television to remote parts of the world constitutes cultural arrogance. Who am I to deprive those in Bamaga of *Charlie's Angels?*

But let me tell you about Bamaga. It is one of the few places in the world that can legitimately be considered the end of the earth. Bamaga is a small town at the tip of the Cape York peninsula, a five-hundred-mile-long finger of land sticking up out of the northeast corner of Australia. To get there, you travel over an arid, baking, unmarked road known (from this day forward) as the Miles of Masochism. This is a rotten road, littered with the corpses of failed four-wheelers. I traveled it with a commercial outfit, Kamp-out Safaris, in a brutish four-wheel-drive bus known appropriately as the Beast. There were seventeen of us aboard, and every once in a while sixteen of us would have to stand outside, shoulder to the Beast, attempting to shove this road warrior out of some steep, muddy river bottom. One hundred miles of masochism a day was pretty good time on that trip, and on the fifth day, five hundred miles out of Cairns, we hit the Jardine River.

Most people who four-wheel it up the peninsula quit at the Jardine, only a few miles from the ocean and the end of the world. There is no bridge on the river, which is wide, fast, deep, and famous for the saltwater crocodiles that visit it. Like American alligators, these unreconstructed saurians like to drown their prey and secrete the victim in some underwater hidey-hole. They return to the feast over a period of days, like a man making repeated midnight raids on the remnants of a holiday turkey. Only days before our arrival a local man had been found washed up on the banks of the Jardine. Perhaps he had simply drowned while swimming the river, but the body was severely lacerated. That might have been caused by snags. The suspicion was that he had been "taken" by a croc.

We all piled out of the bus after storing our gear in the overhead racks. An extension was fitted to the exhaust pipe that made it stick up over the top of the bus like a submarine's periscope. The Beast's tires were deflated for more purchase on the sandy river bottom. The driver, after scouting the river for a couple of hours, revved up the

Beast and made a run at the waist-deep water. The sixteen of us sloshed alongside the Beast, alert for beasts.

If the Jardine defeats most travelers, it is also a kind of cultural dividing point. On the south side, the native people are Australian aborigines: tall, slender, elegant people, chocolate brown in color. Bamaga, the only town of any consequence on the north side of the river, is populated by people from the Torres Strait islands. The strait is a seventy-mile stretch of water between Cape York and New Guinea. The island people are darker and more African in appearance. Most of the young men are built like NFL linebackers; three-hundred-pounders are not uncommon. The older men and women tend toward a certain Samoan immensity.

The Torres Strait islanders never penetrated very deeply into the outback. Unlike the aborigines, they could not adapt to a land where water and game were scarce. But it was the islanders who introduced the drum and masked ritual dancing to Australia. Such is the effect of one people on another.

The first thing I noticed on the short jolting ride from the Jardine to Bamaga was the community graveyard. It was an oasis of flowers and grass in a wasteland of ocher dust. The tombstones were ornate, almost gaudy examples of the monument-maker's art. Many of them had recessed and glassed-over niches, and one of them contained a small crocodile carved out of semiprecious stone. Each tombstone was engraved with a few glowing paragraphs recording a man's or woman's life.

Some of the tombstones were wrapped in dark plastic, secured with baling twine and duct tape. Later, as we set up camp on a windswept expanse of beach, I found myself wondering about those blanked-out tombstones. About that time a group of island men approached camp. They looked like the front line of the Dallas Cowboys, and from them we learned the secret of the wrapped tombstones.

More than two years ago, the men said, their relative, Elikum Tom, had died. It had taken them all this time to pay for the stone and amass enough funds for a great feast. It was the way among the families of Bamaga. Everyone, including us, was invited to the unveiling of Elikum Tom's tombstone, and to the feast.

The ceremony at the gravesite was short, dignified, Protestant in nature. The banquet, given the circumstances, was entirely formal. Long tables had been set up in the dusty courtyard of a rickety tin building that turned out to be the Anglican church. A platter piled with dark fillets was passed, and I took a politely substantial portion. One of the women remarked that most white people didn't seem to care for baked turtle lung. There was a linebacker to my left, one to my right, and the lung tasted like cardboard jelly soaked in fermented blood.

"Good," I choked, "baked turtle lung. Good!"

The banquet ended at about dusk. The tables were moved, and people sat in a rough circle surrounding the dusty courtyard. A man set out a four-foot-long log, painted in black and white checks. Another sat beside him, an empty kerosene tin between his legs. There was a hush, and the two men brought out their sticks. They began beating out a rhythm that was East Indian in complexity. And then, from a corner behind the church, the first set of dancers strutted out: ten men in sleeveless white T-shirts and grass skirts. All were barefoot, and each man wore a strip of cloth around his ankles.

The dance, properly described, was more of a stomp, and the movements were martial, reminiscent of karate katas. There was a great deal of muscle flexing, featuring some awesomely impressive muscles. The women sang to the beat of the drums, sang in their own language, a strange, joyful, high-pitched song. The men wore fierce, rapturous expressions, and each powerful stomp raised a tiny bomb-burst of dust.

The dance might have been almost frightening, except that there were catcalls and a good deal of laughter from the audience, primarily because small children in the back of the column tried to imitate the men. They often fell or stumbled, or simply looked adorable and silly trying to flex skinny five-year-old muscles.

The men danced for fifteen minutes or so, then abandoned the courtyard to a group of scruffy dogs and wrestling children. Soon enough, a group of women in orange blouses and grass skirts glided out from behind the church to dance while the men sang. Little girls fell over trying to follow the movements. There were other dances: teenagers danced, groups of men and women, groups that had obviously practiced more than others. This went on all night—men dancing and flexing, women gliding—until it seemed everyone who lived in Bamaga had performed several times. There was some drinking—the local beer was strong, the rum harsh—and a lot of good-natured bantering: "I a more better dancer than you, Charlie."

People wandered about the audience. Some of them spoke of Elikum Tom. They remembered his adventures, the funny things he had done. His death had drawn all these people together, and made them closer. By dawn we were all exhausted. Out on the beach, by our camp, I could see a florid tropical sun rising over Horn Island, with the provincial center, Thursday Island, just visible behind it.

Soon there will be television on Thursday Island, and the signal will reach Bamaga. People, I think, will still go to wakes like the one for Elikum Tom. They will pay their respects at the graveyard, eat with the family, but I hear them making flimsy excuses, leaving early. I see them dashing home in order to see automobiles crashing into light poles in Los Angeles.

The people of Bamaga will learn more of the outside world, and will know less of their own. They will, sad to say, know more of us than we will ever know of them.

To the Place
of Walleroo Dreaming

I will dream the artist dreaming: In life the artist was a tall, thin man with chocolate brown skin, curly black hair, and sharp, angular features. He was missing a tooth at the front of his mouth, and there were concentric circular scars on both sides of his chest. He wore a whitened bone—the small rib of a kangaroo— through the hole in his nasal septum. Now, in the heaven called Woolunda, he sits in a curious, liquid posture, as if his bones had no consistency to them. There is a feast spread out at his feet, more food than he has ever seen at one time in his life: There is honey, and meat from the kangaroo and possum and emu, there is the fish called barramundi. Dozens of young women lie, decoratively, all about him. They smile and blush prettily. The artist may have any—or all of them—for wife. The artist exists there, like that, throughout past and present and future, throughout the whole of time. His spirit is secure: It is represented on the rock, at the Place of Walleroo Dreaming.

Dreaming the dreams of another people, of a culture now nearly dead, is a treacherous and ethereal enterprise. One must look closely to the artist's sources, and sometimes the search for sources has the quality of the dream itself.

I began to learn of the Dream Time from another white man, Percy Trezise. It was a warm summer evening on the Cape York Peninsula at the far northeast corner of the Australian continent. The Joonging, as the Australian aboriginals call them, the flying-fox people, were camped in a canyon to the west, half a million strong. They came at us just after sunset, when the sky was still rich with florid tropical pastels. Their bodies were dark, fierce against the dying light. They flew straight, like ducks, only slower, and there was none of that erratic darting about that one associates with most bats.

The largest of them had a wingspan well over four feet, and the sound they made was a steady *foof-foof*, two beats of the great dark wings a second. All together they sounded like the howl of a wind-driven rain, like the howl of a distant hurricane before landfall.

"I painted this once," Percy Trezise said. He is a solid, exuberant man, muscular, with gray hair and a gray beard. He jacked three shells into a 20-gauge shotgun, and the dingo bitch, Lahsa, capered at his feet.

We were standing in a clearing beyond the open-sided shed where Percy Trezise paints his award-winning outback scenes. The forest around us was dense with eucalyptus, thin-trunked, stringy-barked trees every ten steps or so. In the grasses of the flat forest floor, between the trees, were dozens of mounds constructed by compass termites. The nests were thin-bladed little monoliths, three to five feet high, and so hard that an ax struck against them raised sparks. The gables and spires along the tops of the blades and the buttresses fanning out below gave them the look of Gothic cathedrals, though they lacked certain essential symmetries. One thought of alternate universes, of a time before men, of the Dream Time.

The major blade of each nest pointed north, due north, toward the sun, so that the temperature within them was intensified and the secretions of the creatures who lived there hardened that much quicker. It is said that aboriginal people used a stick of ironwood and a rock to pound holes in the nests and that murder victims were hidden there. In two or three days the hole would be covered over and the bones would be eaten.

Percy Trezise raised the shotgun to his shoulder, and the dingo whimpered in anticipation. Lahsa was about the size of an Airedale, a solid, beige-yellow animal with white boots and a white tip on her tail. Trezise had raised her from a pup, and she was as affectionate and responsive as any domestic dog. The dingo is one of the few nonmarsupial mammals native to Australia, a wild dog brought to the isolated continent by aboriginal people sometime during the Pleistocene. Placental mammals, the dingoes were more efficient predators than the marsupials that flourished in Australia, and they contributed, through competition, to the extermination of the marsupial Tasmanian wolf and Tasmanian devil. With the white settlement of Australia, dingoes began feeding on sheep and poultry. And, like the coyote in America, they have been eliminated in most areas for all the same reasons.

"The dingoes used to feed on the flying foxes," Trezise said, "but there are so few of them anymore that the foxes are breeding out of hand."

The wall of darkness was on us then, like a eclipse slicing over the land. Trezise fired three times. Two of the great bats thumped to earth. Lahsa ran to the first. There was the sound of ripping parchment, then the cracking of small bones.

I looked at the other fox; it was almost pretty. It had velvety black fur and a long, doglike snout—not the pushed-in face and fangs you find on those bats in your attic—and it was big: a foot and a half long, with plenty of meat on it.

"If I didn't feed her on the foxes," Trezise said, "she'd be out killing wallabies, and we don't have many of those left." The wallaby is a medium-sized fellow as kangaroos go, and stands about three feet high.

Trezise fired three more times, but it was getting dark, and he only pulled down one of the foxes. The rest of the Joonging were settling into paper-bark trees that grew in the small gullies leading down to the Little Laura River. But before they could begin their night's feeding on the blossoms, they had to deal with the kookaburras nested there.

Kookaburras are large, belligerent birds, about half again the size of a blue jay. They feed on snakes and lizards, and their braying fifteen- to twenty-second-long calls are usually described as sounding like fiendish laughter. The vocalization begins with a high-pitched squawk, degenerates into a *hohohoho, hahahaha* sound, then tapers off into infectious chuckles. The sound is at once so human and so obviously inhuman that it seems crazed, maniacal. There hadn't been any of that mocking laughter for more than half an hour, but now the kookaburras were defending their nest sites from the flying foxes, and the darkness all about us was filled with hideous, hysterical laughter.

I felt vaguely somnambulant, surreal, standing among those little Gothic cathedrals filled with the digested and secreted bones of the long dead, standing in the receding rush of the invasion of the flying-fox people. It seemed a good time to ask Percy Trezise if he would, please, escort me into the Dream Time. In the darkness all around, the kookaburras shrieked out their mad laughter.

Percy Trezise grew up in the south of Australia, and in 1938—he remembers the year still—he won a book about aboriginal culture in a school essay contest. The book ignited his imagination and led to a lifelong obsession. After a few unsatisfactory adult years in the south, Trezise moved his family to far north Queensland, to a city at the base of the Cape York Peninsula.

In September 1960—another date Trezise remembers with precision—he visited the Split Rock gallery, south of the town of Laura. A road crew had just discovered the site: a huge sandstone block, nearly a hundred feet high, covered with aboriginal rock paintings and engravings. There were recognizable kangaroos, emus, fish, possums; there were strange, elongated figures, spirit figures called *quinkans*, with upraised arms and strangely shaped heads. They looked like El Greco figures as interpreted by Yves Tanguy.

Some of the paintings were superimposed on others, some had obviously been repainted; some were crudely drawn, others were magnificent, genuine works of art.

There was a history there, Trezise knew, the record of a culture, a record that encompassed countless centuries.

Not much was known about the rock art of the area. Cape York is said to be the second largest wilderness area left in the world. The soil is so sandy and the rainy season so wet that established rivers overflow their banks, and impromptu rivers spring up everywhere, washing out roads and airstrips, toppling buildings. To live in Cape

York is to spend several months of the year in a cold, mosquito-infested bog. Not many people do.

The peninsula measures three hundred miles across at its base and tapers off five hundred miles north to a windy, wave-battered, seldom-visited point called Cape York. The peninsula, which separates the Coral Sea from the Arafura Sea, is a finger of land that sticks up into the Torres Strait as if to prod the soft underbelly of New Guinea.

Two hundred million years ago the area was a vast inland sea, and the sea laid down deep beds of sandstone. Over the millennia the sea fell back. Wind, weather, and rushing rivers carved out mesas and plateaus, so that today the peninsula is a jumble of flat forest, low mountains, and sandstone cliffs. In the cavelike overhangs of these cliffs, aboriginal people made temporary camps, moving with the game, with the ripening of fruits and greens.

Trezise was certain that Split Rock was not an isolated phenomenon. There were too many styles, too many centuries represented. His occupation as a pilot was ideal for preliminary surveys: If you were a passenger on one of the very informal airlines serving Cape York in, say, 1962, your plane would drop to treetop level and skirt a sandy ledge, circle back and do it again, just a little closer. In the cockpit Percy Trezise would be making little notes on his navigation chart.

Trezise turned out to be right. He and his family, notably sons Stephen and Matt, found scores of rock-art sites. The occupation debris at one site was carbon dated to 13,200 B.C. Others had to be more recent. The gold rush of 1873 led to a war of attrition between whites and aboriginals, and Percy Trezise found more than one depiction of a white man, probably dating from that era. One drawing shows a white man wearing boots, a rifle lying by his side. He is stretched out on his back, as in death, and birds are shown picking at the body. So there was an unbroken pictorial record of the culture—a record of thousands of years of human life.

Trezise has a pretty good idea of where the people came from: "I'm willing to bet that some form of early man arrived in Australia at least two hundred thousand years ago. Remember, this was during the Ice Age, when a lot of the water was concentrated in polar caps. There was more land, less water, and island hopping would have been easier. Back, let's see, five hundred thousand years ago you had

Homo erectus in Java. That isn't so far away from here, and if some form of early man got to New Guinea, the next move would have been down into Cape York."

"Books I read," I said, "have man arriving in Australia about forty thousand years ago."

"True. They're *sure* of that. But more and more scientists are beginning to think that one hundred thousand years is a probable date, and some think two hundred thousand is possible. I think we'll find rock art that can be dated to forty thousand years ago."

Discovering the meaning of the figures painted on the sandstone walls proved more difficult than finding them. Trezise decided to take an early retirement, bought the Quinkan Hotel and Bar in Laura, and spent his time painting outback scenes, looking for more galleries, and talking to local aboriginal people. He became close friends with an aboriginal artist, Goobalathaldin, whose name means "waves standing up," and who calls himself Dick Roughsey for the benefit of whites who can't wrap their tongues around his native name.

Roughsey, a painter like Trezise, grew up in the bush and knew the legends and religion of his people. "That's rare," Trezise said. "Did you ask any of the aboriginals you met about the Dream Time?"

I told him that I had spoken to a couple of fellows, Legs and Freddy, at the Quinkan Bar a few nights ago. They worked as hands on the local ranches, and we talked about horses and cattle and rodeos. Legs wanted to know if I had ever met Charley Pride, whom he proclaimed "the best singer in the world." As for the Dream Time, "It was a long time ago, in the olden times."

Trezise nodded. "The culture is rapidly disappearing," he said. "Luckily, Dick had a gregarious personality, and he was able to make friends with some of the old men around Laura. These were initiated men: They had the cicatrix scars on their chests, the missing front tooth, the pierced nasal septums. These fellows wouldn't tell what they knew to the young men, but after a time they accepted Dick and me into their kinship system. And they agreed to tell us what they knew. We were to record it in the white man's fashion so that it wouldn't be lost forever."

The old men showed Roughsey and Trezise the galleries they knew and explained the meaning of the figures. At night around the campfire Trezise taped the ancient legends. In 1969, he published *Quinkan Country*, largely a compendium of the myths. He and Dick Roughsey collaborated on a series of books, which are, in fact, nearly exact transcriptions of the old men's tales: The creation of the world, the saga of Goorialla, the Giant Feathered Serpent, of Gaiya, the Devil Dog, and Joonging, the Flying Fox.

Walleroo Dreaming is a small gallery of rock art set on a plateau not far from Percy Trezise's outback camp near Laura. There are a number of figures that appear to be catfish, crocodiles, and flying foxes. Off to one side, painted in white ocher on the roof of a small overhang, were the figures of an old woman and a giant dog. Not far from that, amid some other crudely drawn animals, was an equally crudely drawn woman lying face-down, with a long, snakelike object connected to the foot. Some distance from these figures, set off by itself, was a magnificent twelve-foot-long drawing of a walleroo. It could be distinguished from any other type of kangaroo by the length of the lower leg and by the peculiar tilt of the head. It was painted in rare white ocher, with an outline of red ocher, an impure iron ore mixed with water. Below the walleroo and off to the side were several sticklike human figures, and just under the belly was another human figure painted upside down.

Several days with Percy Trezise, with his books, with other books, had supplied me with just enough knowledge to dream. "The Dream Time," Trezise told me, "flows like a river through the past and the present and the future." In one of its meanings the Dream Time is that ancient time when ancestral beings created the earth and set down the laws.

These would be the first stories a child learned. Probably the man who painted Giant Walleroo—it was almost certainly a man, for women were not allowed to know the secrets of sacred dreaming—lived four to five thousand years ago, and the creation myth he learned was that of Goorialla, the Giant Feathered Serpent.

I dream the artist as a child, with other children, sitting under a figure of the Serpent at another gallery. An old man is telling them the tale:

In the beginning of the Dream Time all the land was flat, and there were only people. Then Goorialla, the Giant Feathered Serpent, traveled up from the south, and from his droppings he made that mountain you see over there. And his belly dug out the river you see below. Goorialla stopped atop his mountain, and he listened to the four winds for the voices of his people.

When he finally found them, they were having a great bora, and Goorialla hid and watched them dance. Finally he came out, saying, "You are not dancing properly." And he showed them how to make a headdress of beeswax and white cockatoo feathers, how to make arm bands of pandamus palm leaves, how to make pearl-shell pendants that hung from yellow grass stems. All the people—the flying-fox people and the walleroo people, the dingo people and the emu people—rejoiced in the new knowledge, and there was a great bora.

When the dance was over, all the people went into their humpies to sleep, but two young blue mountain parrot boys, the Bil-Bil brothers, had no place to sleep. They went to Emu Woman, but she had too many children. Finally they went to Goorialla, who said, "Wait, I must make my humpy bigger." He opened his mouth so that the top of it was the ceiling and the bottom was the floor, and he said, "Come in now." The two boys went in and were swallowed.

In the night Goorialla began to worry about what the people would do when they found the boys missing; so he went to the only mountain in the world, the biggest mountain there ever was, with great, sheer cliffs on all sides.

The people tracked Goorialla and tried to climb the cliffs, but only two tree goannas, the Wangoo men, could scale the cliff. They made two sharp quartz knives and told the people, "When we do what we are going to do, Goorialla will be very angry. Go and change into birds and animals so he can't find you." The Wangoo men climbed the cliffs, and they cut Goorialla from both sides, neck to tail. The two Bil-Bil boys had changed into blue mountain parrots, and they flew away.

Now a cold wind sprang up; it blew through the empty ribs of Goorialla, waking him. When he saw that he was cut and his dinner was stolen, he thrashed about in fury and agony, and he tore up the great mountain and hurled pieces all over the country. The pieces make up the hills and mountains as we know them today, and all the birds and animals are our relatives. We are descended from the walleroo.

The artist believed in the literal truth of this story, believed that he was related to all living things. He lived with perhaps forty people, all intricately connected by kinship ties. It was a hunting and gathering society, and the walleroo people were nomads in a harsh land. Cooperation was essential for life; religion was even more important.

Percy Trezise traveled the world studying rock art on a Churchill Grant, and he believes the most spiritual work comes out of the harshest land. "I think the work of Australian aboriginal people and of African Bushmen is more religious than, say, the cave paintings at Lascaux in France, which seem to me to be mostly concerned with hunting magic."

I dream the artist as a child, enjoying the myth of the creation of the dingo:

Old Eelgin, the Grasshopper Woman, had a giant dog who hunted men and brought them to her to eat. One day she set the dog on two butcher bird boys, the Chookoo-Chookoo brothers. The brothers fled, and the dog could be heard howling for miles away, and his galloping gait sounded like the roll of thunder. Old Eelgin hobbled along behind, urging the Devil Dog on.

The brothers came to a canyon, and one climbed one side and the other stood across from him. They sharpened their spears and waited for Gaiya, the Devil Dog.

"There he is," shouted the younger boy, but the older said, "No, that is only his tongue."

"There he is."

"That is only his nose."

When the giant dog's shoulders appeared, the boys threw spear after spear, and when Gaiya was dead, they butchered him and called the people together for a great feast. They kept the tail because the spirit lived there, and they sent it back to Old Eelgin, who was still hobbling behind. When the spirit reached the Grasshopper Woman, he was so angry at her that he bit off the end of her nose.

Meanwhile, Woodbarl, the White Cloud, asked for the bones of the Devil Dog. He took them to the top of a mountain and made two small dingoes from them, one male and one female. He breathed into their mouths, and they came alive, and Woodbarl said, "You will not eat people anymore. From now on you will be afraid of people."

The child loved the story, loved it for the drama of the telling: all the howling, the thunder, the suspense of the wait for the Devil Dog. But Percy loved it more for its neatness, for the way it explained why dingoes fear men, why grasshoppers have flat noses and butcher birds have long beaks, like spears.

The story was told at the small cave in the Place of Walleroo Dreaming. There were other story sites, some of them as simple as a cottonwood tree.

The Cottonwood is the son of Woodbarl, the White Cloud, but it is not his first son. Woodbarl loved the daughter of Turramulli, the Thunderstorm, who allowed no one near her. Woodbarl fashioned a spear and threw it through the thighs of Turramulli, who jumped up in agony and chased Woodbarl to the eastern cave, where he lived. Woodbarl's son was killed by a lightning bolt hurled by Turramulli, and after Woodbarl buried his son and cut his head and shoulders in sorrow, he went to the Cottonwood Tree and sang, *"Shoo, uhna gundawooly, shoo."* He sang until the Cottonwood Tree became his new son.

Now the cottonwood tree has yellow flowers, which represent the lightning of Turramulli, and when the seed pods burst open, they show the white cloud of Woodbarl. This is the beginning of the rainy season, when the thunderstorm chases the small white clouds over the land: a handy bit of knowledge to have in a place like Cape York, where the onset of the rainy season means an immediate search for high ground.

Dream the artist as a twelve-year-old boy: For days there has been yelling and screaming, his mother insisting he is too young, his father agreeing, but his mother's brother is boss in the matter, and one night the artist is wakened roughly and taken to a new site by several of the older men. Dream his terror as they pull back his lips and an old man pushes up the boy's gums with a sharpened thumbnail. A stick of ironwood is placed against a front tooth. There is a jolt, and the tooth is gone. Concentric circles are cut in his chest with sharp knives; his nasal septum is pierced with a thumbnail, as are his ears.

After that terrible night the boy and perhaps four or five others spend three months in isolation and enforced silence. The older men explain the sign language used in hunting, and they show the tracks of various animals engraved on rock. In the end there is a crawl through the caves—the tall, thin spirit figures, quinkans, staring down from the walls—representing death and the heaven called Woolunda.

The boys emerge from the cave as newly initiated men, and they are told the sacred names of the animals, the names used only in the most important ritual of the year. It is a time just after the rainy season, when the world is green, the trees heavy with fruit, and the young animals newly born. The men leave camp in the middle of the night and walk through the dewy grass to the Place of Walleroo Dreaming. They sit for a time, just under the Great Walleroo. When the false dawn begins to glimmer in the east—this is the time of dreaming, when magic is on the land—the ritual begins. It is quickly done, for when the sun rises, it burns away the magic like dew.

One of the men pounds a heavy club on the ground, screaming. The others chant the scared name of Walleroo, and they call on Walleroo Dreaming to wake and send his children onto the land. Each man performs a dance: walleroo mating, walleroo feeding, walleroo giving birth. Walleroo Dreaming is wakened by the shouts, and he sees the dance of mating, of feeding, of giving birth; and the new walleroo are set loose on the earth, for the Place of Walleroo Dreaming encompasses all the walleroo ever born and ever to be born. Only the walleroo people can call forth the new walleroo each year.

It is the most important ritual of the year, and it must be performed properly, regularly, or the walleroo will vanish from the earth.

"The giant walleroo in that gallery," Percy Trezise told me, "is a totem. That is one meaning for the word *dreaming.*"

The artist would have been the most talented man of all the walleroo people. At the campsite, near Walleroo Dreaming, anyone might paint on the wall. A man's wife runs away with another man and he paints her face-down, with a snake eating her foot. It is a bit of crude and simple magic: Let her be bitten by a death adder and die in agony.

At the place of Walleroo Dreaming, the sacred site, all the figures are rich in magic, and the upside-down human figure under the belly of the beast is the most frightening of all. "I suspect that it is an inquest figure," Trezise said. He told me a story that had happened recently. Over on Mornington Island, some of the older initiated men had a bitter falling out. Some of them got the clothes of another, something he had sweated in, and they "sang" the clothes. When the victim heard about it, he knew that the spirit figures, the quinkans, would steal his kidney fat while he slept and that he would vomit up any food he tried to eat. The man refused to eat—he knew it was useless—and died some time later. Of starvation.

"I remember," Trezise said, "one of the old men telling me how he fought with a quinkan. He went on and on about this long fight they had, and I could see he really believed that it had happened. So I asked about the time, and where he was, and very slowly it came to me that he had dreamt this thing in his sleep. But he told me the story as if it had happened in real time."

That is the third meaning of dreaming, and it implies a certain terrible suggestibility. A figure drawn upside down—like the one under Giant Walleroo—represents death. The fact that it is in the sacred place, under the totem animal, makes it a very powerful curse, a magic so strong as to be inevitable. Four or five thousand years ago, some enemy of the Walleroo people died—killed himself in one way or another—because of that figure on the rock wall.

I dream the artist angry, as all artists are: He is no mere smudge scribbler. He doesn't concern himself with hunting-magic figures— "Hope I get a wallaby, hope I catch a fish"—he doesn't bother with simpleminded love magic—"This'll make her want me." No. He is an artist, the custodian of Walleroo Dreaming. The man who spent five years collecting white ocher. Who has the largest collection of kangaroo-hair brushes, ever. Who argued ten years for the privilege of repainting the sacred figure. Who applied a talent no other man had to the work. Who produced the brightest, the best piece of sacred art anyone had ever seen. And the stupid, ungrateful, morally blind imbeciles go and paint an inquest figure under Walleroo Dreaming.

One component of the Artist Dreaming is anger; and the artist dies an angry man. He is buried with great honor, and a small kerosene tree is pulled up and stuck upside down on his grave, the main taproot pointing west to show his spirit the way to Woolunda. Big Uncle—everyone's uncle—meets him there. The artist has the scars and the missing tooth that mark him as an initiated man, and he is allowed to enter Woolunda. All others must wander forever and drink maggoty water.

Big Uncle sets about his first task, which is to break all the artist's bones so that he cannot run away. This is a curiously painless procedure, and the artist is relieved to be rid of the rigidity of his skeleton. The feast is spread out before him, and young girls from all over have come, hoping to be chosen as wife.

At the Place of Walleroo Dreaming, the artist's protégé paints another stick figure just below and to the right of the Giant Walleroo. The artist smiles a secret smile. His soul is now secure in the Place of Walleroo Dreaming. Standing there in Woolunda—a tall, slender man, rippling with the lack of bones—he looks exactly like a spirit figure. He is a quinkan.

Percy Trezise and I were drinking beer just before sunset one day, and he said, "There are so few initiated men anymore. The rituals aren't done properly, and they aren't done regularly. I think we're losing something very important." It seemed to him that laws laid down by the ancestral beings concerning hunting were "the world's first set of ecological principles."

"They knew game was scarce and they knew how to conserve. Nowadays, you have the lumbering interests and the cattle ranches and the bauxite mines. You have all these people four-wheeling it up to Cape York. We're losing the wallabies and the dingoes and the walleroo. I never see any emus, and the giant emu is extinct."

Lahsa came in and snuffled at Trezise's leg. "Did I tell you that I did the dingo ritual?"

"Show me," I said.

"Well, it's simple, really." He stood, then walked forward, bouncing twice on each leg, occasionally lifting the right like a dingo marking his scent. There was a rhythmic chant that went along with the dance, and the sacred name of Dingo Dreaming was contained in the chant.

We walked down to the Little Laura River, Lahsa running ahead, then looking back to be sure we were following. She led us to the exposed root system of a tree that had been overturned during a flood in the last wet season. I heard some welcoming yelps. Trezise reached into a hole dug in the dirt amid the roots and pulled out a dead flying fox. There was a fat dingo pup attached to the far wing.

"Tangible results of the dingo ritual," I said.

"Yeah." Trezise handed me the pup. It squirmed comfortably and licked at my hand. "You know," he said, "one of the old men told me that when people stopped doing the ritual, all the animals would die." He reached over and scratched the pup behind the ears. "It's happening," he said.

Coming Back from Gato Island

The false dawn was gray, like ancient, tarnished silver, but in an hour the tropical sun would hang like an immense, burning weight over the remote jungle village of Tapilon. In another hour it would set the surrounding Visayan Sea aflame. All the roosters in all the Philippines—or so it seemed—were battling one another in an effort to squawk and scream that scalding sun into the sky.

The first full minute of counting, I got an incredible fifty-two cock-a-doodle-doos. Nearly one a second. Forty-three the next minute. Fifty the third.

This is a true statistic, personally compiled over two weeks' time: In the Philippine village of Tapilon, near the northern tip of the island known as Cebu, there are, on the average, forty-eight distinct cock-a-goddamn-doodle-doos per minute between the hours of five and six in the morning.

Cockfighting is a national sport in the Philippines, and any red-blooded Filipino with the space owns a couple of game roosters. There were half a dozen living just under the window in the house where I was staying. They set up their various and raucous squawks, and others would answer them on all sides, and others, farther away, would answer *them*, so that the sound assaulted the ear as a receding circular wave. The auditory effect, were it charted, would look much like the ripples made by a stone dropped into a calm pool. And a stone was dropping every minute.

One can stay in bed only so long when the cocks are disrupting the dawn at the rate of forty-eight times a minute. Consequently, this first day in the village, I rose about four hours earlier than I had planned.

I know our Philippine hosts—Anders Taneo and his family— were only trying to help, but I wasn't really ready for three sacks full of giant, poisonous sea snakes at 5:30 in the morning.

Mr. Taneo, a large, round man, more muscular than the average Filipino, had been down to the beach and had purchased the snakes from various fishermen for the edification of the film crew I was working with. He opened a sack and dumped three of them at my feet. They were about four feet long and as big around as my forearm. They writhed about on the clean wooden floor, and I stepped away from them as they made for my bare feet. All had alternating grayish stripes, though some were blue and others were black in the interstices. Anders dumped out another sack. There were eight of them now, all tangled together and slithering about in such a way that you really couldn't keep your eye on all of them. I was in a small, confined room, and there were nearly a dozen venomous snakes sliding about, and I hadn't had any coffee.

"If you want to make a film about our snakes," Anders said, "you must learn how to handle them." He grabbed one behind the neck with the thumb and first two fingers of his right hand. Anders held the snake to his face. The animal's little tongue flicked out at him.

Anders motioned that it was my turn to pick one up. He did this by waving his snake at me.

It was easier than it looked. The snakes were slow on land, and there was a knucklelike swelling just behind the head where you grabbed them. They felt dry to the touch.

"No," Taneo said, "don't squeeze them so hard. You hurt them."

After a short time, I found I could grab them at will, hold them gently, and wear them around my neck, which was the easiest way to carry them. They were poisonous, of course—all sea snakes are venomous—but they seemed passive animals, and I had the impression that I would have to mistreat them severely before they would strike. They were, I thought, quite beautiful, in a dark way, and they were fascinating, as all dangerous things are.

People, too, can be venomous, and they can strike out in murderous ways. But there is another human venom, something a man holds within himself, a venom that can poison the mind.

I had come to Tapilon to learn about the snakes. I ended up relearning a lesson about people, and myself.

I don't know why they call me on these things. I don't even know where Richard Stewart got my name. But late one winter afternoon he called and said he needed a writer for a project in the Philippines. Something about the only sea-snake industry in the world and the divers who catch the slimy beasts with their bare hands. Richard was president of a company called Ocean Realm Productions, and he seemed to be juggling about fifteen projects at once. He was going to shoot a documentary about sea snakes and sell it to ABC and use another part for a video magazine he was working on, and he'd be using a special video camera Sony had given him to test in the field, and his company had built an underwater housing for the camera, and maybe Sony would use part of the film to promote its camera. Richard said he had his entire crew together and all he needed was a writer.

I looked out the window. It was twenty below zero, and snowdrifts were piled up around the house. My dogs had refused to step outside in the morning. They stared angrily at me, determined to hold it until spring. I had never been to the Philippines, but I understood it was warm there.

"Sure," I said, "I'll go."

Looking back over my notes on that call—there were a series of calls, actually—I see that Richard never really said he wanted me to work in front of the cameras. "Maybe you can do a few on-camera interviews" is what he said. I just assumed that when he saw what a handsome, articulate fellow I am he'd be obliged to get me in every shot.

It was a mistaken impression. Manny Punay made much the

same mistake, and that's what led to the threats of piracy and murder on the high seas.

Emmanuel Y. Punay, of Cebu, was a thin, excitable fellow who wore one of those narrow, neat, dark mustaches you associate with cardsharps and door-to-door aluminum-siding salesmen. He was an authority on *Fasciata semifasciata*, the snakes we had come to film. He has written an article on the Gato Island variety for a book about the biology of sea snakes. One look at the book—Manny usually carried a copy or two with him—was sufficient to see that he had invested a good deal of ego in *Fasciata semifasciata*. The very first sentence in Emmanuel Y. Punay's article was an authoritative quotation attributed to Emmanuel Y. Punay.

The book also contained a picture of Manny holding one of his beloved snakes at a press conference in Hong Kong. Manny was wearing snakeskin shoes, a snakeskin jacket, and a snakeskin bow tie. He was smiling in a silly, sinister manner that suggested he really loved having his picture taken with sea snakes.

Manny met us at the Cebu airport and immediately produced a week-old newspaper column. It said that an American film crew was coming to Cebu, that everyone should cooperate with us, and that the resultant film would star Emmanuel Y. Punay.

In reality, the agreement between Richard Stewart and Manny Punay, as I understand it, was that Manny would be paid a certain daily fee to arrange for transportation and provide liaison with the village. Since Manny was a recognized authority on sea snakes, Richard probably promised that he'd appear in the film. He might even have said it would be a very important part of the film. Manny took it from there. He was a handsome, articulate fellow, and he was going to be a television star.

It was dark before we loaded the fifty boxes of gear onto the bus for the five-hour drive through the jungle to Tapilon, where men caught poison sea snakes with their bare hands. There were nine of us: Richard Stewart; his brother Mike, who would provide under-water camera assistance; Brian Friedman, still photographer and boat captain; Mike Van Roy, technician; Tim Cathren, associate producer; Iggy Tan and Tony Perez, Stewart's Philippine business partners; Tim Cahill, writer; and Manny Punay, world-renowned authority on sea snakes.

Manny livened up the tiring ride with jokes.

"A customer says to a waiter, 'Give me a sandwich,' and the waiter says, 'With pleasure,' and the man says, 'No, with catsup.'"

"That's a good one, Manny."

"I know another one. . . ."

Even though Manny was a soon-to-be star, he wanted us to like him, and he was trying to be one of the boys on the bus.

We arrived in Tapilon on the stroke of midnight. It was Independence Day in the Philippines, and there was a celebration in progress on the concrete playground near the school. We clambered out of the sweaty confines of the bus—a horde of children gaped at us as if we were benign extraterrestrials—and two distinguished older gentlemen escorted us to a series of chairs set just below the stage. Another man made an eloquent speech of welcome. He talked about peace and harmony, about mutual respect and the brotherhood of men. The assembled citizens—the entire village of Tapilon—gave us a standing ovation. There was no hint of fawning. The hospitality was genuine, from the heart.

Brian whispered, "Do you feel it?"

"Yeah."

"Jesus," he said, "I've never felt so honored in my whole goddamn life."

After the speeches of welcome, the celebration continued. A series of young girls, in singles and pairs, came out before the village to dance. A group of older women floated onto the concrete and danced slowly, in tandem, moving their arms sinuously, like Thai dancers. Young boys tumbled. Everyone, it seemed, had his or her moment alone before the village.

My favorite dance featured an older couple. He was tall, skinny, with a sour expression. She was short and round and jolly. They started in with a stiff fox trot, moving in the practiced, routine steps of a couple that has been together over the years. Gradually the woman seemed to become aroused. She caressed the man. He drew back, shocked. She began to run her hands over his back, buck her hips against his. He dropped her arm and broke into a stylized run, still moving to the music, a look of sour terror on his face. She kicked off her sandals and chased him. It was a funny, bawdy dance and everyone, American and Filipinos, laughed aloud.

Later, one of the village elders took us to the home of Anders Taneo, where we would sleep.

"I can't get over it," Brian said.

"What?"

"I think I love these people."

In the morning, the rooster hit forty-three crows a minute and Anders Taneo dumped the snakes on us.

There are only a dozen or so men in and around Tapilon who dive for snakes. It is a small industry, the only one of its type in the world, and the snakes seem to be in no danger of extinction or serious depletion. The day's catch is skinned on the beach, and the innards are fed to local hogs. The skins are shipped to factories in Manila, where they are processed and made into such items as ladies' handbags.

We followed the divers out to Gato Island the second day we were in Tapilon. They rode in *bancas*—big, dug-out outriggers powered by 18-horsepower Briggs & Stratton engines, which easily outdistanced our outboard-powered inflatables. It took an hour to cover the twelve miles of choppy sea, and the island loomed on the horizon like the sleeping cat it is named for. It was a little over an acre in area: an uninhabited volcanic peak, capped with a tangle of jungle. Sheer rock walls rose some sixty to eighty feet, then gave way to the inward slope and the jungle. There were caves set into the rock walls at the level of the sea. The water inside the caves was an impossible, fluorescent shade of blue.

The snakes, *Fasciata semifasciata*, lived and mate inside the caves. They trap small fish in crevasses with the coils of their bodies, paralyze them with a bite, and feed on them. They lay their eggs in various nooks and crannies. The best hunting, the divers say, is at night, when they sometimes find themselves in a great tangle of mating snakes, a sensuous, frightening serpentine ballet.

The divers sat in their bancas and finished off the bottles of anise-flavored wine they carried with them. The men of Tapilon believe that alcohol, taken internally and in sufficient quantity, thins the blood and renders a sea-snake bite less toxic. It seems to be a delicate process: drinking enough to thin the blood in case of a bite, but not so much that the diver becomes clumsy and gets bitten.

In recent years, one diver has died from a bite. Most merely feel sick and numb, and the bitten appendage swells for a day or two.

Judging themselves sufficiently inebriated, the divers donned rubber wrist bracelets made from inner tubes, and their homemade wooden goggles with the glass glued to the frame. I followed them into the cave, which was about forty feet in diameter, with a domed ceiling another forty feet high. An improbable number of tiny birds—about thirty million at a guess—were roosting in the cave, and they did not take our entry lightly. They began whirling around above, building up momentum for the swift, swooping dives they made at our exposed heads. The birds emitted high-pitched, batlike shrieks, and the cave echoed with their fury.

A diver hung in the water above one of the larger crevasses. A snake appeared, moving languidly. The diver sank toward it, swimming to a spot directly above the animal. The snake flipped its flattened tail, but the diver seized it behind the neck. He put the snake's head under the bracelet he wore on his left wrist and hung there, underwater, for a full minute and a half. He got the second snake with one lightning movement of his right hand. With two snakes in the bracelet on his left wrist, he swam out to the banca and passed the unfortunate beasts to a man who put them in a sack.

Stewart got it all on tape, and for the moment, the shoot seemed to be going, well, swimmingly.

I can pinpoint the exact moment when Manny Punay stopped wanting to be one of the boys. We had interviewed some divers in the morning. I was asking the questions and wasn't doing very well.

"Tell us how you catch the snakes."

"I grab them."

This was no good. My question would be edited out—no on-camera interview for me, handsome and articulate as I am—and the tape would show only a man describing his rather unique occupation to the camera. Manny said he thought the man was frightened by the crowd that had gathered around us, and especially by my interview technique. "He will talk to me," Manny said, and he proceeded to speak for two minutes, telling the man exactly how he caught poison sea snakes with his bare hands. The diver nodded happily, relieved that he didn't have to do any of the work.

Manny didn't seem to realize that the format called for his

question to be edited out, and that a smiling man nodding on the screen wasn't going to tell the audience very much. Still, none of us wanted to cut the interview short and make Manny look foolish in front of his friends and relatives.

That night we set up a monitor and reviewed the day's footage. As usual, there were fifty or sixty villagers in attendance. When Richard got to Manny's interview, he skipped over it in fast motion so that colors smeared themselves across the screen and the voices squeaked comically. The audience laughed.

Manny was sitting beside me. "They cut me out?"

"Not you, Manny. The diver wasn't any good."

Manny's face hardened. "They cut me out," he said bitterly. "This is my village. These are my relatives. Here my honor is paramount. They want the people to laugh at me." Manny was silent for some minutes. "Do you know," he said finally, "when a Japanese wife is raped, she commits hara-kiri. When her honor is gone, you see, she can no longer face her husband."

I got the idea that Manny had taken the incident for a mortal insult.

That night we had dinner at Anders Taneo's house. Manny was sitting next to Richard, and he was drinking more than his share of rum and beer.

"No," he screamed suddenly. "This is my village. You cannot speak to me like that. My honor is at stake."

"Okay, Manny," Richard said.

"I call the shots now."

"Okay, but I call the shoot."

Manny stared at Richard. He was smiling, but the smile seemed born of some deep pain, and it wavered on his face in a frightening and grotesque manner. "You have your boats," he said, "and you can go to Gato Island. But I assure you, you will not return from Gato Island. You will not return from Gato Island."

There was a stunned silence at the table, and we adjourned soon after. We all knew that there were pirates in the Visayan Sea. You could read about them in the paper: how they board fishing boats, kill the crew, and steal the catch and the boat. It seemed to me that Manny had threatened our lives.

A man thinks that because he travels and has friends of many different colors in many different countries, the venom isn't in him. Then a disappointed fellow with too much rum in him ruptures the poison sac with the tiniest pinprick of fear.

"It's scary as hell," Mike Stewart said. "I mean, they're always smiling at us. They seem to like us. Can he really turn them all against us?"

"I like these people," Brian said. "I want to come back here. I don't believe this."

"All he'd need is one banca," I said. "Any banca can outrun our inflatables. One banca, one man, one rifle."

"Ahh, he was drunk," Brian said.

"Yeah. He couldn't have been serious."

"Right."

But the sac had been ripped open, and the poison was festering. They were different, not like us, inscrutable. You had to look behind the smiles, because there was a dreadful darkness there.

There was a compromise reached during the night. Manny demanded money: roughly ten times his agreed-upon fee. And because Richard had to borrow from his crew, Manny felt that the money bought back his honor.

I had seen him late that evening, made a special effort to seek him out and perhaps smooth things over—or at least clarify the threat. I was haunted by a local peculiarity, the Filipinos' need for something sociologists label S.I.R.: Smooth Interpersonal Relationships. Fillipinos do not care for confrontation. Even when the content of what must be said is unpleasant, it is expected that everyone concerned will be polite, will smile. The corollary is frightening: When a Filipino becomes angry, the fury is unmoderated and can be deadly.

"Manny," I had said that night, "what exactly do you mean? It sounds"—and here I laughed a bit to show the absurdity of it—"it sounds like you're saying we'll all be killed if we go to Gato."

"These are my people. This is my beloved *barangay* [village]. Imagine, going to Gato Island without me."

"Are you saying we'll be killed?"

"You will not, I assure you, return from Gato Island."

I wasn't sure then that any amount of money could buy back the honor Manny obviously felt he had lost. But no, the problem had been worked out. Still, that morning as we launched the boats, as I joked with the children and looked into their faces, even then the venom was pumping along with the blood, so that I looked at each face differently.

"Goodbye, Joe," one of the kids called. "Goodbye."

If you were looking for it, if you had spent a bad night, you could see something conspiratorial, something sinister in each smile.

"Goodbye, Joe. Goodbye."

Manny went out to Gato with us that morning, as if nothing had happened. We shot until dusk and started back in the inflatables long after the divers had left in their bancas. Our outboards were experimental models that ran on gasoline at low rpm and diesel when the engine was running hard. In theory this was a money-saving feature. The problem was that the seas were too high. Every time we ran in diesel range, the boats swamped. We had to run on gas, at low rpm, and each of the inflatables carried only a small can of gas. All the diesel fuel in the big tank was useless.

When the biggest inflatable ran out of gas, we had to tow it with the smaller one. It was dark now, and there were some lights on the horizon that might have been coming from shore or might have been coming from fishing vessels. I don't want to overdramatize this—Mike Stewart, Brian, and Manny felt they knew where we were—but as far as I was concerned, we were lost at sea. Worse, it seemed to me that we would run out of gas soon. When that happened, there was no telling where the current might take us. It was a big, empty ocean out there.

At first I thought the fire I felt was sunburn, but when I found myself chilled, shivering uncontrollably, and sweating at the same time, I knew that I was suffering from heat exhaustion. I lay on my back, legs draped over a sack of snakes we were bringing back for the fishermen. They felt cool under my thighs, and when they moved, they were slow and deliberate, as if rearranging themselves in sleep.

The moon above was a sliver, but you could see the ball of it, faintly. It laid a path out across the water. There were clouds in the distance—great, swollen tropical towers—and they hung dark below the stars. There was lightning in the clouds, and it rumbled across the sky in immense, white-hot sheets.

The boat stirred up a phosphorescence, and our wake was a

glowing, living thing. All around us, on all sides, the sea was deep and dark and warm as blood. I drifted off—the moment of sleep felt like surrender—and my body jerked me awake. A star fell from the sky. It streaked across our bow, miles above, then dropped slowly, and more slowly still, so that it seemed to fall throughout time. There was a shower of red, and the star grew in size. It was immense in my vision, an ominous wonder that hung motionless, as in a fever dream. Slowly the redness faded to green, and it shrank and fell until it was only a thin green ray that disappeared into the dark Visayan Sea.

I thought: So here we are in a small boat lost at sea. I have been working all day under the tropical sun, and now I am shivering with the heat. Such fevers often produce a special clarity. I thought: If all this happened in the United States, there would have been no fear, and this . . . distortion . . . arose out of that difference. But it was not the United States, and we were in a small boat lost at sea. That thought came back to me, fever bright, and there was a crystalline ringing in my ears.

We were several hours overdue. In the United States, my friends would have been looking for me. There would have been lights on the beach. . . .

We saw the lights an hour away. There were dozens of them—the people of Tapilon—standing on the beach, carrying kerosene lanterns. When I stepped out of the boat, my knees buckled. A man I had never seen before helped me to my feet.

We are all in a small boat lost at sea.

3

Animal Lore

Rime of the Ancient Porcupine

This is a tale of murder most foul, of a crime against nature and man, of instant retribution. It is a tale for those who would believe that there are more things invisible than visible in the universe, and nonetheless true for the fact that it happened in the ancient times, which is to say, about 1939. It is a tale of storm blast and wondrous cold, and ice as green as emerald, a tale, in short, of a bad winter in the north country. The ice then, we might conjecture, was here, the ice was there, the ice was all around. It cracked and growled and roared and howled, as Samuel Taylor Coleridge would have it, like noises in a swound—which is a swoon—something unconscious, a frigid, brittle dream. However, this tale is no dream, but a true and locally well-known story. In the bad winter of 1939, the unholy deed was done. It happened no more than three miles from my house, tucked away in a pocketed groin of the Absaroka Mountains.

To understand the nature of the crime, however, it is first necessary to know a bit about the porcupines of the northern Rockies. They can be pestiferous animals. Sometimes called quill pigs, porcupines are actually large rodents. Vegetarians all, they enjoy the tender layer of tissue beneath the bark of living trees. When especially hungry, or perhaps in a destructive mood, porcupines may completely girdle and kill a tree. They have been known to splinter used ax handles and canoe paddles for the salt and oil they contain.

Porcupines also relish rubber. A friend of mine once parked his car at a mountain trail-head. When he returned after a week of backpacking, he found that the car wouldn't start. Some animal had gnawed through the rubber on his generator coil, shorting it out. My friend decided to wait until morning to walk the ten miles down the old logging road to the main highway and hitchhike ten more miles into town for a replacement. That night, camped by the car, he heard a satisfied scratching and a moist munching under the hood. It was, of course, a porcupine, and the beast regarded him balefully, his large nocturnal eyes glinting in the glare of the flashlight. My friend levered the porcupine off his engine block with a long branch he was saving for his fire. He might have hammered the animal to death with the same branch, but that is not done, not here in the northern Rockies.

It took a full day to get back with the part he needed. He replaced the coil, and since he was already a day late for work, he drove the car hard down the logging road. About three miles from the main highway, the temperature gauge pegged at high and steam began spurting out from under the hood. My friend was more than a little irritated to discover that in his absence the porcupine had returned and eaten a hole through the underside of his bottom radiator hose.

We have more than our share of porcupines out here at the Poison Creek Ranch. About once every six months, one of my dogs, to its detriment, tries to eat a porcupine. The dogs kill skunks with great regularity, and they return to the house with their heads held high, proud and malodorous. But when they've been quilled by a porcupine, they skulk about outside the front door, afraid and ashamed to come in for the doctoring they need.

The porcupine does not run from a dog. He will, instead, present his backside. My dogs, like a man who continually burns his mouth on the first piece of pizza, do not learn from history. They suppose an animal's arsenal is invariably located about the head, since that is so in their own species. The porcupine does not throw his quills but drives his powerful tail into the dog's mouth, leaving dozens of barbed and needlelike quills in the dog's tongue, and in the roof and bottom of its mouth.

The quills, which are modified hairs, range in size from half an inch to three inches. Since they are barbed, the quills will, with time, work their way into the dog, eventually reaching the brain and killing it. For that reason, every quill must be quickly and carefully removed. I do this with needle-nose pliers I bought especially for the operation. You want to roll the dog onto its back, under a bright light, get its mouth open, and pull out the quills. The dogs are never enthusiastic about this operation, and one of them once blackened my eye with a front paw trying to push me away. These days, I put a quilled dog into a large burlap sack, which I tie around his neck. It takes half an hour of intense and sweaty struggle to stuff a pain-crazed eighty-pound dog in a gunny sack.

I could, I suppose, wait for a fresh snow, track the porcupines, and blast them into eternity with the 12-gauge, but, as I say, that is not done in the northern Rockies. Since the days of the mountain men here, porcupines have been sacrosanct. Like the albatross in the old poem, a porcupine is considered a pious beast of good fortune, and for very practical reasons. A man or woman lost in the mountains hereabouts can usually find and kill a porcupine. In winter, especially, they show up as dark lumps in the crotches of bare trees. They do not run from man and may be killed with a branch or even a stone. The flesh, especially that of the tail, is rich and fatty, and the calories it contains may sustain a man for days. Of course, rabbits may be easily trapped, but their flesh is lean, its calories quickly burned away. There are documented tales of men who have eaten several rabbits a day while lost, men who died of what is known as "rabbit starvation."

So porcupines are slow-moving, ambulatory sources of food for the lost and injured, and that is why the killing of such a beast in any but the most dire circumstances is considered a dangerous and wanton act capable of generating the worst of luck. And in the bad winter of 1939, in the dismal sheen of the snowy cliffs, no more than three miles from my house, a man committed that very crime; and like the albatross in the old poem, the porcupine was avenged and death fires danced at night.

The man had built a wooden frame house, and he set it up on

blocks so that he would not have to dig a foundation. As the long white mountain winter set in, the man discovered a major flaw in the design. Various small animals took to living under the house for shelter and warmth. Every night there was a commotion of yips and squeaks and howls. Every night, the sickly sweet fragrance of skunk drifted up into his kitchen. The fellow was having trouble sleeping and eating, and as the drifts piled up over his windows and darkened the rooms, as the terrible psychic weight of cabin fever descended upon him, he developed a fanatical hatred for the squabbling things that lived under his house.

And so it happened that this man found a huge porcupine one dreary winter day. He was sitting on the lowest branch of a bare and icy tree, and the man who built his house on blocks looked upon that particular porcupine as the disturber of his sleep and the despoiler of his appetite. Perhaps he chuckled as he dug out the kerosene and matches. Quickly, he doused the porcupine, struck a match, and tossed it onto the animal, which erupted into a colorless flame. In his agony of fire, the porcupine ran to where he lived, ran to the area under the house. The flaming porcupine, this dying animal, set the wooden house aflame. It burned to the ground in a matter of hours.

The tale is true and can be verified. In my mind's eye I see that man, standing there thigh-deep in a drift, shivering in an icy wind and looking mournfully at the last glowing, gloating embers smoldering away in the ashy puddle where his house used to be. It was a long and bitter trek to the nearest shelter, and I like to think that this man, who set a porcupine afire, walked like one that hath been stunned and is of sense forlorn. A sadder and a wiser man, I imagine, he rose the morrow morn.

Life and Love

in Gorilla Country

T he most imperial creatures in the Garden were easily twice my size, and had they been so inclined, they could have batted the life out of my body with a casual backhand slap. I was a guest, not entirely welcome but tolerated because I abided by the rules. I stayed low and still, in a proper worshipful attitude. When I came upon a family of them on my last day in the Garden, Ndume, the one I knew best, the leader and patriarch, sighed as if to say, "You again?" He didn't exactly frown—nothing that intense— but he compressed his lips slightly, and a small vertical ridge formed in the shiny black skin just above his nose. It was an expression of mild annoyance.

I thought I read some small curiosity there as well, so I crawled forward a bit. Ndume's expression softened, and I grunted twice, a polite custom among his kind. He returned the greeting, a deep, double guttural rasp. Neither of us moved for quite some time. He sat, and I lay, in a deep green tangle of luxuriant vegetation. A drifting mountain mist cooled and dampened our faces. It was not polite to stare, so we both shifted our eyes frequently. A residue of morning rain glittered on the leaves. When I looked again, Ndume was holding his chin in the palm of his hand. He seemed to be in a contemplative mood. I smiled at him, careful not to show my teeth, for this is an aggressive and impolite thing to do. Ndume smiled back, grunted courteously, and rose up onto all fours. He moved toward me, smiling vaguely and shifting his gaze in a well-bred manner. Despite the gleaming pelt of shiny black fur, I could see muscles the size of melons rolling in his upper arms. Ndume is a "silverback," so called because of the saddle of silver hair—a sign of sexual maturity—across his broad back.

His odor was sharp: musky and sweet with a faint sour tang. He could have reached out and touched me. Instead he cocked his head slightly, like a man trying to solve a tricky but trivial puzzle. There was a rolling, cloudlike fog in the Garden now, and we regarded each other, man and gorilla, through a swirl of dreamlike mist. His eyes were a deep golden brown under the heavy black ridges of his brow. I felt unreal, strangely insubstantial, out of time, as though the mist between us was the stuff of millennia.

The Garden is Volcano National Park, which stretches forty-six square miles across the upper slopes of a chain of volcanoes known as the Virungas. The dense cloud forests there are the last refuge of Ndume, of Mrithi and Peanuts, of Mtoto and Picasso and Brutus: of an estimated two hundred mountain gorillas. These are the highest-ranging gorillas in the world and are generally thought to be the most magnificent of their species.

I had come to the tiny central African country of Rwanda braced and equipped for the Virungas, which rise to almost fifteen thousand feet, and I spent most of my time tracking and watching gorillas at an average altitude of ten thousand feet. The fact that the volcanoes are only a few miles south of the equator has no bearing on the weather. At ten thousand feet in the Virungas, "equatorial" often means cold and wet. The best new rain gear couldn't stand up to the constant and torrential downpours. It was like working in a meat locker under the spray of a fire hose.

The gorillas themselves don't much care for rain, and their day is designed to take maximum advantage of the sun. After a good thirteen hours or so in their night nests—curious-looking, carefully bordered piles of matted vegetation—the great beasts rise, feed for a few hours, drowse for an hour or two during the warmest part of the day, then feed for another four or five hours so that they will have enough energy to put in another thirteen hours of nest time. Food is abundant, and the gorillas are perfectly adapted to the forest; all they really seem to crave is the occasional sunny day.

Ndume strode off into the forest just as the sun broke through the clouds and began to burn off the mist. We were on the lower slopes of a volcano called Visoke, just above Lake Ngezi. The temperature rose to seventy degrees, and the eleven gorillas of Ndume's family were settling down for their afternoon siesta. Two infants, both less than two years old, and two juveniles, both about four, lay together in a furry heap. One of the juveniles stripped the leaves off a vine and stuffed them into his mouth. An infant reached up, grabbed the juvenile, and pulled him backward. The juvenile's mouth was open, and his face shone with a kind of idiot joy. His play chuckle, a *heh-heh-heh* sound, was barely audible. It resembled the sound a child might make laughing helplessly in church.

The largest juvenile, a six-year-old female named Picasso, climbed a small tree and stared down at me. Slowly the tree began to topple, bending until the trunk broke with a sharp crack and Picasso rolled into the dense vegetation on the forest floor. I was never able to decide whether gorillas are extraordinarily bad judges of which trees will hold them or whether they simply regard riding a breaking branch as an exciting and efficient way to get down to the ground.

Ndume clambered up the thick trunk of a huge hagenia. These are immense, gracefully expansive trees about forty feet high. The crotch formed by the trunk and the great lower branches is often large enough to accommodate several adult gorillas. Ndume found one such platform, rolled over heavily onto his back, one long arm dangling, and let the warm sun bake his chest and legs. One of the juveniles climbed up to be with Ndume, settling carefully into the big male's armpit. An infant found a soft spot to sleep in the middle of Ndume's huge belly.

There were yellow flowers blooming on the senecios and on the vine-entangled hypericum trees. Below, the surface of Lake Ngezi was as still and blue as the sky above. The chain of volcanoes stretched out, noble and massive in the distance, ranging all the way to Uganda in one direction and to Zaire in another. The infant crawled over the silverback's chest and pulled at the hair under the juvenile's chin. The two dissolved into play chuckles and rolled over Ndume's belly, wrestling indolently as the patriarch yawned, showing his massive canines.

I felt, in that bright, aureate moment, that I was watching one of the loveliest scenes on the face of the earth. It seemed like a tableau out of time: the lazy frolic, the drowsy family at peace in the provident forest, the special beauty of the lake and the mountains. I found myself thinking of the dawn of man, of the Garden of Eden.

The sensation was almost physically seductive, and I wanted the moment to last forever—especially since I carried with me a fund of ominous knowledge. What I knew tinged the idyllic setting with a sense of doom. For all the serenity of the place, I could not help dreading the specter that haunted it—a specter that one writer has called "the black suction of extinction." The signs of it were glaringly apparent. Ndume, for example, has no right hand. Chances are that he lost it in a poacher's trap. And chances are that his predecessor, a patriarch named Stilgar, was also a victim of poachers. If so, it is likely that the poachers cut off his head and hands, boiled them to remove the flesh and then sold the skull and skeletal hands to tourists.

Poaching is an emotional and well-publicized issue, but the gorillas face an even greater danger. They are caught up in a grave and perhaps insoluble crisis that has grown out of the history of Rwanda and involves painful decisions about the very survival of the gorillas and the people of the area. Unlike most cases involving the extermination of animals, the situation in the Virungas is not one in which the needs of the animals and those of the people are mutually exclusive. In the long run, there is an identity of interest for all the inhabitants of the region. Most lives, however, are conducted in the very short run.

Long, long ago, the inhabitants of the area were the Twa, aboriginal Pygmies who survived primarily by hunting. They were conquered by an agricultural people called the Hutu. These farmers viewed the forest as an enemy and set about clearing it to raise crops. Around 1000 A.D. the Tutsi (sometimes called the Watutsi) arrived from the north. The Tutsi were herdsmen who by and large left the forest alone and frustrated the agricultural ambitions of the Hutu, whom they quickly enslaved. In 1959 the Hutu, bearing centuries of anger, finally rose up against the Tutsi. One of the revolutionary slogans translated roughly as "Let's cut these people down to size"— a reference to the fact that the Tutsi are the tallest people on earth. The Hutu meant their slogan literally, and legless Tutsi bodies choked the forest streams. Thousands of survivors fled to neighboring countries.

Since then, the Hutu have restored the subsistence farming ethic and have changed the face of Rwanda. Vast stretches of primal forest have been cleared to make way for self-contained family farms that average a mere 2.5 acres and that barely keep people alive. Now, with land growing scarce, local farmers are looking to Volcano National Park for more cropland. Just twelve years ago, forty square miles—or almost half of the park—were turned over to cultivation. That single act was the most important factor in the reduction of the mountain gorilla population from an estimated 450 in 1960 to about 200 in 1981. The advantages to the people were illusory and short-lived for the simple reason that the countryside that nurtures the gorillas also nurtures the people. The vegetation of the Garden acts as a spongy reservoir, releasing water to the rivers in the dry seasons and storing moisture during rainy periods. It is hardly a coincidence that the smaller rivers below the areas cultivated twelve years ago are now dry and that local people report that the water stopped flowing at just about the time the cultivation began. Further cultivation will cause more sedimentation and erosion, then drought and famine. If the Virunga watershed is destroyed by cultivation, the gorillas will surely perish. But so too, eventually, will the people.

The government of President Juvénal Habyarimana understands this equation, and it is firmly committed to protecting the park. But the pressures for more farmland are going to be very great in the next few years. You can feel it at the edge of the park: the need and the press of hungry humanity. The farms, called shambas, roll bare and treeless right up to the forest, and as many as 780 people work and live on each square mile.

On the last day I visited the creatures of the Garden, Ndume had chosen to feed and doze no more than a hundred yards from the place where the shambas began. I sat somewhat above him, watching him watch the people hoeing potatoes or harvesting pyrethrum. Children shouted in play, men drove goats with whistles, and women called to one another across the fields. Ndume, with his long, handsome, sensitive face and troubled soft brown eyes, sat still and silent and stared into the teeming shambas below.

Early one May morning, I was standing by the night nests of a six-member family known as Group 13. A trail led away from the nesting site, and Mark Condiotti, who works for the conservation organization known as the Mountain Gorilla Project, was showing me how to track the animals. It wasn't all that difficult. A group of twenty men crawling on their hands and knees might have made such a path through the thick undergrowth. Occasionally we passed through what amounted to a leafy tunnel: the vegetation was trampled below but undisturbed at a height of about four feet.

We found ourselves in a thick stand of bamboo. There was a strange, unsettling, subaqueous quality to the light, a sense of shimmering twilight, and through the ten- and fifteen-foot-high stalks we could just make out several bear-size black shapes, moving slowly. I cleared my throat several times quite loudly.

The sound is called a double belch vocalization, DBV for short. Gorillas make the sound by a rasping inhalation and exhalation of breath. Humans make it by clearing their throats. The first time the sound is short and emphatic; the second sound follows immediately and is softer, more drawn out.

DBVs are sounds of reassurance. Gorillas move slowly, and any abrupt action might be interpreted as a threat, so they make the sounds before changing position or when moving into the proximity of another individual. It is a convenient way to signal lack of aggressive intent, and it's a handy thing for human visitors to know.

We were looking for Mrithi, Group 13's silverback, but we ran into Mtoto, a charming three-year-old. She spotted us and batted her chest—*pockety-pock-pock-pock*—then gave us a slow sideways glance. We smiled, without showing our teeth.

Mtoto stood and walked across some broken bamboo stalks. She pounded her protruding belly and occasionally glanced in our direction to see how intimidated we were by this terrifying display. Mtoto weighed about thirty pounds. One of the bamboo stalks broke under her, and she fell onto her back. She passed wind in several prolonged toots, then lolled her head over a piece of bamboo and stared, her soft brown eyes sinking absurdly into the top of her head.

The clouds broke and sunlight pierced the bamboo grove in several oblique shafts like light streaming into a cathedral. Mtoto strutted off to join the others, who were moving even more slowly now. They seemed sated and ready for their afternoon siesta. We found Mrithi in an open, grassy glade. He stared at us, pounded the flats of his hands on the ground four times, then walked away, leading his group deeper into the shimmering world of the bamboo grove.

Gorilla faces read like human faces: the animals smile when they are content, frown when they are not, and display an infinite number of nuances. Some have long hair, some short, and a few of the males sport little goatees. I spent about thirty hours no more than ten feet from the gorillas and met almost forty individuals.

Personalities varied as much as appearances. The juveniles tended to be bold, curious, mischievous; the adults were more restrained. Beethoven, Group 5's silverback, is immense, a dignified aging patriarch, a William Howard Taft of a gorilla. Brutus has the slicked-back hair of a 1950s juvenile delinquent and a mean, pinched face. He is the one gorilla in the Garden who attacks humans—and I was determined to meet him.

I liked Mrithi as much as any silverback I've met, and I visited him several times. But he is a gorilla who lives in the bamboo, and some researchers think this dark and visually limited world makes the animals who live there more aggressive toward strangers. Mrithi charged me twice, but one of those charges veered off so quickly that I could see he was not coming for me at all. One of his favorite tricks is a forward charge of about eight feet, followed by an abrupt attempt to push a stalk of bamboo down on his victim. Unfortunately, the bamboo was often tangled above, and Mrithi was unable to dislodge it. Worse, small pieces of vegetation ended up falling onto his own back. He is not, I'm afraid, the most intimidating silverback alive— that would be Brutus—and Mrithi's ineffectual rages always reminded me of the cartoon character Elmer Fudd.

Still, when a silverback pounds the ground, you want to respect him, and so we waited several minutes before tracking him again. The second time we found him, Mrithi treated us to a halfhearted series of cough-grunts, an *eh-eh-eh* vocalization sometimes called a pig grunt because of its slightly swinish resonance. The sound is a warning.

"He's still excited about the interaction with the other group a few days ago," Mark said. "We'll try one more time, and if he retreats, I think we ought to leave him alone."

The "interaction" was a brief fight between Mrithi and the silverback of another group. Rosalind Aveling, who, along with her husband, Conrad, handles tourism and education for the Mountain Gorilla Project, had been tracking Group 13 that day. She noticed that Mrithi led the group through the bamboo without allowing them to feed, which was unusual, and that he was guiding them directly into an area occupied by a second family of gorillas.

Suddenly Ros heard an outbreak of screaming and hooting. She hurried toward the sound, but the gorillas had gone. In the flattened greenery on the sloping forest floor, Ros found silverback dung. Next to the dung was a patch of fresh blood.

About thirty yards farther on, Ros found Group 13. They were bunched closely together on top of a ridge. The second group was huddled below, in the depths of a ravine. Mrithi was strutting along the top of the ridge, beating his chest and hooting. The silverback below responded with chest beats and hoots.

No one knows for sure why Mrithi chose to lead his group directly into the teeth of the second group that day, but a factor to be considered is Ijicho, Mrithi's flighty and attractive constant companion (almost) and the female lead of this little soap opera. At about eight years of age, Ijicho is just starting her regular four-day-a-month estrous cycle, and she was in heat on the day of the altercation. Female gorillas often pass over to other groups, and Mark thinks that Ijicho tried to join the second group and that Mrithi had been obliged to follow her.

A. H. "Sandy" Harcourt, the director of the research center at Karisoke, doubts that Ijicho would have traveled such a distance to change groups, for records indicate that most transfers take place while two groups are in sight of each other. Personally, I hate it when science gets in the way of a good story, and I like to think that Mrithi rose one morning to find Ijicho gone. I choose to believe that he followed her out of a sense of burning loss and implacable rage, that he fought for her and won.

Ijicho was in estrous the next day, but no copulation was observed, and the day after that, Ijicho approached Mrithi boldly as he lay in his day nest. She stared into his eyes and made a light, moaning vocalization. Mrithi sprawled grandly on his back and emitted a dismissive neighing sound. I like to think he was punishing her for her attempt to abandon him.

On the last day of Ijicho's cycle, I was pleased to find that she and the others had settled down into a pleasant open field full of succulent thistles. Gorillas are particularly fond of these prickly plants and seem to consider them a great delicacy. Mrithi sat cross-legged in his nest. He folded his arms over his chest, and his black fur glistened like metal in the warm afternoon sun. His head and upper body were immense. He looked like some pagan idol, a god of immense strength and insatiable appetite.

We were fifteen yards away. The silverback uncrossed his arms, scratched his head, and sighed. The thistles were delicious, the glade was open to the sun, and he was ready for his nap.

About half an hour later, Ijicho rose from her own nest nearby. She approached Mrithi, moaning in a low, guttural fashion. He woke up, and they stared into each other's eyes for several seconds.

"They're courting," Mark whispered.

Ijicho stood on all fours, her face on a level with Mrithi's. They continued to stare.

"I think we're going to have a copulation," Mark said.

Ijicho reached out with her right hand, a slow, tentative movement. Mrithi rose up onto his knees. Simultaneously, Ijicho turned away from him, presenting her backside. He entered her and began stroking. His great bulk—Mark estimated his weight at 350 pounds—covered the female, who seemed far less than half his size.

Mtoto, the mischievous juvenile, moved closer to the silver-back's nest. Mrithi began stroking faster. His lips were pursed, and he began hooting—a relatively high-pitched *hoo, hoo, hoo*—in time with his strokes. Mtoto studied the action. I thought I read both bewilderment and fascination in her eyes.

It was over in less than two minutes. Ijicho simply wandered away and began browsing on thistles. Mrithi sat up in his nest and stared at the humans with a blank and unfathomable expression. He looked entirely regal.

"They copulate nearly every month," Mark said. "She's been going through some adolescent sterility. God, I hope she's pregnant this time."

It was too moody a day to sit in a graveyard, any graveyard, but this—the final resting place of nine mountain gorillas, with nine rustic wooden markers—set the mind diving into some dark and chilling waters. Yellow-green moss clung to the trunks of the surrounding trees. A lighter green variety drippped like beaded drapery from the top, outermost branches. A fine mist hung in the air and drifted, silver-gray, through the green world above. Somewhere below, thunder rumbled.

The graveyard is located at Karisoke, behind the big house where Dr. Dian Fossey lived for thirteen years until she left in 1980. It was Fossey who discovered that gorillas could be habituated to the presence of humans. And it was she who changed the public's perception of gorillas: the "savage apes" became "gentle giants." Fossey was often pictured with Digit, a magnificent silverback, and the two were often seen touching. Those photos struck an emotional chord. There was a mystical echo of God and Adam reaching out to touch and understand each other, as in the Sistine Chapel. Part of Group 4, one of Fossey's study groups, was slaughtered by poachers in 1978 after Digit himself had been killed trying to protect his family. His mutilated body was found later.

It began to rain lightly in the graveyard at Karisoke. Not far away, on a day like this one, I had gone with photographer Nick Nichols and Conrad Aveling to see the notorious Brutus. We all knew that if Brutus continued to charge and bite people, someday he might kill someone.

Ever since George Schaller's pioneering work with the mountain gorilla in 1960, it had been known that no gorilla will attack a man who holds his ground. No gorilla except Brutus. The records at Karisoke indicate that he has injured three people in twelve years; local people put the number at six or seven, and they tell lurid tales of entire calf muscles being stripped away from the leg by those great teeth.

We started at about noon. Our information was that Brutus had last been seen at the ten-thousand-foot level of Visoke, on the Mount Karisimbi side. Down below, in the mud-hut village of Bisate, someone was pounding a drum. It was, from this distance, less rhythmic than mechanical: thump . . . thump . . . thump . . . thump . . . and so on until, it seemed, the end of time.

After hours of painful climbing through chest-high nettles, it was a relief to enter a sloping hagenia meadow. To our right, great dripping branches hung cantilevered over a gaping canyon, which looked as if it were carpeted in green velvet at its greatest depth. Thunder rolled, and the drums thudded out their mechanical counterpoint.

Finally, we found a nest that was bigger than any I had seen before. The dung it contained was, by careful scientific measurement, ten centimeters in width. Enormous. "Brutus," I said and stared down at the dung feeling foolish and afraid.

Just then the sky ripped apart and rain hammered down endlessly, relentlessly, while thunder rolled and the drums of Bisate continued to thump away. Gorillas hate rain. It makes them evil tempered, and Brutus was grouchy on the sunniest of days.

No one knows why Brutus has become a savage and atypical gorilla. He has ranged close to the shambas for years, and the locals used to make money by taking curious visitors up to see him. These inexperienced guides knew nothing of Fossey's habituation methods: they were noisy, apt to run, clumsy, and aggressively impolite. Perhaps Brutus has been pushed beyond the limits of gorilla endurance. Perhaps he is angry at the whole damned human race. He too sits at the edge of the park, but he is not silent. He roars down into the shambas, and the people below tremble at the sound.

The trails kept turning back on themselves, and after four hours we decided to give up on the search. Conrad wanted to try one more path, but Nick and I sat, exhausted, on the rim of Brutus's nest. The sound we heard started off at a high pitch, like a cock crowing— provided the cock in question weighs over four hundred pounds. It rose in pitch and volume so that it sounded for a moment like something ancient and reptilian. In the forest, above the spot where Conrad must have been, we could see the foliage parting rapidly on a downhill vector, and the scream dropped into a lower register, as will a donkey's bray. It seemed then as if there was more than one voice raised, and Nick shouted, "Christ, Conrad's being mauled!" We sprinted up the hill, and the scream now sounded like leopards or lions, like dragons in combat. It broke off into a piercing, defiant yowl, and its echo reverberated out of the green velvet depths of the ravine.

But Conrad had stood his ground, and Brutus had stopped about five yards away. Later, we pieced it together. Brutus had been sitting in a field of nettles, waiting out the rain. Gorillas sometimes seem so depressed by the rain that they neglect to seek shelter; they sit, shivering and miserable, with the water drumming on their heads and a clear mucus running from their noses. When Conrad approached on a trail that led directly to Brutus's field of sorrow, the gorilla took it all out on him. He charged directly downhill, screaming and roaring, lips pulled away from his black tartar-covered teeth, wet hair plastered to his head.

All I ever saw of Brutus was his black shape as he lumbered back up the hill, muttering and cursing as much as gorillas can be said to mutter and curse. He turned to roar once more and disappeared into the jungle. Off in the distance, the clouds parted over Karisimbi and the mountain shone with a red-orange spectral glow.

"He stopped this time," I said.

"Yeah," Conrad said. "Maybe he's been reading Schaller."

Maybe. Sitting in the gorilla graveyard, I found myself smiling at the memory of Brutus. So he's not your average silverback. I like to think of him ranging close to the shambas, howling and screaming and roaring at the people below. I like to think that he *knows*; and I like to think that those echoing roars have a significance beyond anger and defiance.

No one knows if the gorillas will survive. Researchers believe that with proper management, poaching can be stopped and the Virungas can be spared. Given these conditions, the gorillas will survive, and they may even multiply.

I looked down at one of the graves. It had not been tended in some time. Thistles had grown up around the marker, and when I moved them, I read the name Digit. I thought of Group 13, of

Mrithi and Ijicho feeding on thistles like gourmands, making love in a field of thistles on a special sunny day. It seemed to me that thistles were a fine and appropriate funerary flower for a gorilla like Digit. I hoped Ijicho was pregnant.

The Clown Owl's Bitter Legacy

I was camped up by Elbow Lake making a bowl of Mountain
House instant applesauce when it occurred to me how much I
loathe and despise Woodsy Owl. Mountain House advises users
to pack out the foil package—good for you, Mountain House—but
they ruin the effect by including a drawing of Woodsy. The clown
owl, in this peculiar depiction, was carrying a backpack and wearing
a hat with—get this—a feather on it. An owl with a feather in his
hat is obscene. It's like a man walking around with a severed human
finger stuck in his hatband.

Later, I conducted my own informal, unscientific survey and
discovered that most people are basically neutral about this lackwit
owl, this driveling goody-goody. But ask yourself: Would I rather
have a drink with the Crime Dog and get some gravelly voiced
advice on how to take a bite outta crime, or would I like to stroll
around Central Park with some nincompoop fowl?

Woodsy Owl, to my way of thinking, has no dignity. He is
supposed to be a symbol of our great parks and wild lands, and yet he
looks like he ought to be leading cheers in some bush-league
baseball park. Even then, in my mind's eye, I see all 750 people

attending the game howling in rage and flinging beer cans at this fat, shambling, grounded fake.

At this very moment, I have a phone number on my desk. Just one quick call and I can find out how the bird was born and who is responsible for the noxious muppet. But how much more satisfying to speculate. Woodsy clearly is the product of some committee. Take the matter of size. Why is the bird bigger than most kids and smaller than most adults? I see a bunch of people sitting around a table discussing this very matter.

"Yeah, well, he ought to be like a big brother to the kids, see, but not threatening to adults."

"Right, perfect. And he ought to *skip* everywhere he goes so the kids will identify with him."

"We'll give him big floppy yellow clown's feet."

Can you imagine someone trying to make Smokey the Bear wear clown feet? Smokey had size, dignity, and a legend to match the Lone Ranger. An actual bear cub, Smokey was found badly burned after a disastrous forest fire. Compassionate rangers nursed the lone survivor back to health, and one gets the impression that it was Smokey himself who decided to devote his life to the fight against fires set by careless campers.

Everything about Smokey had meaning. He wore a hat and pants to show that he was an orphan, to underscore the fact that he was raised by rangers. Mom and Dad were mere spots of bear grease, long since absorbed into the mute forest loam. There was a certain sadness in Smokey's gruff, gentle warning: "Remember, only you can prevent forest fires." But for all his enforced domesticity, despite the pants and hat, Smokey never wore a shirt. He wanted you to know that he was a bear—a great big powerful bear with a score to settle, an orphan's rage burning in his massive chest. You got the distinct impression that if you were careless with matches in the woods, Smokey might show up on your doorstep one day and rip your lungs out.

There is absolutely no threat factor in this new bird. Here's Mom and Dad out at the campsite, having martinis in the Winnebago. Junior and Sis are playing tag outside among the redwoods, and they stop for a Twinkie. Junior tosses the wrapper on the ground. Here comes fat, floppy, feeble little Woodsy. "Hoo, hoo, give a hoot, don't pollute."

"Dad, come quick. There's a little guy out here in a funny suit and he's bothering us."

The camper door slams open and there's Dad. "Get away from my kids," he bellows, "you perverted little creep." Dad turns back to the door. "Milly, get the sheriff on the CB and tell him there's a dwarf in a chicken suit molesting children out here." Now Dad takes a few threatening steps toward Woodsy. The forest is silent. Sis tosses *her* Twinkie wrapper on the ground.

"Hoo, hoo, give a . . ."

"Get outta here!" Dad towers over the trembling bird, and Woodsy decides, what the hey, a couple more Twinkie wrappers aren't really worth a beating. He turns and skips away in floppy-footed terror, skips because it is his only mode of locomotion, and the skipping so irritates Dad—convinces him finally that he's dealing with a dangerous pervert—that he launches a furious kick to the bird's backside, lifting him a foot or two off the ground.

"Yay, get him, Dad," the kids cry as Woodsy skips stiffly off into the forest dragging one floppy yellow foot.

Now if you really need some flying thing to remind you not to pollute, I suggest Rodan, the winged reptile who used to battle Godzilla in those Japanese monster movies of a decade ago. That was one fearsome pterodactyl, Rodan. Almost as big as Godzilla himself, Rodan had fearsome talons and a great, ripping beak.

An effective series of TV commercials would have Rodan flying unseen above a group of careless backpackers camped too close to a mountain lake, tossing litter in all directions. Next shot: Sergio Leone-type close-up of Rodan's burning red eyes, sound up on an awesome scream. Below, in subtitles, the words appear: "I'm extinct because of you, you bastards with your Kelty packs."

Commercial two gets to the meat of the matter. Same site, same careless campers. A good-looking young woman tosses a cigarette butt into the lake. Sound up on the Rodan scream, a whooshing from the sky. Montage of the campers' faces staring upward in horror. Cut to: the girl swept off the ground by giant talons, her screams fading in the distance. Cut to: a long shot of Rodan picking, like a vulture, at something moist and pink on the ground. Close-up of the great scaled head rising in murderous triumph. The sound of the Rodan scream. Subtitles read: "Don't pollute or I'll rip you to shreds."

Unfortunately, instead of some perfectly acceptable and effective reptilian terror, we're stuck with this bonehead. Woodsy—or some little guy dressed up like him, anyway—does come around to some of the grade schools here in Montana. He hands out seeds for spruce trees. The kids are supposed to plant them. Fine, except that this is a semiarid grassland where no spruce grows. What a way to help kids appreciate nature. Plant a seed, kill a tree. Every spring a child asks, "Mom, why does Woodsy lie to us?"

The rare spruce tree that makes it will grow slowly. By the time the child is ready to leave home, the spruce may be chest high, a twisted, stunted, grotesque caricature of a tree, something out of an Edgar Allan Poe story, a haunted, crippled, gnarled thing: the clown owl's bitter legacy.

The Shame of Escobilla

P eople often speak of holy places—areas that are awesome or harsh or tranquil—but you seldom hear of a place that is evil. I know of one. It is located on several acres of low tropical hills, in the Mexican state of Oaxaca. The hills are green and there is a view of ocean, and these acres represent evil in a very pure form.

Here the senses are assaulted. An odor of death and putrescent meat rises up from these hills. Animal bodies are piled four and five feet deep, left to rot and dry under a blazing sun. As many as fifty vultures pick at the purple and black meat. They work with a joyless efficiency, steadying the carcasses with their talons as they yank at the soft flesh with their powerful beaks. The weight of all those bodies rotting generates an intense heat, so that when a breeze springs up, the air becomes artificially warm, heavy with death and decay. Standing in the path of such a breeze, one is left feeling fouled, hopeless, unholy.

Everywhere there is the constant droning of flies. The air is black with them. Working among the vultures and the flies in the awful stench are the most unfortunate people of the local villages: there is one man with a horribly contorted spine, another whose right eye is a mass of scar tissue. These men stumble over the rotting reptilian bodies like sinners confined to some virulent lower level of hell.

The final evil is there also. Not only are mature animals slaughtered and left to rot in the sun, there is also an immense pile of eggs—the next generation—and these, mixed with the entrails of their mothers, are rotting too. The entire pile is covered with maggots, a heaving mass of hissing malevolence.

That pile and those rotting bodies may signal the last time sea turtles will mass on the beach at Escobilla to lay their eggs. The carnage is being carried on despite the good intentions of the Mexican government. The motive is simple and timeless. It is sheer greed.

Two hundred million years ago reptiles owned the earth. There were turtles then as there are turtles now. It is thought that they developed from a marsh-dwelling lizard that hunched its shoulders forward, protecting its head with hard scales, in case of attack. Over millions of years these animals developed a shell, called a carapace, and a horny undershell, called a plastron. The body itself twisted into a strange configuration to conform to the confines of the shell.

About 90 million years ago, several species of turtle took to the sea. The stumpy, cylindrical legs became thin, flattened flippers. It was the last radical move these living dinosaurs ever made. As the stem reptiles gave rise to birds and to mammals, as the last brontosaurus thundered to earth, the turtles plodded on, survivors.

Today there are seven generally recognized species of sea turtle. One, the Pacific or Olive Ridley, an eighty-pound animal with a shell the size of a manhole cover, is found in the warmer waters of the Pacific from southern Japan to Baja California. Like nearly all reptiles, the Ridley lays eggs, and these the females deposit in the sand on certain small stretches of isolated beach. In many places, nesting females are slaughtered out of hand, even before they can lay their eggs, and in other spots locals may collect nearly 100 percent of the eggs laid. For this reason, the 1975 reptile *Red Data Book* lists the Pacific Ridley as endangered: "In danger of extinction and whose survival is unlikely if the causal factors keep operating."

In Mexico, the government has established an enlightened program of turtle conservation. Beaches are patrolled, egg poaching is illegal, and reasonable quotas have been set for harvesting the animals. On the beach at Escobilla, about two hundred miles south of Acapulco, nesting female Ridleys come up out of the surf between the months of July and November. The massings occur about once a month, on certain star-swept nights when the moon is entering its last quarter and when the winds blow inland from the sea. Local people call this an *arribazón*, and some say that as many as two hundred thousand turtles have laid their eggs on one four-mile stretch of beach in previous years. If this estimate is even close, Escobilla is the site of the largest arribazón in the Americas.

On Saturday, October 1, 1977, I stood on the beach at Escobilla in company with an ABC-Sports TV crew filming an *American Sportsman* segment. The show concerns itself with celebrities and their adventures with and reactions to animals. The arribazón was fine meat for *Sportsman*. One of the celebrities was *Outside's* Jack Ford, who had informed me of the expected October arribazón. The ABC crew was gracious enough to make room for me on their charter flight from Acapulco to Puerto Ángel, an hour's drive from the beach.

No one lived on the sand itself—no fresh water—but nearby there was a compound composed of a *palapa* and several red tents housing eleven Mexican marines who patrolled the beach to prevent egg poaching.

We arrived in time to see the *morriña*, the hatching of eggs laid during a previous arribazón. The beach was pocked with small depressions. As I watched, the sand would suddenly collapse into itself and, miraculously, a small black flipper would appear, the black dot of a head would emerge, and finally the hatchling—not quite the size of a quarter and all black like some child's toy stamped out of hard rubber—would move off resolutely toward the sea. Ten, twenty, thirty, and more would dig their way out from the same spot.

The eggs were about the size of Ping-Pong balls. When I found one hatchling struggling to break the shell, I peeled it away. The turtle was curled over a bright, yellow-orange yolk to which it had been connected by a kind of umbilical cord. The hatchling pulled away from the yolk—the little mark on the bottom of the plastron is called a yolk scar—and crawled off toward the water.

All up and down the beach, tiny turtles were making their way out to sea. There were half a dozen men walking the beach with white styrofoam boxes, collecting the hatchlings. I saw dozens of boxes containing about two hundred animals apiece, and was told that the men were doing something scientific that had to do with the preservation of the Ridley. No one seemed willing to tell me any more than that.

Later, I sat under the palapa watching the sunset with Juan José de la Vega and Bob Nixon. De la Vega, twenty-nine, is director of the Cosmographic Society, a Mexican conservationist group. He wears his hair to his shoulders, sports a wide gold bracelet, and speaks good English in a relaxed, offhand fashion. Nixon, the writer for the *Sportsman* segment, is blond, crisply efficient, and, at the moment, he was clearly unhappy with Juan José for what appeared to be good reason.

De la Vega had proposed the segment to Nixon, indicating that the turtles of Escobilla were in danger, that a man named Antonio Suárez, owner of a company called PIOSA, was slaughtering the animals out of hand. "Soon," Juan José said, "there will be no more arribazónes at Escobilla."

The problem was that Nixon and I had just learned that the men with the styrofoam boxes worked for Antonio Suárez, that this same Suárez had footed most of the bill for a new laboratory for the study and preservation of the turtles, and that this lab was supposed to put hundreds of thousands of hatchlings into the sea each year. The next day, Sunday, officials from the Mexican Department of Fisheries and the governor of Oaxaca would be on hand at a ceremony to dedicate the lab and, incidentally, honor Antonio Suárez and his contribution to the conservation of the Pacific Ridley turtle.

I'm pretty sure Nixon felt as I did: Juan José had attacked Suárez out of sheer lust for publicity. I told de la Vega as much, to his face.

Oaxaca was in the midst of a terrible drought, but dedication day, Sunday, dawned pale and cold, and a wet wind howled in from the sea bringing torrential rains. The important visitors would first inspect the PIOSA slaughterhouse, then move on to the nearby lab. Official cars bogged down on the muddy road from Puerto Ángel to the slaughterhouse, and a large banner welcoming the governor wrenched loose from a tree and whipped itself into tatters.

People dashed from the cars to the shelter of the slaughter-house. Workers, dressed in green T-shirts and shorts, stood nervously about, surreptitiously ogling the important visitors. There was a pile of live turtles, helpless on their backs, in one corner of the room. They barely moved. Occasionally a flipper would jerk in a sad, spasmodic gesture.

In the center of the room was the killing table. It was a long, wooden affair accommodating ten turtles, and the front was canted down at a slight angle. The turtle was lifted onto the sloping surface, and the neck was placed in a semicircular scoop on the ledge at the downside of the table, so that the head was held stationary, in midair. The weight of its body against the ledge prevented the animal from moving. The turtles had lost their green sea color and looked as gray as the sky outside. The eyes were solid black and without expression.

One of the workmen drew a curious, silver gun with a wide red-skirted barrel. The Mexican camera crew moved in for a close-up. The gun was placed on top of the turtle's head. We heard a muffled thump. The animal's head jerked up, the black eyes bulged, a great lump formed at the throat, formed again, the mouth opened wide, snapped shut, and the eyes turned fluid and pale. Great gouts of dark blood burst from the turtle's head. Another man carried the dying animal to a spot near a short conveyor belt. A grooved tube caught the blood and carried it out of the slaughterhouse and about twenty yards down the beach into a cove.

"On killing days," Juan José whispered, "the cove is red with the blood of these turtles."

"Sure, Juan," I said.

The conveyor belt carried the turtle to another room where it was placed on a slaughtering table. Every turtle I saw gutted that day was a female, and all of them had eggs in their oviducts. The eggs and entrails were placed in a large plastic bucket. Later, I was told, the eggs would be taken to the new lab and buried in the sand and new turtles would grow from these eggs.

It was not, all in all, a very pleasant hour. When one of the ABC cameramen expressed some disgust with the carnage, a young Mexican biologist who spoke fluent English blistered him with an eloquent torrent of words. She was a plump, darkly attractive woman wearing very thick glasses. Mexico, she said, is a poor country. These turtles are a natural resource. They graze on their own, in the sea, at no expense to the people, and return every year for the slaughter. She and the other biologists would help set quotas so the turtles would survive, even prosper. "But you don't want us to harvest these animals," she said. "Then what will we eat?"

She referred not only to the twelve pounds of meat recovered from each turtle, but also to the money made by the fishermen, by the people who worked in the slaughterhouse, and by those who fashioned the turtle leather. Even the bones of the slaughtered animals were left to dry, then ground into fertilizer. "Why don't you go back to your own country," she concluded bitterly, "and film your own turtles?" Her eyes glittered angrily behind her glasses.

Monday we went to see the lab. It was a sterile, newly constructed building only half a mile north of the slaughterhouse. I counted ninety-six small sea-water tanks containing about two hundred hatchlings apiece, and ten larger tanks holding five hundred hatchlings apiece. About twenty-five thousand turtles in all, exactly the same size as the ones we had seen at Escobilla, and all, I was told, hatched at the lab.

We couldn't find a biologist in charge, but the workers said the hatchlings would be kept a week or two, maybe three, then released at sea, beyond the breakers. At Escobilla, I had seen the surf pound in and watched as the tiny hatchlings had been tumbled back onto the sand for hours. I had seen some eaten by crabs and was told that certain fish massed beyond the breakers and fed on the hatchlings as they swam out to sea. The turtles in the lab would be spared many of the usual causes of infant mortality.

On the beach, in front of the lab, there were eggs buried in the sand, and these were penned to discourage such predators as dogs and coyotes. In another area I saw a large, open-sided building containing hundreds of the styrofoam boxes. Each was filled with sand and held over one hundred eggs. There were two kinds of eggs buried in the sand and contained in the boxes: those laid naturally and taken from the beach at Escobilla and those taken from the oviducts of slaughtered females.

Two large tanks, containing mature males and females, had been constructed for the study of mating behavior.

A plaque on the front of the main building said that the lab was dedicated to the preservation and study of the turtles and that it was built by the government, by the fishing unions—called *co-operativas*—and by private enterprise. That last meant PIOSA— Pesquera Industrial Oaxaqueña Sociedad Anónima—and Antonio Suárez. PIOSA had put up most of the money for the lab. Even Juan José admitted that. The lab seemed a perfect example of enlightened self-interest.

It wasn't until much later that night that certain things began bothering me. Some of the men working at the lab were the same men I had seen collecting turtles at Escobilla for that unspecified "scientific" purpose. Many of the men working at the lab were the same men I had seen gutting turtles at the slaughterhouse the day before. They all wore the same green T-shirts and shorts.

We had come to the lab unannounced. When we got there the men were taking the hatchlings out of the tanks and putting them in the boxes. We asked why. The tanks, we were told, were dirty, and since the pipes weren't working, they had to be emptied, cleaned, and filled with new sea water. This made sense. Except . . . looking back on it, not one of the tanks was refilled until it became apparent to the workers that we meant to stay for some time.

It was Monday. The governor and the officials had left. Was it possible that the turtles we saw—the ones supposedly hatched at the lab—had been brought in from Escobilla? For a day? For the governor's visit and the dedication? No, it hardly seemed possible. I was thinking like Juan José.

Still, it seemed worth another visit to the lab.

Slaughterhouse cove is a shove-off point for the turtle fishermen. They leave in shifts, two men to a thirty-foot skiff powered by a forty-horsepower Johnson outboard. It is a forty-minute run north to Escobilla, and, during nesting season, when the females are massing a mile out for the arribazón, there are turtles everywhere, as far as the eye can see. As many as a hundred animals may be contained in an area the size of a city block.

Like all reptiles, the Pacific Ridley is dependent on external stimuli to regulate its body temperature. Primarily vegetarians, they feed on sea grasses in the early morning, then pull to the surface to bask in the warmth of the sun. As their body temperature rises, metabolic activity increases, digestion occurs more rapidly, and the stomach is emptied in preparation for another meal. When basking, the turtles are very nearly somnambulant. And easy prey.

I watched as a fisherman grabbed the loose end of a long rope tied to the gunwale of the boat and plunged into the water, a foot and a half behind a turtle. He grabbed the top of the shell with one hand and pushed down on the back of the shell with the other, forcing the animal's head and front flippers out of the water. Quickly, he slipped a noose over one flipper. His partner grabbed the rope at the gunwale and pulled the animal to him, heaving it up into the boat and flipping it onto its back.

Fishing this way, I was told, a two-man team can catch twenty-five turtles in an hour and make two runs a day. There are a score of boats working on the best days.

The fishing itself seemed almost too easy. Certainly it was a good deal easier than in previous years, the fishermen told me, when turtling had been banned during the nesting season and the animals could only be found far out at sea. Now they were massing for their own slaughter, and many more were being killed—killed during nesting season, in most cases, before the females could lay their eggs. Still, as a high official in the Mexican Department of Fisheries pointed out, the new lab was putting so many new hatchlings into the sea that, in effect, "less were being killed."

I spent some time diving with the Mexicans. The turtles, I found, were virtually harmless when approached from the rear. They made no effort to escape or dive until literally touched. I came on them like the Mexican divers and rode them along the surface for several yards. The leather on the back of the neck felt surprisingly "dry," like the skin of a snake or lizard that you always expect to be slimy. Their faces, even while basking, had a pinched, disapproving cast and their mouths were turned down, like a child's drawing of a scowling person. They seemed unimaginably ancient.

I was joined, during one dive, by half a dozen dolphins. They frolicked, undulated beside me as I swam. The turtles, by comparison, seemed joyless, dreary beasts, altogether too intent on brute survival. I thought of them as the constipated accountants of evolution, and was, in turn, thoroughly and contemptuously ignored by them. On one occasion, diving with a fleeing turtle, a dolphin actually buzzed the slower animal in a silly, playful manner. We—the dolphin and I—were the mammals: fast, giddy, intelligent. In evolutionary terms we were children teasing our elders.

An unsettling thing happened when we returned to slaughterhouse cove after the first day of diving. The manager of the slaughterhouse asked us all to leave, and he threatened force if we didn't. Why had they been so anxious to have us film the dedication on Sunday, but wanted us out of there on Tuesday? Looking back on it, I should have connected it with our visit to the lab on Monday, and my misgivings about what I had seen.

Back at the hotel, Jack Ford and I talked about our dive over a beer. Ford had happened upon a pair of copulating turtles, and had a story to tell.

The male species is the worst sort of opportunist. Knowing, instinctively, that the females must mass for nesting, he lies in wait. Intercourse takes place in the water. The male secures himself to the top of the female's shell with two curved nails, each located on the inside of a front flipper. Turtles have five fingers, and that curved claw, located about halfway up the appendage, corresponds to our thumb.

Having nailed himself on at the top, the male curves his longer, heavier tail under the female's shell. The penis is housed in the tail and extruded from the anus.

"They weren't moving," Ford said, "they just sort of wallowed there in the swells. They really didn't look like they were having any fun. I watched them for about forty minutes, but they may have been connected for hours. . . ."

"They're turtles," I said, "they do everything slowly."

"When the male pulled out," Ford said, "I got a look at his equipment." Jack spread his hands the full width of his chest, then described the diameter of a baseball with the thumb and forefinger of both hands. "They are very well-equipped animals," he said.

Local fishermen are equally impressed, and their stories of bizarre copulatory feats among Pacific Ridleys bugger the imagination. It is thought that sperm is stored in the female's genital tract and can continue to fertilize eggs for years, and that a nesting female may mate several times a day on the way to a nesting site. A female crawling onto the beach may exhibit scratches on the neck and her shell may be broken near the head where the male has held her.

But it is the size of the male equipment and the long copulatory periods that the fishermen expand upon. And this has led to the myth that eating turtle eggs is good for the human male. The eggs are said to put lead in the old pencil.

In Spanish, eggs are *huevos*, and egg poachers are called *hueveros*. Poaching is a crime, and the hueveros of Escobilla were not delighted with the idea of an interview. I had rented a Volkswagen bus and a driver in the town of Pochutla and was trying my luck at the *cantinas* along the highway near the beach. No one, at three cantinas, believed that people actually poached eggs. They asked where I had ever heard of such a thing. A surprising number of people I talked to didn't even live in the area. Some citizens expressed great amazement when told that less than two miles from where they sat, turtles occasionally came up on the beach by the thousands.

My driver for the day, a slick young Mexican with shiny hair and a mustache, lost his patience after a few hours. In his capacity as a public driver, he said sadly, he had sometimes picked people who he believed might have been carrying eggs. He had seen one such man walking on the highway, and, if I wished, he would drive back and ask him if he wanted to talk. The young man in question wore a straw hat with an extravagantly folded brim and a shirt which was cut off below the pectorals to reveal an elaborately muscled brown stomach. For fifty pesos he agreed to talk for an hour.

The man, whom I'll call Alfredo, said he had already heard that a gringo was asking questions. He chose to ride on the floor of the van and directed us onto a dead-end road shielded by rows of corn.

Alfredo said that a number of local people poach eggs, but that the hueveros are not organized as such. On a moonless night people just seem to gather at the Escobilla bridge; and, after much discussion, about ten are chosen to work that night. They split up into pairs and walk through the jungle, off the trail, finally crawling up over the cactus dunes. One man lies in the dunes, near the cover of the jungle. The other creeps out onto the beach.

Even on moonless nights, the star glow on sand and sea makes it light enough to work. Poking into the sand with a sharp stick, the huevero feels, more than hears, a muffled pop when he hits the first egg in a nest. Digging with his hands, he empties the nest of its hundred or so eggs, filling a small sack that he takes to the man in the dunes, who places them in a large sack.

If the soldiers come—you can usually see them flashing a light—the man in the dunes fades into the jungle with the large sack. The huevero on the beach drops his small sack and runs for the jungle at top speed. The soldiers wear boots and carry heavy rifles. The odds are pretty good that the huevero will make the jungle.

Working this way, two men can steal as many as eight thousand eggs in one night. Eighty nests. His share of the take, four thousand eggs, Alfredo could sell to a driver for fifteen hundred pesos, about seventy-five dollars. He was chosen to go to the beach four times a year, tops. His poaching income came to three hundred dollars in the best of years. His annual income from growing corn, Alfredo said, was five hundred dollars. He was responsible for a family of ten, and the temptation to steal eggs was very great.

Alfredo was not proud of night work. He wanted me to know that many of his eggs were given to the poorest families, to widows, for instance, with starving children. In the past, Alfredo said, when there was a drought like this year, hungry people could go down to the beach and the soldiers would let them dig up a limited number of eggs to eat. Now, PIOSA was killing all the turtles and the soldiers would not let starving people dig for eggs. Everyone, Alfredo said, knew that the turtles would soon be gone. He had lived near Escobilla all his life, and he thought he had a right to earn some money from the eggs before PIOSA killed all the turtles.

Later, over beer and mescal at a cantina far from Escobilla, I talked with my driver. He wanted me to understand that he had never done such a thing, but that he had heard how the business worked. A driver with a legitimate load makes a space and caches forty thousand eggs or more. There are checkpoints along the major highways, so egg smuggling is a sweaty affair. In Acapulco or Mexico City the eggs are sold under cover of darkness to a man in the marketplace. The driver can make as much as two pesos per egg, so a single forty-thousand-egg load can bring a driver about four thousand dollars, tops.

In the more cosmopolitan cities, a turtle egg sold in a restaurant can cost as much as nine pesos. The eggs are said to be somewhat oily and they are often served fried, five or six at a time, and covered in chili sauce to mask the taste. Sometimes eggs are served raw, in the shell. The top is peeled off, a squeeze of lime is added, and the entire mess is dumped into the mouth. The eggs are eaten primarily by wealthy and ignorant men who cannot sustain an erection.

The second visit to the lab was a revelation. All the tanks were empty. There were no hatchlings. There was no sea water. Nothing.

The large tanks outside, containing the mature turtles, were empty. One misshapen adult female lay on her back, dead beside the tank. She had been left there to bake in her own shell.

Ten styrofoam boxes, like the ones we had seen at Escobilla, were stacked by the side of the building, apparently forgotten. There were two hundred hatchlings in each box and all were dead or dying.

The only person at the lab, an old man eating his lunch under a tree, explained that all the hatchlings had been dumped at sea. As for the styrofoam boxes, somebody must have forgotten them after they *brought the hatchlings in from the beach at Escobilla on Saturday*, the day before the dedication. Sure, he said, it would be okay if Juan Jośe put the hatchlings out to sea. Somebody had just forgotten to do it. The mature adults, the man said, had been taken to the slaughterhouse.

That night I apologized to Juan Jośe de la Vega.

Had all twenty-five thousand hatchlings been brought in from Escobilla? To impress the officials and the governor? To put on a sideshow for the Mexican TV cameras and the Mexican people?

Hunting was now allowed during nesting season, and if officials at the Department of Fisheries can be taken at their word, it was this lab that they expected to compensate for the carnage. But it was apparent that the lab wasn't functional.

Even if the lab were functional, a good argument can be made that it might have been worse than useless; that some projects would yield an incredibly poor rate of return and that others might actually contribute to the extirpation of the species. From reading, I had learned that there were similar labs all over the world, and some interesting work has been done at them. For instance, there was the matter of burying eggs taken from the oviducts of slaughtered females: experiments conducted on Green Sea turtles, with similar nesting habits, showed a 14 percent hatch rate among replanted eggs from slaughtered females, compared with a 63 percent rate in eggs from undisturbed nests. More to the point, Juan José had opened ten boxes at the lab and examined ten eggs, all from slaughtered females. In all cases the yolks had turned milky and had begun to disintegrate. Few, if any, eggs from the slaughtered females would ever hatch.

As for dumping the hatchlings at sea, the authorities are divided, but according to Dr. Archie Carr, one of the world's foremost herpetologists, it may be a useless endeavor. The struggles of the first day may be an integral part of the life cycle. Hatchlings in tanks may become pen happy and find themselves unable to feed at sea. Dumping could put the hatchlings in an unnatural current. Finally, whatever mechanism it is that tells females to return to the beach of their birth must surely be implanted at birth. It is quite possible, even probable, that none of those twenty-five thousand dumped hatchlings would ever see the beach at Escobilla.

Time was running out for the ABC crew. Their original concept— one hundred thousand turtles on the beach—was scrapped in favor of good footage of at least one turtle laying her eggs in the sand. Walking the beach each dawn, I was able to count an average of twelve new tracks and nests a night. Twelve nests, separated by four miles of beach and twelve hours of darkness. Even with a wooden sled towed by a burro and several hired men to carry equipment, the crew was very lucky to get good nesting film. As it happened, the turtle that was finally filmed came up onto the beach no more than four hundred yards from our campsite.

She arrived unseen, riding a breaker, then crawled over a strip of wet sand and up the gently sloping beach. Adapted to sea life, she moved laboriously on land. Her flippers were spread out to their full extent on the sand, and they made awkward semicircular patterns in the sand as she dragged the weight of her body the forty or so yards she needed to get above the tide line.

Every few minutes she stopped. Her lungs, designed for breathing in the buoyancy of the sea, were compressed by the weight of her body. She exhaled. The throat pumped and she inhaled. It sounded, eerily, like the amplified breathing of a man surfacing after two minutes underwater.

It took her twenty minutes to select a nesting site. Settling herself into the sand, she curled one of her back flippers and flung sand almost directly over her head. Within minutes, her head and carapace were covered in thick, clinging sand. She stopped to draw a few ragged, tearing breaths. Her body was tilted down at a slight angle, the backside sunk into the hole.

The television lights exploded in the night, but the turtle, driven by instinct, was oblivious. The body contracted, the head sank into the sand, and two strong cords strained in her neck. She was scratched and raw there where some male's claws had dug into her during copulation. The cloaca contracted and a moist white egg dropped eighteen inches into her nest. Another followed, then another. She lifted her head to draw another breath and then the contractions began again.

"She's crying," someone said. Tears were rolling out of her eyes and tracking down the sand that clung to her face. No matter that the tears are only a way of eliminating salt from the system: the mother's labored breathing, the seemingly painful contractions, her tears had turned the filming into a wrenching emotional experience.

A hundred or so eggs were laid, two or three at a time. The back flippers curled more delicately than one would have thought possible, and the mother spread sand over her eggs in a gentle, loving gesture.

At this moment, the Mexican biologists approached the lights. Producer/director John Wilcox shouted to a translator, "Tell those people to please stay out of her track." The plump woman exploded. "We speak perfect English," she said. "We are biologists. We have a right to study this animal." Bob Nixon jogged over to talk to her.

Having covered her nest, the turtle lifted herself up onto the tips of all four flippers and fell on the sand, packing the eggs and disguising the nest. She repeated this ludicrous dance a dozen times or more, then, backing away, she flung more sand over the area with her front flippers. Satisfied, she started back out to sea. I followed her down with a flashlight. When the first wave hit her, she seemed to relax. The sand came off and her sea color shone in the light. The backwash pulled her out a few feet, a second wave hit her, and she was gone.

The question of how many turtles there were out there haunted me. The biologists—the people who were supposed to know—had been willing to argue over one animal.

ABC's charter plane was ready at the Puerto Ángel strip when word came in from Escobilla that there were turtles in the breakers. It was a sign that had preceded other arribazónes. I elected to pass on the flight and stay another night on the beach with Bob Nixon, assistant cameraman Gordon Waterman, and Juan José de la Vega.

The night was mild, a gentle breeze blew in from the sea, and the moon was in its final quarter. This had to be the night. That day there had been turtles in the surf.

Our group built a fire. The marines built one of their own and another was started by the biologists. They were measuring out ropes which would be used to encompass a certain area. Stakes had been driven into the ground all along the beach to divide the area into like sections. The biologists would count the number of turtles nesting between the ropes and multiply by the number of stakes for an estimate of the total number of nesting turtles. Clearly they expected the arribazón.

A few marines stopped over for a drink of mescal. We had filled several soft-drink bottles with that white, searing liquor at the nearest cañtina. The marines were happy. This would be the night. We sang some songs.

We shared our mescal with a local man who had lived 150 yards from the beach for ten years. As little as five years ago, he said, each arribazón took seven or eight days. There were four a year and the beach was black with turtles. Now, he said, there were fewer turtles. Too many had been killed by PIOSA. He thought there would be no arribazón.

I ate some sandy peanut butter on Bimbo bread, drank more mescal, and walked the beach. It was seven, eight, nine o'clock. In previous years the turtles had begun coming in directly after sunset. Still, there were songs from the campfires.

Our group talked with representatives from the Department of Fisheries and with fishermen from the co-operativa Reforma Portuaria. I was able to piece together this version of the events at Escobilla:

There are seven co-operativas, or fishing unions. PIOSA pays the fisherman by the turtle, and the fishermen are licensed by the

Department of Fisheries, which also checks the union records to see that the quotas are not exceeded. Each co-op has an equal number of turtles it can catch each month. When José Lopez Portillo assumed the presidency of Mexico, he promised to develop industry. Last year fishermen from five of the co-ops, seizing the opportunity, went to a Mexico court and asked that the traditional ban on turtling during the nesting season be lifted. During other times of the year, they said, the turtles were too far out to sea and it was difficult to catch many in the small skiffs. The ban on fishing during the nesting season, they said, was depriving them of their livelihood. The judge agreed with the fishermen. The ban was lifted and the Department of Fisheries raised the yearly quota for Oaxaca.

Victor Valdez, of the co-operativa Reforma Portuaria, said that two of the co-operativas, including his own, had opposed the lifting of the ban, arguing that such untimely hunting would decimate the turtle population. Most fishermen, Valdez said, know this. But everyone is poor, and now, for a few years, a fisherman can nearly double his yearly wage, and with less work. Another fisherman said that he knew that leaders of the five co-ops, bringing suit to lift the ban, received money from Antonio Suárez and that Suárez had pressured them to bring the suit.

Juan José nodded. "Last year," he said, "the Cosmographic Society made a film about these turtles. We interviewed the judge who lifted the ban. We asked him how many turtles there were at Escobilla. It was very clear that he knew nothing of the situation here and it was a very embarrassing piece of film for him and for PIOSA. Antonio Suárez later invited me to lunch. He wanted to 'buy' our film. He offered me eighty thousand pesos." De la Vega refused, and the film was shown on Mexican television.

I passed him the mescal and stumbled through my fourth or fifth apology to him in the last few days. He waved it off with good grace. "I knew if people came here," he said, "they would see for themselves what is happening."

The business of lifting the ban and raising the quota is an experiment. The lab is a safety valve for that experiment. Even if the biologists decide that the Ridleys are being extirpated, officials can rest easy because the lab is supposed to put some huge, astonishing number of turtles into the sea each year. I have that statement directly from a high source at the Department of Fisheries.

We talked, finally, with some of the biologists. They had their own mescal and were excited about the arribazón, and the discussion was not as bitter as it had been earlier in the week. None of them, to a person, would answer my questions, but we talked enough for me to form some impressions. They were, I think, sincere in their desire to set reasonable quotas: ones that would eventually increase both the harvest and the number of turtles as a whole. They had been hostile because foreign conservationists put pressure on the government and the government responds by firing biologists. I felt that they truly believed that if they filed a strong enough report, the government would reinstate the ban on turtling sometime during the next four years.

I thought about the Mexican TV cameras and all those officials whose only taste of Escobilla had been seeing twenty-five thousand hatchlings at the lab. It had been very impressive. I had no great confidence that the ban would be reinstated.

It was ten o'clock and still we had seen no turtles. I wondered if the local people were right, that there would be no arribazón. The Ridley, I know, is the only turtle to nest in such great numbers, and I wondered if it could be the numbers themselves that triggered the arribazón.

If that were so—and this theory is a layman's guess—it might explain why there had been normal arribazónes July through September, but not in October. Each of the seven co-operativas was allotted 1,500 turtles per month, for a total of 10,500 animals. In July 10,500 turtles were taken, but by August the cumulative total was 21,000, and in September that number rose to 31,500. Now, in the first week of October, the count was rapidly approaching 40,000 animals, and nearly all of them females, laid across the killing table at PIOSA.

By midnight there were still no turtles. The songs from the campfires became louder, more brittle, drunker. There were the sounds of voices raised in anger.

I took another four-mile walk. Bob Nixon spoke with the woman biologist. She had been drinking, he said, and seemed to be very depressed, almost near tears. "If you want to see the arribazón," she said, "go to the dump." In the firelight, behind her glasses, her eyes glittered, wetly.

* * *

The dump is located on several low hills just southeast of the slaughterhouse. When the turtles have been slaughtered, when the twelve pounds of good meat have been stripped from the bone and the leather has been stripped from the head and chest, the remains are dumped onto these hills like garbage and left to dry in the sun before the bones and shells are ground into fertilizer.

The stench there—the odor of death—was unholy. It clogged my nostrils and sent bile rising in my throat. Vultures retreated reluctantly as I approached. Here and there I saw flippers stripped of their flesh, their five fingers, like yours and mine, jutting up out of black putrescent meat.

There were eggs there too, where no eggs should be. Mixed with the bowels of their slaughtered mothers, they were heaped into a sprawling pile and covered with maggots. I suspect someone will tell me that PIOSA only chooses the finest eggs to go back in the sand or on those styrofoam boxes, and that these were rejects. But I saw that pile with my own eyes. There were thousands upon thousands upon thousands of eggs, all rotting in that evil heap.

I was, quite literally, sick to my stomach.

On the telephone, Antonio Suárez is a very persuasive and charming man. He is proud that, in his capacity as director general of PIOSA, he employs some one thousand persons who fish for turtle, shark, red snapper, and lobster.

He denied that he ever offered Juan José de la Vega money for a film.

He denied that he offered the leaders of some co-operativas money, or that he pressured them in any way, to bring suit against the ban on turtling during the nesting season.

He said that it was not true that he was responsible for depleting the species.

"It is my opinion," Antonio Suárez said, "that the turtle is a resource we ought to take advantage of, but that we ought to protect the species, that we ought to have quotas, and that we ought not to protect a bigger quantity than the species can support, and that we may always repopulate the species."

Suárez was proud of the new lab and said that it was true that he had paid for most of the construction costs. He said the lab had dumped *20 to 30 million hatchlings into the water in the months of*

July through September! He said that the Department of Fisheries had checked on this number.

It is possible that Suárez misspoke himself. Officials at the Department of Fisheries said they had no such data. And, in late November, one high-ranking biologist involved with the lab admitted *that it had not been functioning when I was there. He said he expected it to open by February or March.*

Suárez was quite specific about the October arribazón. He said that while arribazónes are always larger from July through September, some fifty thousand Ridleys had laid their eggs on the beach in October. Again, this is somewhat at odds with information received from the Department of Fisheries. In late November, officials there said there had been no October arribazón.

People I know and trust were on the beach at Escobilla during the entire month of October. The moon entered its last quarter twice and the winds blew in the sea, and, for the first time since anyone who lived near the beach could remember, there was no October arribazón. Only 90 million years of evolution going to waste on the beach at Escobilla.

> *Author's note:*
> *The above article appeared in the February 1978 issue of* Outside *magazine. I had gone to Mexico expecting to see one hundred thousand turtles spread out along a moonlit stretch of beach, and the story I envisioned would be a prism through which we could look 90 million years into the past. When the turtles failed to appear, I wanted to know why. This was a reluctant investigation, but the evidence of greed and fraud couldn't be ignored. A reporter has mixed feelings at such times. It was a great story, but the research left me feeling angry and helpless.*
> *In the years that followed, I monitored the situation on the beach at Escobilla from afar. (It was made known to me that I wouldn't be a welcome guest in that part of Mexico.) Some well-meaning people working on behalf of the turtles felt the article was counterproductive. Carlos Nagle, a consultant for the World Wildlife Fund who*

works with the Mexican government on environmental problems, thought a more tactful, diplomatic approach would have produced better results. Indeed, after publication of the article, American scientists had their research permits revoked, and Nagle found poisonous pieces of cut-up jellyfish on the beach where he walked barefoot. "I cursed you and your magazine for four years," Nagle told me mildly. "Mexicans are sensitive to American cultural and economic intrusions. They are proud. The outcry over that article: it was like walking into someone's house and telling them they had to rearrange their furniture."

Does such an article simply leave the reader feeling helpless while making the job tougher for those who are fighting for a diplomatic solution? Juan José de la Vega didn't think so. "That article was the best thing that ever happened to the turtles," he said. "It made the public aware of the problem. Mexican people have no desire to see an entire species of animal vanish from the earth."

And José Toro, the American Justice Department attorney who was to finally secure an indictment against Suárez, agrees with de la Vega. "These investigations are not conducted in a vacuum," he told me. "It was public pressure that made the investigation possible, and the pressure came as a direct result of that article."

As a journalist, I have to believe that a problem in the spotlight is one that is not going to be hidden away; I have to believe that people exposed to such a situation will care, and that something can be done.

Four years later, in 1982, I tested that belief. Here, in part, is that followup to the original article.

A few weeks after the *Outside* article was published, I received a letter from Dr. Peter Pritchard, vice-president for science and research at the Florida Audubon Society. Dr. Pritchard, having recently returned from a fact-finding mission to Escobilla, wrote: "When I was there in late November, they were still killing five hundred to seven hundred turtles per day, and *every one* was a female containing eggs. . . . The local PIOSA *jefe* told me that the story behind the opening ceremony of the research facility and the subsequent draining of the tanks was simply that the plumbing system was not ready for dedication day, so they had hand-filled the system just for the ceremony, then emptied it again. They still did not have their plumbing system in operation when I was there, but they were 'working on it.' . . . I, like you, was revolted by what I saw. . . . The feds say that they will clamp down and close the season if the turtles show a diminution in numbers. Unfortunately, it may be too late then—the Kemp's Ridley, on the other coast, has shown no recovery even after a decade of full protection. . . . Open season during the breeding time is a sure recipe for disaster."

"The Shame of Escobilla" was reprinted in the IUCN (International Union for Conservation of Nature and Natural Resources) Marine Turtle Newsletter. Dr. Pritchard wrote a commentary, and I quote from him again, not only because his comments are cogent, but because it will later be important to know exactly where he stands. Reflecting on his visit to the slaughterhouse, Pritchard wrote, "I found the sight of the beautiful female Ridleys, fresh from the sea, being bashed in with iron bars and deftly eviscerated, one after the other, five hundred or more per day, a disgusting and demoralizing sight, and I found the idea of creatures being butchered in this way when they were gathering to lay their eggs totally unacceptable, both emotionally and biologically."

Pritchard had questioned the director of the Mexican Department of Fisheries, who had, apparently, been quite frank. PIOSA, he said, had been allowed to fish during the breeding season, had been allowed such dangerously high quotas, because it would be logistically difficult and extremely expensive to field a small army of enforcement personnel in remote coastal Oaxaca. It was thought that if Suárez got the quotas he wanted, he would, in turn, see that those eggs laid naturally or buried at the lab would be adequately protected from poachers. Pritchard's commentary went on to question the concept of the lab itself and mentioned that the Suárez/PIOSA operation constituted the largest butchery of turtles in the world.

In the summer of 1978 ABC aired its *American Sportsman* segment on the plight of the Olive Ridley. Producer/director John Wilcox and associate producer Bob Nixon had put together a powerful and emotional documentary. It was all there on film: the lab with thousands of turtles in the tanks and the media standing around looking suitably impressed, followed by empty tanks only two days later. There was a final shot of the dump, that foul boneyard, and all those eggs, the next generation, rotting away in that maggot-infested heap.

A small groundswell of public support seemed to be building, and the Environmental Defense Fund took good and proper advantage of it. They threatened to sue the United States federal government: The EDF demanded that the Olive Ridley and two other species of sea turtle be declared a threatened species under the Endangered Species Act. Threat of suit was enough. The Olive Ridley was declared to be endangered. The effect of the action was to prohibit importation of any of the protected turtles or of products derived from them.

Things started to go bad for Antonio Suárez in the spring of 1979. In California, Charles Clark, a Marine Fisheries Service agent, came across a shipment of freezer packages labeled "chunked Tabasco River turtle." Clark examined the meat. It was not light-colored, like freshwater turtle. It was dark, beef-red, fibrous: more like sea turtle. Clark notified Charles Fuss, the special agent in charge of law enforcement for the National Marine Fisheries Service in Saint Petersburg, Florida. Fuss had been getting similar reports about sea-turtle meat for sale in Florida. But as a result of the federal action taken the previous July, all six species of sea turtle found in the Western Hemisphere had been declared endangered or threatened. Fuss geared up an investigation.

There were twelve agents on Fuss's investigative team, and it was a rare case of near total cooperation between government agencies: There were people from the Fish and Wildlife Service, from the U.S. Customs Service, from the National Marine Fisheries Service, and from the Wildlife and Marine Resources section of the Justice Department.

The interagency team talked with turtle experts. It was perfectly legal to import Tabasco River turtle (that has since changed), but, according to José Toro, a special attorney for the Justice Department, the investigators were looking at nearly 190,000 *pounds* of it.

And there were not enough Tabasco River turtles in all of Mexico to account for that much meat.

One element of the investigative team, working with customs declarations, followed a paper trail to a seafood exporter in Mexico. The man had no knowledge of the shipments pouring into Miami International Airport. Investigators determined that export papers had been stolen from the company's office, that signatures had been forged in what appeared to be a criminal conspiracy of some proportion.

Meanwhile, Sylvia Braddon, a research chemist with the National Marine Fisheries Service, was working to identify the meat in those packages of "Tabasco River turtle." The technique she used is called isoelectric focusing. It involves passing a strong charge of electricity through a small sample of meat for several hours. Eventually the protein "focuses," forming a microscopic pattern of blue lines, distinct for each species.

In order to identify the species involved, Braddon would have to test the lines developed from the suspect meat against those from the meat of every other freshwater and saltwater turtle in the world. Luckily the investigators had a pretty good idea of what kind of meat they were dealing with: 190,000 pounds seemed to implicate the most prolific turtle butcherer in the world, Antonio Suárez.

Peter Pritchard provided one of the samples of Ridley meat used by Braddon. The thin blue lines from Pritchard's sample matched exactly those from the meat in the suspect tins.

So it was Ridley meat. The fact that only one man in the world would have that much Olive Ridley meat to sell doesn't cut much ice legally. There was still a blizzard of paper and a forest of middlemen between Antonio Suárez and all that illegal meat.

It was a very difficult case, but José Toro had a plan.

I knew nothing about the investigation of Antonio Suárez in the late summer of 1979. The story had pretty much died down as far as I knew; so I was surprised to get a strange and urgent call about Suárez a year and half after the publication of the story.

The man on the phone sounded like a guy who knew his Raymond Chandler and who subscribed to *Soldier of Fortune* magazine; the kind of guy who might weigh three hundred pounds, smoke cigars, and talk out of the side of his mouth. He was calling from Los Angeles, or so he said, and he claimed to represent a group of wealthy southern California conservationists with the money to "provide extraordinary solutions to extraordinary problems."

"The slaughterhouse," he said, "it's located on a pretty remote stretch of beach, isn't it? You give us the layout, we could be in and out of there in twenty minutes. We'd be in Mexico in ten, twelve hours, tops."

"You're not . . . are you suggesting some sort of, uh, paramilitary operation?"

"I'm suggesting that we talk to these bastards in the only language they understand."

"Well, you know, I'm not really sure that, uh"—this lunatic was talking about bombing Mexico!—"we'd be able to, uh, do much good, uh, that way!"

There was a pause while the man seemed to consider his options. "All right," he said finally, "you tell me. How do we stop this guy Suárez?"

I wish I could say I pegged him immediately, but it was only after he hung up that it occurred to me that the guy was neither a militant environmentalist nor a flaming nutcase. He sounded more like a very clever professional investigator. "Okay," he kept saying, "if that won't work, how do we get Suárez?"

If indeed the man was an investigator of some sort, then he was pumping me for any nasty information I might have on Suárez. The most prolific turtle butcher in the world must have been a very worried man.

Events slid around the bend and went careening downhill for Suárez in November 1979. Suárez had been meeting with Pritchard—the two men would spend eight hours at a crack, arguing their way through a long lunch—and Pritchard invited him to the United States to speak at the First World Conference for World Sea Turtle Conservation. According to Pritchard, Suárez had initially thought that those who opposed him were obstructionists, sentimentalists who didn't like killing, vegetarians, hippies. "But," Pritchard told me, "he was impressed by scientists, by reasonable men with facts at their fingertips." Pritchard saw the conference as a process of give-

and-take, a learning experience for Suárez, who he felt was coming around to a more rational approach.

The Justice Department's José Toro, unknown to Pritchard, attended the conference for entirely different reasons.

"Mr. Suárez," Pritchard told me, "was very nervous. He was speaking in the largest room of the United States State Department to five hundred of the most knowledgeable sea-turtle experts in the world."

Worse, members of the World Wildlife Fund had put copies of the *Outside* article on every seat. Two unidentified men, described to me as "large and probably Mexican," went from seat to seat, confiscating the reprints. No matter: the WWF people handed out more reprints as the delegates entered the room. They had also arranged showings of the ABC *Sportsman* segment.

Suárez spoke before an unresponsive and surly crowd. As he stepped off the podium, he was surrounded by federal agents and handed a subpoena. Apparently he panicked. Suárez fled. He flew back to Mexico, leaving his clothes and luggage in his hotel room.

"I knew," José Toro told me, "that there was a great quantity of Olive Ridley meat involved, and that seemed to point to Mr. Suárez. We had no legal proof, however, and the subpoena only involved his records. I went into the investigation with an open mind, but when Mr. Suárez fled, we began concentrating on him."

Toro and other agents took up the paper trail once again. Names on letterheads submitted to United States Customs led to a group of Cuban businessmen in Miami, and inquiries there led to another group of Cubans in Mexico City. There, Toro, who was born in Puerto Rico and of course speaks fluent Spanish, began looking for the man any investigator wants to find: the fellow with a gripe.

On Toro's list of people he wanted to talk to was a man named Martin Zacarias. It looked to Toro as if Zacarias had once been involved in the conspiracy but had been somehow muscled out of the business. There were three separate meetings in Mexico City, and because Zacarias was no longer involved in the business, Toro felt justified in granting him immunity in exchange for information. On the third meeting, Zacarias produced a sample customs document, written in pencil. It contained the precise wording used in the customs declarations for the illegal meat.

Zacarias said that the sample document had been drawn up during a meeting in Mexico City sometime in December 1977. At that meeting he and other individuals present had conspired to fraudulently mislabel Olive Ridley meat and export it to the United States. One of the individuals present was named Antonio Suárez.

Taking this information to the grand jury in Miami, Toro was able to obtain an indictment against Suárez, PIOSA, and five other individuals and corporations. Suárez hired the best lawyers he could find and returned to the United States only after plea negotiations had been completely worked out. On October 28, 1981, Suárez pleaded guilty to all charges and paid a total of fifty thousand dollars in fines.

Antonio Suárez eventually quit the turtle-slaughtering business. "No," Toro told me, "that was not part of the plea negotiations. I think that we denied him the United States market, and perhaps the business is no longer profitable." Toro, who shares a Latin background with Suárez, thinks there may be something else involved. "Antonio Suárez," Toro said, "is a very proud man, very concerned with dignity. He is very Latin in that respect. I think it was devastating to his ego to stand before that judge, to be declared guilty, to acknowledge that he engaged in criminal acts. I think for him the worst humiliation came at the arraignment, when they took him downstairs for fingerprinting and mug shots.

"You could," Toro said, "almost feel sorry for him."

So the butcher of Escobilla was driven from the beach in humiliation and disgrace. The good guys won, the villain was crushed, and the turtles were saved for all eternity.

That's the way I'd like to end this report. But the turtles are not yet saved, and Antonio Suárez may not have been a total villain.

According to Dr. Peter Pritchard, "It was easy to see Suárez as evil incarnate, and that is how I saw him at first." After talking with him for a while, Pritchard saw that Suárez truly believed industrialization was the only way to preserve the turtles: If turtles were worth more to local people than eggs are worth to poachers, then poaching would stop on the beach.

What Suárez didn't believe was that harvesting during the nesting season was harmful to the population as a whole. "He was beginning to come around to our point of view," said Pritchard. "Hard facts, statistics, scientific research impressed him. That is why I invited him to the sea-turtle conference in Washington." That is where Suárez was served with the subpoena.

"I knew nothing about that," Pritchard said. When Suárez fled, Pritchard raced to the airport. He wanted to assure Suárez that he had not betrayed him. "We didn't talk for some time after that," Pritchard said. "He did call when he made the decision to quit the business, though. He was very concerned about what the world thought of him. He didn't want to be known as the man who was killing off an entire species of animal. I remember I once asked him what he thought about the *Outside* article. I thought he would scream and yell, call it a pack of lies. Instead, he looked very sad. 'They judged us harshly,' he said. He was sensitive to that judgment."

Perhaps the person whose opinion counted most with Suárez was his daughter. "He loves his daughter," Pritchard said. "He dotes on her. He told me once that if she even told him to quit the business, he would at once, without question. One day he called me. Now I'm sure there are many other reasons for his decision, but he said, 'Peter, Fernanda asked me to stop killing the turtles.'"

Suárez sold his turtle operation to Propemex, a government-owned company that continues to kill the animals at a furious pace. "Suárez," says Pritchard, "was the strongman, el Chingón, the man in charge. You could reason with him. Now you see bureaucrats who shrug their shoulders and pass you on to other bureaucrats."

Carlos Nagle, a consultant for the World Wildlife Fund, puts it more bluntly. "If what you really wanted was to save the turtles, then you have to see what happened to Antonio Suárez as a tragedy. He was a typical poacher on his way to becoming a game warden. He is a very intelligent man, and he could see the long-range consequences."

But Suárez is gone, and the bureaucrats of Propemex are the new butchers on the beach.

The situation, however, is anything but hopeless. Things are not the same in Mexico as they were in 1977. Then, the only conservationists on the beach at Escobilla were Juan José de la Vega and Boris de Swan of the Cosmographic Society. By 1981, during the largest arribazón of the year, more than 150 conservationists hit the beach, like commandos. Aside from Juan José and members of the Cosmographic Society, there were representatives of two other growing environmentalist groups, Amigos del Universo and Bioconservation.

"The marines," Juan José told me, "made it possible for us to be there. I can't praise them enough. When the arribazón started, they provided a plane for us. We flew down from Mexico City and got on the beach only a few hours after the first turtles crawled on the beach." The conservationists spread out, with people taking stations every fifty yards. They stayed two weeks. "Poachers don't want the eggs after a week or so," Juan José said. "They hatch in forty to forty-five days, but hatchlings begin to form inside very quickly. No one would eat an egg with a turtle head in it."

As the conservationists helped the marines patrol the beach, the navy patrolled the water out beyond the breakers. New Fisheries regulations require all fishing to stop for seven days after the start of an arribazón.

More than seventy reporters covered the operation. The public saw what was happening on television and heard about it on radio. Nine of the most influential newspapers in Mexico ran front-page articles on the plight of the turtles. Two documentary films were produced, and both were eventually shown on television. John Ruiz Healy, a popular reporter on Mexico's *60 Minutes*, did a devastating report on poachers and sellers.

People like Juan José see the media in Mexico as major allies. "The public is now aware of the problem," Juan José told me, "and this is a dramatic change from when you first came to Escobilla."

Ricardo Mier, of Bioconservation, adds, "It is a paradox, but the ecology movement seems to be growing here, and growing very rapidly, in spite of the current economic crisis. I think this is because we can now clearly see that true value lies in natural resources and not in pesos or dollars."

As the public becomes more conscious of the slaughter on the beach at Escobilla, more pressure is put on the Department of

Fisheries to reinstate the ban on fishing during the breeding season, or, failing that, to lower the quotas allowed Propemex to more reasonable levels.

The current quotas are absurdly high. Here are some numbers; it doesn't take a marine biologist to analyze them.

• 1973: Juan José de la Vega sees his first arribazón. More than 100,000 turtles lay their eggs on the beach.

• 1981: The *total* number of turtles arriving on the beach for *all* arribazónes, July through November, is 50,000.

• 1981: The total number of turtles allowed to be killed, according to quotas set by the Department of Fisheries, is 89,000.

The number of turtles arriving on the beach in 1981 was only a tenth of what it was only a decade ago. And although fifty thousand turtles reached the beach in 1981, almost twice that number were killed before they could lay their eggs. And 1981 was the sparest year for arribazónes in recent memory, which probably means that fewer turtles reached the beach than ever before, throughout the whole of time.

Juan José de la Vega says the memory of 1973, when he saw one hundred thousand turtles lay their eggs on the beach in a single night, is a treasure no one can take from him. He likes to relive it now and again. He stood alone, surrounded by all that . . . biology, and the moon was full and bright. A gentle breeze was blowing in off the ocean, and the smell of the sea was strong. All around, on all sides, as far as the eye could see on this bright night, there were turtles: turtles coming in out of the ocean, turtles laying their eggs, turtles returning to the mystery of the sea. Juan José had a sensation of a time before man, a sense of the fecundity of the sea and land. There was something deep and full expanding inside of him, something other people feel only inside a church.

There is an image that lives inside my memory as well. It is a vision of that slaughterhouse dump, those acres of death. The breeze I recall was heavy with the stench of rot, warm with the weight of decay.

Propemex is still dumping bodies there, and, according to Dr. Pritchard, still dumping eggs. These eggs are said to be too immature to be buried in the sand; either that or too fouled with the mother's intestines during the slaughtering process.

So these eggs are dumped where the bodies of mothers are left to rot. But many of the eggs are not fouled; many are not immature. Many of them live, and hatchlings emerge to crawl over the rotting bodies of their slaughtered mothers. They crawl frantically, through the stench of death, toward a sea they will never reach.

4

The Home Front

(See the USA . . .)

In the Wind

Ill Wind at Poison Creek

It was, my friends used to say, a "local color" sort of a house that I
lived in up on Poison Creek, just east of Livingston, Montana.
The former owners, one could deduce from the various wounds
in the walls, used to shoot the place up every once in a while.

The bathroom door didn't offer much privacy, but it was a
triumph of local-color decorating. The hole in the outer portion was
relatively small, about the size of a silver dollar, but the shotgun
pellets had spread out from impact so that the hole on the inner side
of the door was a ragged, splintered abyss of some two feet in
diameter. The shot had proceeded across the linoleum floor and
spattered up against the tub. There were pocks on the outside curb of
the porcelain and a good deal more of them on the inside edge.

It was rumored that the previous owners, a fine local couple,
had had something of a marital spat and that she had attempted to
make her point with the family bird gun. The husband retreated to
the bathroom, prudently locking the door and hunching down in
the bathtub, there to ponder the vicissitudes of life on the ranch. He
was, it was rumored, uninjured by the blast, though the shot that hit

the inner side of the tub must have gone ricocheting about inside in an annoying fashion.

Living there on the ranch at Poison Creek as I did for some years, I came to understand that the spat in question must have occurred during one of the periodic excesses of the Livingston Wind Festival, which extends from January 1 through December 31, as befits the third-windiest town in America.

Livingston is windy because it is only sixty miles north of—and four thousand feet below—Yellowstone Park. It gets cold down there in the park. In the winter, trees burst in the impossible silence of fifty-below nights, burst with the sound of a rifle shot because sap stored in the trunk has frozen solid and expanded. The park is actually the caldera of an ancient volcano: two million acres rimmed with mountains. The cold air trapped in the caldera is denser, heavier than warm air, and it wants to fall, like water, into lower, warmer regions. The Yellowstone River has carved a canyon out of the northern rim of the caldera. The winds and the water, both propelled by gravity, flow down Yankee Jim Canyon, toward Livingston. The wind, like the water, picks up speed during its four-thousand-foot drop into Paradise Valley, south of Livingston, and this valley, sunk between two parallel mountain ranges, becomes a natural wind tunnel. Just before Livingston, the mountains come together to form a little gun sight of a canyon. Here, the Yellowstone River narrows and flows faster. The same thing happens to the wind, and it bursts out of the confines of the canyon to batter the town, tear branches off of trees, punch windows out of houses, and fray the tempers of Livingston's ordinarily saintly residents. In Livingston, if you want to see at night, it is necessary to point your flashlight at least ten yards upwind.

The wind is, in fact, so constant that Livingston is the first town in the country to own a wind-powered utility company. True, all those windmills out on the flats are something of a joke around town; but to be entirely fair to the windmill designers, the program is still in the experimental stages, and some failures are to be expected. Even so, I enjoy taking my out-of-town visitors past the wind farm, which sometimes looks like a graveyard for small planes, with its broken propellers and twisted metal shards lying about on the wind-flattened plain. "What the hell is that?" my visitors ask.

"New windmill," I say, with a surge of perverse pride. "Supposed to withstand gusts of a hundred fifty miles an hour. Blew down Saturday."

The windmills don't actually "blow down" but suffer malfunctions from a variety of causes. One was shorted out when struck by lightning. The short caused the windmill to spin on its own, sucking power from the very grid it was supposed to feed. I'd drive by it on a rare, calm day and see the big propeller spinning furiously. The fact that I would eventually have to pay Montana Power for the privilege of laughing at a huge outdoor fan, a Frankenstein fan, spinning madly, expensively, out of control on a godforsaken flat in the middle of nowhere was, ultimately, not such a hot joke.

Another failure happened during a power outage one bitterly cold day. The turbines are designed to stop generating during an outage so that linesmen won't be fried during repairs. The turbines detach from the blades, which spin free, and a "snubber" mechanism adjusts the pitch of the blades to lose the wind, causing them to stop. Unfortunately, the cold had thickened the hydraulic fluid in the snubber. The propeller spun free, completely out of control, eventually throwing a blade, which put the whole affair out of balance and set it shaking out there on the flats. It shimmied for hours in a dance of wind-driven hysteria until it crashed to the ground, a victim of its own mad polka and metal fatigue.

Lessons learned in the howl of the Livingston winds will, I'm sure, eventually make the wind farm a paying proposition. And if we couldn't laugh about the wind, we'd be reduced—as many of us often are—to tears, spittle-spewing rages, and arguments punctuated by the boom of shotguns.

The wind here averages sixteen miles an hour; twenty-one miles an hour in the winter, with frequent gusts in the eighty- and ninety-mile-an-hour range. (In the "windy city" of Chicago, by contrast, wind speeds average out at nine miles an hour.) A blow of twenty-one miles an hour is a serious matter: It is perceived by the body as a form of constant and unrelenting attack. This is because we all live inside a little sac of personal air that exists just beyond the flesh, a kind of necessary insulation from the world at large. In a windless situation, our airy aura is about a third of an inch thick. When the wind reaches twenty-one miles an hour, it blows away most of that familiar personal air. In a twenty-one-mile-an-hour blow, a person retains only 1/25th of his or her usual insulation, and that person is subsequently irritable, bad-tempered, thin-skinned.

Science bears me out on this: One study showed that, on the average, the number of schoolyard fights doubled when wind speeds hit forty miles an hour. In Italy, the effects of a hot, dry wind called the sirocco are well known. Lawyers along the Adriatic routinely "plead the sirocco" in cases in which someone has stuck an ice pick into his wife or neighbor for no particularly good reason.

In Israel, the desert wind of the spring and fall is called the sharav. Its physiological and psychological effects have been calibrated by a pharmacologist named Felix Sulman. Examining the urine of wind-sensitive patients under normal conditions and then during the sharav, Sulman found that when the wind blew, one group (43 percent) showed huge increases in the excretion of serotonin, a blood-vessel constrictor. These high levels of serotonin tended to cause migraines, sleeplessness, nausea, and intense but unfocused "irritation." A second group of sufferers (44 percent) showed a severe drop in adrenaline secretions, which caused apathy, depression, and "exhaustion." A third group (13 percent) suffered from both exhaustion and irritation. In other words, the wind either pisses you off or beats you like a gong. Or both.

The house on Poison Creek was just down the east side of the Absaroka Mountains, about four miles from part of the new wind farm. When the winds would die for a while you could walk out into the strange stillness and hear them conspiring, regrouping atop Livingston Peak: low, malevolent whispers up there at 9,314 feet. Then the clouds would darken and begin to roll down the flanks of the mountain toward Poison Creek. The wind would hit the house like an avalanche; it would set the TV antenna humming like a giant tuning fork, and the house would vibrate to the antenna's tune and set the dogs howling in helpless emulation.

It was a siege then, and it could last for days, angering you, beating against you, stealing your insulation and your equanimity. On the third or fourth day of a big blow, I'd find myself lying on the couch exhausted, angry, and I'd think of my predecessors in that house: I could see them lying there, as I was, too tired to rise; I could see them firing angry shells into the wall and screaming, "Shut up, damn you, just shut up!" I could see them bickering over petty matters; I could envision the shotgun aimed at the bathroom door; I could hear its boom over the hum of the antenna, the howl of the dogs, the eternal roar of the wind.

First-time visitors to Poison Creek would be drawn to that splintered door, examine it in respectful silence, and then ask, usually in an awed whisper, "What in God's name did this?"

Invariably, I'd tell them, "The wind."

The First Fear Fandango

L ast year, at a dinner party, the subject of high-school nicknames came up. I said that I had never had one, but that, if the truth be known—I must have been shithouse at the time—I'd really like to be known as the Falcon. Everyone around the table burst into hysterical laughter.

"Oh boy," these supposed friends of mine said, "the Falcon." And that set them all off on another choking orgy of whoops and guffaws.

Well, the fact is, I've been doing a little sky diving lately, and when one learns to fly, when one begins to swoop and soar in the wind thousands of feet above the rolling, golden hills of California, then, by God, he's earned the right to Falconhood.

Not that the first jump was all that graceful. That time Falcon dropped in a kind of terror, and he danced the first fear fandango. The plane banked above, the earth lay three thousand feet below. Instantaneously, all the gears and levers, all the intricate wiring of the Falcon's body reached flash point and burst into a magnesium-bright, adrenaline-fueled flame. There was nothing to fight but the wind; and so the Falcon fled, running hard and without hope in the indifferent, empty sky.

It was a long time ago, before we had taxes or bowling or bubble gum, and the theory runs that we lived an arboreal life, swinging through leafy treetops in the equatorial forest. There followed, it is said, a prolonged dry spell, and the forest dwindled. We climbed down from the trees onto the savanna, adopted an upright posture, and became nomadic food-gatherers and cooperative hunters. Later we became farmers, city builders, philosophers, artists, winos, and sex therapists, all of which led, in a straight unbroken line, to the very summit of our culture, the styrofoam coffee cup.

But sometimes in our dreams we fly. We exist above the ground as we must have in the equatorial forest. In our waking moments, when we fall, we startle and grab. At the top of the stairs, when we catch our foot in the rug and pitch forward, a hand goes out to the bannister, the side wall, grandma—anything, seen or unseen. The instinct may be inbred, something we developed in the trees, before we were men.

Indeed, it seems that children are born dreading a fall. Eleanore Gibson performed an elegant experiment that seems to confirm this. Gibson constructed a "visual cliff" consisting of a flat board on one side and a steep drop-off on the other. A solid sheet of glass, heavy enough to support a small child, covered the deep side. Infants old enough to crawl, six months and over, were placed on the center of the board and called by their mothers from different sides. Although they crawled freely over the flat board, the children refused, uniformly, to venture out over the deep side. Gibson concluded that the development of depth perception—at least the sort of self-protective mechanism that keeps us from falling off things—does not depend on prior experiences. Falling is something we fear instinctively, and it may be our oldest and our first fear.

All this relates with devious exactitude to sky diving, the sport of jumping out of a perfectly good airplane with a sack of brightly colored nylon on one's back. Veteran jumpers refer to their terrestrial brothers and sisters as "whuffos," which is the first word of the oft-asked question, "Whuffo they jump out of airplanes?"

Well yeah, whuffo?

In the very early stages—the first ten jumps or so—I think we are dealing with junkies—adrenaline junkies. The phrase comes from the mountaineer/photographer Galen Rowell, who uses it to explain why he habitually hurls himself into life-or-death situations. And so it is with sky diving. The sport is a form of staring into the abyss, of confronting our oldest and deepest fear. From the moment you leave the plane until the moment you pull the rip cord—an interminable length of time that usually lasts about thirty seconds— you are effectively dead. It's all the fun of suicide without the messy consequences.

Those consequences—"You mean that big red spot used to be a guy?"—tend to weigh heavily on the mind when one considers taking up sky diving. It is a risky sport, and while I take risks— especially for money—I spend a lot of time computing the inherent necrological density. To this end, I did a bit of research this summer after a couple of smirking, desk-bound editors insisted that I write a personal account of sky diving. From a parachuting handbook by Dan Poynter: "In the United States, over the last eight years, an annual average of thirty-five people have been fatally injured while parachuting . . . it is interesting to compare numbers with other activities: last year over 200 people perished scuba diving, 900 bicycling, over 7,000 drowned, 1,154 succumbed to bee stings, and 800 were even hit by lightning."

I took training for my first jump at the Pope Valley Parachute Center, a drop zone about two hours north of San Francisco. The first order of business was to learn the proper touchdown technique. The landing shock, we were told, would include some horizontal movement and would be roughly equivalent to jumping off a Cadillac doing about three miles an hour.

Our instructor, Bill, a short, sandy-haired man with a dry, almost sour sense of humor, spent a full hour teaching us how to fall from a four-foot platform. It seemed to be his theory that an action, repeated often enough, is stored as memory in the muscles.

There were twelve people in the class, and they ranged in age from the early twenties to late thirties. One young woman was about five feet tall and weighed maybe 150 pounds. She was the sort of blond often described as "perky." She looked like someone who ought to be named Betty.

Every time Betty jumped off the four-foot practice platform her face twisted into a pinched, apprehensive grimace, like someone who, for some reason, has elected to jump into a vat of vinegar. This was a constant source of amusement to a young gas-station attendant out of a hot, dusty central-California agricultural town. He had driven over a hundred miles to Pope Valley in a hot muscle car and pretty much figured he was going to burn up the sky with his natural ability. He combed his thick black hair straight back from the forehead and looked like somebody who ought to be named Duane.

Every time Betty got up on the platform, poor Duane had to stifle a laugh that invariably came snorting up out of his nose.

We learned the arch: legs apart, arms outspread about shoulder level, spine bowed until you can feel the strain at the small of your back. The arch is assumed upon exit from the plane. It puts all the weight in the stomach and forces the body into a horizontal position, facing the ground. The classic demonstration of the efficacy of the arch involves a badminton birdie. Dropped with the tip down and feathers up, it falls straight to the earth and is stable. The sky diver wants that stability in the air; his arms and legs are the feathers, his belly the tip. When the birdie is turned upside down, it flips over in its fall. A sky diver who arches his back the wrong way, like a hissing cat, will also flip over, and the opening chute may come up, say, between his legs and foul.

We examined the jump plane, a red, white, and blue Cessna 182 with room for the pilot, three student jumpers, and the jump master, Bill. We practiced getting into the "go" position, which involved stepping out onto the wheel and hanging from the wing strut. Betty said she wasn't sure she could hang from the strut since she couldn't even do one pullup. Duane rolled his eyes skyward so that we could all appreciate how hopeless Betty was. Bill said that nobody should worry about hanging on to the strut. The problem, he said, was getting people to let go.

We learned that our standard, round twenty-eight- or thirty-five-foot canopies would have a forward speed of about nine or five miles an hour, respectively. (More advanced-class chutes do about fourteen, and square canopies can do about twenty.) We learned how to steer the chute with toggles attached to directional lines, how to tell a bad chute from a good one, what to do in the rare case of a water landing, and spent half the afternoon working on emergency procedures. Bill would get a student up in front of the class, strap a harness on him, and yell, "Go."

The student was to make like a badminton birdie, and count "Arch thousand, two thousand" on up to five thousand. The static line, attached to the parachute, deploys the chute in about three seconds. If, by the count of five, there is no opening shock, the main chute has malfunctioned, totally. You must immediately pull the rip cord on the reserve chute strapped to your belly.

"Go."

"Arch thousand, two thousand . . ."

"Bam, opening shock. Whatta ya do?"

"Check to see if it's a good chute."

"It's bad. Whatta ya do?"

"I cut away the main chute." The procedure is to unsnap the capewells—two hinged metal plates near each shoulder on the harness—revealing two thick wire rings. Thumbs go in the rings, you pull, and the main chute goes free. Meanwhile, you look down, sight on your reserve-chute rip cord, and pull.

Betty stood up in front of all of us, nervously arching, which is not the most flattering thing you can do when you have a few pounds to lose.

At this point in his session with each student, Bill would begin throwing insults—often hitting close to home. Apparently he thought that real anger and confusion were as near as we were going to get on the ground to the feeling of dropping from that wing strut. "God, are you *fat*," Bill told Betty. "Do you belong to Weight Watchers? Because if you don't, you should."

Duane started off on a series of horsy snorts that lasted for a full thirty seconds.

"Lost forty pounds this year," Betty said through clenched teeth.

"Who are you talking to?" Bill yelled. "There's no one up there. You got a bad chute. Whatta ya do?"

Duane was curled up in his chair, head buried between his knees, and his back was shaking like a man in the throes of intolerable grief.

Later, during a break, I talked with Betty. Her face was round, even a little puffy, but it was clear that she would be very pretty a couple-dozen more pounds down the line. I imagined that sky diving had something to do with her weight-loss program, that it was simply another method of demonstrating to herself that she could do anything she put her mind to. Betty was the least physical person in our class, and most of the rest of us, with one notable exception, had come to admire her perky determination.

"The only thing I worry about," she said, "is if he tells me I can't jump." Bill had made it clear at the start that he would allow no one to jump until he felt certain they could handle it. "I told everyone at work that I was jumping," she said.

"But what if you chicken out?" I asked.

"Oh, that's fine. People understand that. But to be told you don't even have the choice . . . that's the worst thing."

I was in the second planeload of students to jump that day. With me were Betty and Duane. No one talks in the plane. The mouth is too dry and there are too many things to think about.

I remembered an old newsreel I once saw of a blimp disaster and its horrifying climactic moments. The airship was in dock, but something happened and it began to lift off. Two workmen grabbed at a hanging line, trying to hold the blimp down with their weight. It rose rapidly, and quite soon both men were too high off the ground to let go without risking serious injury. The camera tracked them as they hung there, helpless on that rope. One man's arms gave way and he fell, hurtling out of the frame. The other held on for several more seconds until he too fell, but this time the camera followed him as he plummeted toward earth. There was nothing for the man to do, and he must have known, with sickening certainty, that he was dead; but something called on him to live, to do something, and so he *ran*. The sequence is terrifying: the man flails his arms, then pumps his legs, like a sprinter in a dream. And he ran until he died.

Bill had told us that we'd have a tendency to run in the air. It was a natural reaction, like that of the man in the newsreel who ran to his death. I promised myself I would hold the arch and not run, not give in to the misinformed bleating of instinct.

It didn't happen that way. I was first out of the plane. Bill opened the door. The wind howled past. He spotted the area where he wanted to cut me loose, told me to sit down and swing my legs out—they blew toward the back of the plane with a frightening jerk—then told the pilot to cut the engine.

I stepped out onto the locked wheel, grabbed the strut, then hung there, arching hard. We were three thousand feet in the air, and everything below seemed to be carved in microminiature. We were going about seventy miles an hour.

I was supposed to look at Bill, but I didn't think I did a very good job of that. He shouted, "Go!" I let go of the strut and arched. Everything happened very fast and very slow at the same time. I was supposed to shout out my count—arch thousand, two thousand, and so on—but I was as silent as a stone. Those movies you see with guys falling off cliffs and screaming all the way down have nothing to do with reality. People who fall from great heights have too much to think about. They don't scream.

Having blown my count, I arched all the harder, arched, in fact, until I could see the plane overhead. A good sign. I had been possessed of this idiot fear that as soon as I let go of the strut I'd be chopped in half by the tail of the plane. It was no use telling me that if the plane was going seventy, then someone hanging from the strut was also doing seventy, and would drop out of harm's way well before the tail passed overhead.

Now, all this happened in the first second. I had held my arch admirably, which pitched me forward so that I was looking straight down, three thousand feet. Some autonomous voice shrieked inside my head. I was falling, I was going to land *on my head*, I was going to end up as a crimson crater in the field below. Another more conscious voice reminded me that I had promised to hold the arch. So I compromised. I arched from the waist up. Everything below took off at a dead run.

No one really knows why this happens, why we feel compelled to sprint away from the long fall. We are frightened, certainly; and our instincts tell us, in such situations, to fight or flee. Since there is nothing up there to fight, we run.

Fortunately, on the static line, your chute will open, you will not die, but giving in to a sprint is hilariously funny to those watching you from the plane. It is rather like one of those cartoons where Wile E. Coyote, having eaten a year's supply of mail-order pep pills, pursues the Road Runner at speeds he himself can barely believe. The Road Runner and Wile E. are moving so fast they are only a blur in our vision. But then the Road Runner stops—"beep

beep"—standing stock still on the edge of a cliff, and it seems as if the law of inertia has no dominion over him.

Too late, Wile E. Coyote perceives the cliff and attempts to stop. His heels plow twin trenches in the dirt. Nonetheless, he is carried over the precipice, and he experiences that moment in which everything moves very fast and very slow at the same time. He turns back toward the face of the cliff, his horrified eyes bulging in his head. He hangs there, motionless in the void. Absurdly, he begins to run. He gains an inch, two, three. A gleam of hope enters his eyes. Then gravity asserts itself and things begin happening very fast. Wile E. falls more rapidly than one might have thought possible. He falls, in fact, so fast that he leaves an inexplicable puff of smoke in his former position, and he makes a whistling sound all the way down to the mute canyon floor.

And so, a second and a half out of the plane, I was running like Wile E. Coyote, dancing the fear fandango. Then, suddenly, there was a jolt on the chest strap and I was brought upright under a bright green canopy, a good one I was relieved to note, all round and shaped like a jellyfish. Over the nearest range of hills—in California's summer they are smooth and golden, looking almost like suede from a distance—there was a great blue lake shimmering in the late afternoon sun. The sky was silent, like the inside of a vast cathedral, and I could hear the beating of my own heart.

The steering toggles were exactly where Bill said they would be and turning the chute was as easy as driving a car. I looked down through my feet to the five-acre plowed field where I hoped to land. A gentle breeze wafted me toward the small target area and I sailed with it, occasionally checking the altimeter mounted atop my reserve chute. At 2,500 feet I was still above the wrong field, one with bulls in it; 2,000—I was coming in over the plowed area; 1,800—a problem was developing. In all that five acres there was one tree, and it was between me and the target. At 1,250 feet I seemed to be hovering, motionless, above that damned tree. The wind was with me—I could see that from the windsock—and my chute had to be making five miles an hour; but still I couldn't seem to clear the tree that was becoming a very large and distressing sight.

At 500 feet we had been instructed to turn our chutes into the wind and prepare to land. Bill had said that if there were obstacles, turn to the nearest open space. Never try to fly *over* an obstacle under 500 feet. And there I was, dropping out of the sky directly into a tree. You land in one of those, you're supposed to cross your legs. Straddling a branch is no fun for man or woman. You're also instructed to cover your face and neck. Jagged, upward-thrusting branches can blind you, pierce your throat. I thought about these things and decided, quite definitely, not to land in the tree. I rode the chute to 450, and finally 400 until I was sure I was clear of the tree. Then I turned into the wind.

The parachute, which was doing five miles an hour, swiveled neatly into a ten-mile-an-hour wind, giving me a ground speed of five miles an hour, backward. I was still tracking toward a target I could no longer see. At about two hundred feet the ground stopped swaying and became hugely immobile. I picked a spot on the horizon and forced myself to stare at it.

There is controversy about this. Some instructors prefer to have first-time jumpers look at the ground; but Bill insisted that people who stare at the ground tend to do one of two things: they either stretch one foot down to the dirt, like a swimmer testing the water in a pool, or they protect themselves by drawing their knees up to their chests. Both moves break legs. Because Bill had been right about that strange run—the first fear fandango—I tried hard not to watch the ground, which is like trying to walk a mile with your eyes closed. Even though I was staring at a nearby hilltop, I could see the good brown earth looming up under me in the lower periphery of my vision. In a moment, I thought, I'll hit. I was, understandably I think, apprehensive about that, and so I began barking, a perverse reaction that rather surprised me.

The sound was something like that made by a sleeping dog when he is partially awakened by, say, the distant backfire of a car. The dog has no desire to investigate, but he feels that he must note the intrusion, so emits a halfhearted, drowsy bark—mmmmm-woof—and drifts back into his dream.

So there I was, at fifty feet, and I discovered, to my horror, that I was humming in a shaky, scared sort of way. "Mmmm . . ." The hum went up a notch in pitch: "Mmmmmm . . ."

I hit, rolling over onto my back in the prescribed manner and barking like a sleeping dog. "Mmm-ooooffff."

All at once, to my utter amazement, I was up on my feet, running around the canopy so the wind wouldn't drag me across the field. I had landed a few hundred yards from the target, on the very bosom of that sweet, brown, plowed field.

After my chute had opened, the plane banked, came back around, and dropped Betty. I saw her come in low over my head, turn into the wind, and land closer to the target than any of the other first-time jumpers. Duane was still up there, last one out. We waited for a time, Betty and I, but we never saw his chute. Bill was up there, stunting under his more maneuverable square canopy; but otherwise the sky above the field was empty. By the time we gathered up our equipment and got back to the hangar, the Cessna was landing, ready for another load. Duane wasn't on the plane.

Bill clapped me on the back. "You did about fifty miles before your parachute opened," he said.

"Yeah," I said, "and I blew my count too."

"Well, you did okay for the first time. Give yourself an eighty-five and remember what you did wrong."

About that time we caught sight of Duane. He was on foot, pulling his equipment over a fence about a mile away. By the time he got to the hangar, he was sweating profusely and he didn't seem to want to talk to anybody.

"Man," Bill asked him, "what did you do *right?*"

"I did all right," Duane muttered sulkily.

"All right?" Bill was incredulous. "All right? You wouldn't let go of the strut. That's why you landed all to hell and gone. I was yelling at you."

"Yeah, yeah, yeah," Duane said.

Later, I ran into Duane as we were both hanging up our jumpsuits, and I couldn't resist sticking it to him a little. "Had some trouble letting go of the strut, did you?"

"What?"

"Geez, you must have landed three miles away."

"Yeah, yeah, yeah."

"You should have seen her," I said, nodding toward Betty, who was smiling serenely and accepting congratulations. "She damn near landed on the target."

"Yeah, yeah, yeah," Duane said. He was staring at the ground. "Look, I gotta go."

*　*　*

In the next couple of weeks I jumped about a dozen more times. By my fourth static-line jump, I was arching well, stable in the air, and pulling a dummy rip cord. On the fifth jump I thought I did everything right, even to the point of not barking on touchdown. The sixth time out I pulled my own rip cord, a bright metal handle—about the size of a Cracker Jacks box—located just about on my right pectoral muscle. It was a pretty fair jump. I arched for the thousand count, then looked. You always have to look. It's no good pulling, say, the latch that loosens your harness. The handle was right where it should have been. I pulled and it came out smooth as eggs through a hen.

On the seventh jump I was instructed to go to a five count before popping the chute. In practice, a five-second delay plus the pull may take up to eight seconds. In that time the sky diver reaches speeds of over a hundred miles an hour and will cover some eight hundred vertical feet.

The sensation becomes that of flying. You can control it. It's like standing on the edge of a high diving board. Lean out and you can feel the point at which you will fall, tumbling over in a front flip. In free fall, from the arch position, a simple downward movement of the head accomplishes the same thing. Bring one arm in, under your body, and you'll do a barrel roll.

Eventually, such acrobatics become second nature. Aside from flips and rolls, experienced divers can go into an hellaciously fast headfirst dive, or modify that position to track horizontally across the sky. Starting from the classic 7,200-foot level, on a thirty-second delay, they reach terminal velocity—about 190 miles an hour—in about twelve seconds, provided they are in the "slow" arch position. At subterminal velocity, maneuvers feel a bit mushy; but once at terminal, the greater wind resistance makes a well-executed roll feel crisp and controlled.

Experienced sky divers make a door exit—no more clumsy hanging from the strut—and can track across the sky in a fast dive toward another sky diver who may be in the slower arch position. At some point above his man, the tracking sky diver will flare out into an arch, then "dock" with the first man by grabbing both his wrists. When four sky divers do this, they form a star, and bigger stars and formations may be accomplished with six and eight and even twenty sky divers.

This is called "relative work," and it is the highest expression of the sky diver's art.

On my eighth jump the rip cord stuck—it wouldn't come out with a one-handed pull—and it seemed to me that I handled the situation with a good deal of grace. Observers on the ground insist that they heard a loud and obscene word come booming down out of the sky, but I tend to discount this because I remember what I did and what I thought. With no hesitation, I reached over and gave the handle a vicious two-handed yank. Moving both my hands to the right had put me out of position, so I arched hard and was falling stable when the main chute deployed.

The experience taught me that I will not panic or freeze during an airborne emergency. Consequently, on subsequent jumps, I've been able to forget myself a little and take a tiny sip of the rapture of free fall. Experienced divers court this sensation—it is more sophisticated than those first few adrenaline-charged jumps—and often they must remind themselves to pop the chute. Some veterans have run that rapture all the way to earth wearing two good chutes that they never pulled.

In my case, during that eighth jump with the tight rip cord, fear turned itself inside out and I made the important transition from falling to flying. And if, in fact, I did shout something nasty during that flight, I prefer to think of it not as an obscenity, but rather as the Call of the Falcon.

Balloon Drop

The pilot hit the big propane burner and threw fire into the throat of the balloon. "Hold us down," he called, and half a dozen folks leaned their weight onto the outside of the basket. The pilot wanted plenty of lift. He was going to be hauling two men and a hang glider—five hundred pounds of dead weight—under the basket. "Okay, let go."

The balloon rose a foot or two, then moved gently to the northwest, so Barney Hallin and I had to walk a few steps with the glider to avoid being dragged. And then we were off the ground, rising rapidly. Double loops of nylon webbing, tied inside the basket and to the king post of the glider, held us fast.

The baseball diamond below began to shrink in the silence of the sky, and people who'd parked alongside the road to watch honked their horns in applause. The Gallatin Valley, an agricultural area just outside Bozeman, Montana, was a green checkerboard sprawling among mountain ranges on three sides. The morning sun, low in the sky, pierced dark clouds to the south and east, sending shafts of slanting light to the hayfields below.

We were at one hundred feet now—not really high enough to

use the parachutes—and terror lent a sharp edge to the beauty of the green world, hard and flat below. Barney was hanging beside me inside a triangle of aluminum tubes called the control bar, centered under the long boomerang wing of the glider. He'd fly the beast. I was along for the ride.

In 1982, Barney Hallin set the Montana distance record for hang gliding.

"It was only eighty miles," Barney said, as if to dismiss the record. "People soar eighty miles every day down in the Owens Valley." Hallin was too modest. The thermals of the Owens Valley provide perhaps the best hang-gliding conditions in the world.

Barney's achievement, in far from optimal conditions, had fascinated me for two years. He started in the wind tunnel known as Paradise Valley, passed through a gunsight canyon along the Yellowstone River, flew almost directly over my house, then skirted the east side of the Crazy Mountains, where he caught some lift at the base of a flat cloud and rose to fifteen thousand feet. His route took him over the eleven-thousand-foot-high ridge of the Crazies.

"There are all these glacial lakes up there," Barney said. "You get above the meadows and the wildflowers, up to the gravel and talus, and the Crazies are dotted with lakes. Some of these lakes were blue, but some were yellow, some were shades of red and orange. I don't know where the colors came from. Maybe it was the position of the sun or reflections off the canyon walls, but they were beautiful."

Listening to Barney talk, you wanted to be up there with him, gliding in the silence of the wind at fifteen thousand feet, looking down into the emerald and ruby lakes, all those shimmering jewels, up there on top of the Crazy Mountains.

It's not an impossible dream, just a damn difficult one. Ten years ago I took a hang-gliding course. Every Saturday morning for a month I drove one hundred miles to a seven-hundred-foot sand dune, spent an hour assembling a rental glider, then carried the thing up the sand, on my back.

Every Saturday, I blasted off the top of the dune at a dead run, and felt a sudden thrill on that last light step before the kite left the ground. Then I was airborne, and the glider would list to the left or the right and catch a wing tip in the sand. There was a long, abrasive slide during which I discovered such things as sand burns. In the four Saturdays I spent trying to learn to soar, my longest flight was a minute and a half. I never failed to crash spectacularly upon landing.

"It's easier now," Barney told me. Like any religious fanatic, he was out to convert the world. "We have better gliders, better harnesses. Quick-deployment chutes have made the sport a lot safer." Even so, you can't just strap yourself into a glider and fly. You still have plenty of dues to pay in the form of time and bruises.

"I could fly tandem with you," Barney said. "You could get an idea of what it is to soar." He wanted to convince me that another round of black-and-blue Saturdays would be worth the pain and frustration. "We'll do a balloon drop," he said, and here we were, at seven o'clock on a Saturday morning, rising into a cathedral of light shafts with the ground receding below us.

Even at the supposed safety of 150 feet—hang gliders have been saved by the new chutes at that height—I had a vision of cartoon catastrophes. The parachutes, 24 feet in diameter, were packed in little bags inside a Velcro pocket on our chests. To deploy the chute, you yank it out of the Velcro by a nylon loop, then toss the bag into the sky. The chutes were attached to our chest harnesses by 30 feet of nylon webbing, and when they reached the end of that, they'd pop open like those huge nylon flowers that blossom out behind speeding dragsters at the track.

My vision of doom went like this: The glider accidentally releases early, and there is no time to pull it out of its dive. The chutes are tossed into empty air, there's a screaming fall, then impact, followed by chutes popping open above, just the way Wile E. Coyote's Acme parachutes always opened a second too late in *Roadrunner* cartoons.

At three hundred feet, half a minute later, I felt a little better: Not long ago, two hang-glider pilots in Sheridan, Wyoming, had used their chutes to survive a midair crash at three hundred feet. We continued to rise smoothly at about three hundred feet a minute.

Barney and I were lying flat, hanging face down inside the triangle at about ten thousand feet, when the pilot shouted, "Now!" I pulled the release ring attached to a modified sailplane release mechanism. Barney had both hands on the base of the control bar. It seemed, then, as if we hung there, immobile, for perhaps two seconds. Then the glider tipped forward, and we were in a free-fall vertical dive.

Barney was pushing out on the bar below us, trying to lift the nose of the glider and get some air under us. We wanted to avoid a tumble. The nose of the glider, having dropped straight down, wanted to keep going, to flip over. The whole kite could turn upside down, and the two of us would bang down onto the fabric of the glider as we tumbled, and then the thing would break, with us in it: the wings could just collapse in on the glider like the wings of a caddis fly folding over its back.

The glider was a UP (Ultralight Products) 185 Comet 2—a two-man version of the kite that has set the world record, one of the hang gliders you are most likely to see at world competitions—and it was specifically designed to prevent a tumble. Barney brought the Comet out of its dive in less than one hundred feet, and I was clutching the control bar, catching my breath, when he said, "You're flying her."

I glanced over at Barney Hallin, and he was hanging in the harness with his hands dangling. Like any novice pilot, I took the glider out of its mild dive—"We're going to die!"—by pushing up on the bar. "You'll stall her like that," Barney said. "Move over to the right a little and pull in on the bar. We'll circle the balloon."

Barney moved with me, and our weight caused the glider to bank to the right and accelerate into a diving turn. There was a sudden, comfortable instinct at work in the feel of a soaring glider. It was clear that if I stayed to the right, with the bar pulled in, we'd go into a spiraling dive. It seemed entirely natural, after banking into our turn, to move to the left inside the triangle and push out slightly on the bar. The glider leveled out as we swept past the balloon.

Barney then had me do a left turn, and we swooped and dived around the balloon, which, unlike the glider, was at the complete mercy of the wind. For twenty minutes we worked with the glider, circling downward with the balloon in air that Barney said had a "lot of sink" to it. I was flying almost in control—soaring was a lot easier than taking off and landing, which is what I knew—and the earth below seemed to glow in the odd pastels I have seen when flying in my dreams.

* * *

At one hundred feet, Barney had me kick out of the cocoon harness so that I was dangling feet down from the hang strap. We were circling into a "no-wind" landing, doing perhaps thirty miles an hour. Not an optimal condition. Light-wind landings are the best: You just head into the breeze, push up on the bar, and stall down into a "no-step" landing. On a windless day, you have to power up on the control bar—"flare out"—at thirty miles an hour. Barney flared hard and stalled her, and we hit the ground running at about five miles an hour. My feet got tangled up with Barney's, and we fell forward and the nose of the glider buried itself in the earth. It was the sort of landing I distinctly remember from my hang-gliding lessons.

The balloon ride had cost four hundred dollars, but even then, lying on the ground with a puffy lip and a mouthful of dirt, I had no doubt that the sensation of soaring, of dreamflight, was worth it. And Barney was right: There's a better, cheaper way to pay your dues. It only hurts for about six months' worth of Saturdays. After that, you've earned the jewels atop the Crazies.

Fear of Falling

I am hanging from a rope.

Well, not hanging precisely. The rope, at the moment, is quite slack, but it is fastened to a fixed point above, and the only way to keep it slack is to exert various pressures against this chimney of granite, this vertical hole in the mountain. My back is pressed up against the rock on one side; my knees are flat bang hard to the granite on the other. I am not accustomed to exertion in the fetal position, and muscle systems I had been completely unaware of all my life burn and shriek. This is torture of a refined sort, and I see—in the fullness of pain; in the clarity of fear—Man as he was before he was Man. Here we are gibbering in the trees, beasts without words, knowing only that falling is death.

Scientists have proved that humans fear falling almost from the moment of birth. One experiment, conducted with infants barely able to crawl, elegantly proved the point. The infants were placed on a sheet of glass and encouraged to crawl over it to the waiting arms of their mothers. When a solid-colored mat was placed under the glass, the babies crawled straight to their mothers, but when the mat was removed, revealing a drop-off, the infants would not venture out onto the glass. The experiment had to do with perception, though I think it demonstrates that falling is our first and most primitive fear.

And that is the wordless and primal message the autonomous nervous system now wants to impart to my conscious mind. "Get off the rock," it says, "or you will surely die."

The only way to get off the rock—without falling—is to climb, crablike, up this vertical hell-hole, this chimney erosion carved out of the granite in Yosemite National Park. Rock climbers, masochists who enjoy pain and fear, call this particular chimney "the Iota." It's a piece of cake for almost any climber with the exception of novices like myself. I am concerned, at the moment, with the psychology of the rope. It could just as well be tied around my neck as fastened to the sling about my waist. The rope does not comfort me.

There is a dialogue in progress here: The rational mind insists that this is a new rope—damn thing cost $120—and there is a good bit of built-in elasticity so that if—please God, no—I should fall, the jolt will not tear my innards out. The worst that can happen, the absolute worst, is that I'll scrape up against the rock and end up looking like parts of my body have been scrubbed with a wire brush. This I know in my mind—but my body does not agree. "You asinine fool," it howls, "you are going to fall, you are going to die."

I have been trying to get up out of this chimney for nearly thirty minutes now. Sometime back, two other climbers shot by me as if I were standing still, which, in fact, I probably was. They stopped only for a word of encouragement: "Go for it." And then they were gone.

At any given time, there are several hundred climbers in residence at Yosemite. In the early days of the sport—say the late fifties—they came for the big walls, for El Capitan and Half Dome and Sentinel Rock, those great glittering slabs of granite two thousand feet or more high. As more and more climbers "bagged" the big walls, certain members of climbing's aristocracy began working on "problems." They took on smaller, but more difficult, walls.

Climbs, and climbers, are rated on a number system. A 5.0 climb is just a tad more difficult than a steep uphill walk. In the late sixties, a 5.7 climber was considered a pretty fair rock jock. These days, some of the world's best climbers are attempting routes rated 5.12, "problems" that would set Spider-Man to whimpering in fear.

These climbers—the very best—make Yosemite their home for the summer and early fall. They are the new matadors, the ultimate in grace under pressure, and Yosemite is their arena. I have always admired rock climbers, and have often wondered what it was that pushed them. The only way to find out, I reasoned, was to give the sport a try.

And so here I am, hanging on the rope, contemplating the fragility of flesh. Two more moves to the lip of the chimney now. And then one more—I am at my limit, exhausted—except the last move is a doozy. I must place my hands up above my head and pull my body up, up, more now, more, up over the lip at least to my waist so that I can bend over the lip and throw a leg up. That's all. The muscles in my arms have burnt my bones to ashes. There is no strength left, and so I—no, no, no—start to fall, and that is when— oh, yes, *now*—my adrenal glands do their stuff, and from out of nowhere, I feel a blinding burst of absolute energy and I am up, over the lip of rock. Safe. My heart booms like thunder inside my chest. I am lying on my back, staring into the impossibly blue sky, and it is as if I can see beyond the blue, see into the depths of space, see the brittle glowing stars whirling forever in their galactic polka.

It is a moment of absolute clarity, such as we've all experienced at one time or another. Here you are driving along the highway, for instance, and a car darts over into your lane. It's a '71 Dodge Swinger, crumpled left fender. Older woman at the wheel. White hair, black dress. Her eyes are wide, her mouth is open. She is about to scream. You swerve right, up onto the shoulder. Gravel rattles against the undercarriage, and the right wheel catches some grass, rocking the car. The Dodge shoots safely by outside, but you are rocketing toward a mailbox, painted white. The little red flag is down. Swerve left, spray gravel, screech, and swerve back onto the highway.

After a heart stopper like that, most people will pull over, turn off the engine, watch their hands shake for a few minutes, and replay the entire episode in their minds several dozen times. Seldom have they seen anything so clearly: the woman's dress, her eyes, her mouth, the total lurch and swerve of motion. Everything seems extraordinarily brilliant. And the entire affair took perhaps five seconds.

I was stuck in the Iota for nearly an hour, but there was the same crystalline clarity about the experience, and I had, for just a moment, a true sense of what rock climbing is all about.

Our bodies, it would seem, are stingy with regard to certain juices that can have all sorts of beneficial, not to say delirious, effects. Only unpleasant things like danger or the proximity of death or final exams open the floodgates.

Each of us possesses adrenal glands; they are two tiny, triangular meatballs located at about the north pole of each kidney. The average adrenal gland weighs less than a fifth of an ounce and measures about an inch across.

The outer 90 percent of each gland is called the cortex and is of no interest to us here. The inner 10 percent is called the medulla. In times of stress, the adrenal medulla is stimulated to secrete two hormones: adrenaline and noradrenaline. Together, these substances can, quite quickly, prepare a person for effective emergency action: Respiration increases, the heart beats stronger and faster, and the blood is pumped to those areas of the body that most need it. Additionally, the central nervous system is stimulated.

The effects of adrenaline and noradrenaline may be felt subjectively as fear or anxiety combined with increased mental alertness. It has been found that those who exhibit fear under some specified stress tend to have high concentrations of both adrenaline and noradrenaline in the blood. However, those who are prepared to stand their ground tend to display even higher concentrations of noradrenaline.

This noradrenaline is wondrous stuff. It affects those systems in the brain that are concerned with emotions, especially euphoria, well-being, and alertness. After its release, noradrenaline is absorbed back into certain nerve endings, where it is stored for future use. (These accumulations in the nerve endings may be more important in the immediate response to stress than the adrenal glands themselves.) Drugs that inhibit the absorption of noradrenaline by the nerve endings are antidepressants. They make you feel good by keeping the noradrenaline sloshing around in your brain.

Amphetamines, it is thought, may actually cause noradrenaline to be released from the nerve endings. Amphetamines act as mood elevators, help decrease fatigue, and produce increased initiative and confidence. They also augment the ability to concentrate.

So there is is: noradrenaline, the basis of what many people in the so-called "thrill sports" mistakenly call adrenaline addiction. It explains why many otherwise sensible individuals habitually hurl themselves into truly frightful situations, and why—having survived, say, a three-day avalanche-ridden climb at elevations over ten thousand feet, they come down from the hill acting like one of the rarest of God's creations: a really happy speed freak. It is, in short, a good and proper reason to confront our most primitive fear.

May 13, 3:00 P.M., Yosemite Valley

I am five hundred feet up a nearly perpendicular slab of granite, climbing a route known as the Grack. The temperature is hovering around eighty degrees; sunlight comes blasting off the quartz, and the rock itself is hotter than a desert highway in August. I am certain that an egg thrown against the wall would fry well before it oozed its way five hundred feet to the boulders below.

The Grack is rated as a 5.7 climb, well above my ability to lead or climb solo. Consequently, I am roped into a belay system: One of American's star rock climbers, Doug Robinson, is sitting on a ledge fifty feet above me, holding the rope in the prescribed manner and bracing for my inevitable fall. I am standing on an inch-wide ledge. Every muscle in my legs is twitching rapidly up and down, like the needle on a sewing machine. I can relieve the pressure on my legs somewhat by standing up straight and leaning into the wall. Unfortunately, this sort of full body contact with the blistering granite makes me feel like a strip of bacon in a frying pan.

My experience in the Iota has helped. I have discovered, in the past few years—as editors began sending me out to fulfill a lot of adolescent fantasies—that a period of intense study and preparation helps get the noradrenaline pumping in those tough situations in which the tough should get going.

Scientists here proved this. Preparation is not only a form of life insurance, it also maximizes the noradrenaline experience. In clinical tests, monkeys placed under sudden stress showed increased levels of adrenaline and noradrenaline in the blood, as expected.

But, when the monkeys were prepared by a warning system and then placed under stress, the adrenaline level remained the same, *while the noradrenaline level increased*.

Still and all, in order to generate a little noradrenaline euphoria, you are going to have to put up with a lot of adrenaline and the anxiety it causes. Risk is a push me–pull you, manic-depressive, psychological roller coaster, and, at the moment, on my tiny ledge five hundred feet in the air, I feel very low indeed. I have been an hour and a half on the rock and I am exhausted.

Doug Robinson sits serenely on his ledge. This climb is child's play for him, no more difficult than taking a flight of stairs. He is smiling out over the valley and thinking of a cheery little book he wants to write about it all, called *Short Pants and Sunny Granite*.

I am thinking about two not-unrelated subjects. First, I am planning my attack on fifty feet of wall. Second, I am considering the neurotic problems of one of my dogs. Since puppyhood she has consistently cowered from people and other dogs. Twenty-seven inches high at the shoulder, she spends half her waking life walking around all crouched down with her belly an inch off the ground. When cornered, she rolls over and wets herself, as if to say, "Beat me, I'm useless." I am thinking about this particular dog because I have never before appreciated her approach to stress. I am thinking that there must be some sweet, almost sexual satisfaction in her life of constant surrender. If only my ledge were wide enough, I'd consider rolling over myself. It would be up to Doug Robinson to figure some way to get 210 pounds of urine-stained deadweight off the wall.

As for attacking the rock, I have a bad case of precommitment jitters. This is the toughest pitch yet, and it looks like ten or fifteen minutes of solid misery. You have to keep up a rhythm, and there is no place to rest. Starting such a pitch is like launching into a fistfight with someone who outweighs you by fifty pounds. You have to see the thing through all the way to the end, and stopping for any reason whatsoever will result in a brutal beating.

Where I stand, there is a crack in the Crack that is maybe a foot wide. The surrounding rock is as slick as polished marble. The first move involves placing both hands in the crack and pulling in opposite directions, as if your intention is to split the wall down the middle. Next, the feet come up as close to the hands as possible. You want your weight over your feet for increased stability.

The next move is to inch one hand up a bit inside the crack. The second hand follows, then one foot comes up, then the other. Only one hand or foot moves. Three points should always be stable on the rock.

Within five moves, no more, my exhaustion fades. The wall is a problem that can be solved. The crack has narrowed considerably, and there is no leverage in attacking it like the Incredible Hulk separating steel bars in a prison cell. Here, just one hand goes into the crack and a fist is made. This is called crack jamming, and it is the first time I have ever attempted it. Doug Robinson insists that he has never heard of anyone who lost his footing on a crack jam and consequently yanked his arm out of its socket and off his body.

Another fist jam. Another. Now the crack is thinner yet. An open hand goes inside, sideways, and is maneuvered about and flexed in any manner that will hold. I actually feel as if I'm getting stronger.

As the crack narrows, hand jams give way to knuckle jams. Here the crack will admit only the index finger, which is then curled and flexed. Feet come up close to the finger in the rock and rhythm dictates that the next knuckle jam is placed . . . now . . . then another, and another, until the crack disappears altogether and I am a mere five feet from Robinson and the sit-down ledge. Between us, all is slick, glittering granite.

Here, though, is a tiny nubbin, a pimple on the polished surface, and I can just get the very tips of two fingers on it, while the toe of my boot falls on another nubbin, giving me just enough height to reach up and grab the ledge. I pull myself up and half-sit, half-lie on the burning rock while my heart bangs away at my rib cage and my breath comes in great superheated blasts. There is something at the back of my throat that tastes of blood and bile. Below, Yosemite Valley stands out all green and hard-edged in that peculiar penetrating vision one acquires while the noradrenaline is pumping. For the moment, I am one of the Gods. Invulnerable.

When I get my wind back, Doug starts climbing again. I have three more pitches like the last one until I can honorably get off the rock, and the adrenaline is beginning to take over from the noradrenaline. I was a fool to ever agree to start this climb. I want off—*off!*—and lying there on my back, it is my full desire to whimper like a beaten dog.

May 13, 11:45 P.M.,
The Mountain Bar, Yosemite National Park

I am working on my fourth beer. Something very curious is going on: Despite the fact that I spent half the afternoon promising myself never to get on a wall with Doug Robinson again, the two of us are planning tomorrow's climb. I feel very good indeed. At present there is nothing to be anxious about, and my exceptionally high spirits probably have to do with an excess of noradrenaline in my system.

All around us, others are planning their own climbs. Most everyone in the place is a climber. According to Doug, there are about thirteen hundred of them in residence, and about two-thirds of them are here tonight. A few of them probably went out and scared themselves badly today. The others, like Doug, did a few easy practice climbs, in preparation, no doubt, for other, more fearsome attempts. For every climber, no matter how accomplished, there is a climb somewhere that is just at the limit of his or her abilities.

They are lucky that way. In sports like football, an athlete who has competed in his event a hundred or more times must "psych" himself up to get the adrenal hormones flowing. This problem of diminishing hormonal returns is called habituation. When scientists subjected rats to stress applied repeatedly and in a rhythmic manner, the levels of adrenaline and noradrenaline in the blood dropped consistently. In this regard—I don't want to hear about any others— I am like those rats. I was, for instance, nowhere near as frightened on my tenth skydive as I was on my first.

Habituation forces the true adrenaline junkies to continually push their abilities to the limit. That is why the best climbers are always looking for a more difficult route to the top of this or that peak, and why divers risk nitrogen narcosis and the bends to set deep-diving records, and why the Federation sends the *Starship Enterprise* out into the void with instructions to "boldly go where no man has gone before."

All around me, climbers are frightening themselves with tales of their most nearly fatal climbs, or remembering friends who perished on some godforsaken wall: typical adrenaline-junkie talk. I've been asking around about knuckle jams: I know I can get a sweet, sharp rush if someone tells me about losing a finger that way.

It is midnight and the bartender calls time. No one wants to leave and it is getting rowdy in this den of addicts. Eventually the Park Police step in to clear out the bar. Their attitude toward the climbers is the attitude of all police toward all junkies.

And so we step out into the brisk night air, shouting and shoving one another, regarding the police with amused tolerance. People who spend the best part of their lives confronting the first fear aren't much frightened by uniforms.

Into the Eyewall

"A little nervous?" the master sergeant asked.

"Scared's more like it," I said.

My notes were spread out on the table in the briefing room at Keesler Air Force Base in Biloxi, Mississippi, and my eye kept falling on the least-reassuring bits of information I had collected. Like this sentence: "In a single day a moderately intense hurricane often releases as much heat energy as would be released by the simultaneous detonation of 400 twenty-megaton hydrogen bombs."

"Listen," the master sergeant said, "I flew my first penetration in 1976, and it was like my first combat mission. If it wasn't for them five other guys I woulda stood in bed."

"It can be pretty terrifying," a captain said, "but oh God, when you've got one of those well-defined babies out there . . ."

"A classic, like Allen or Camille or Freddy . . ."

"And you're banging through the eyewall for that first fix, you feel like a kid climbing to the top for the first drop on his first roller-coaster ride."

"Horrifying."

"But beautiful, some of them."

"Next to sex," the master sergeant said, "it's the best thing going."

I was sitting around the table with members of the 920th Weather Reconnaissance Group and their flight arm, the 815th Weather Reconnaissance Squadron, the men and women known as the Stormtrackers. In another hour I'd fly with the 815th, and they'd get a fix on Hurricane Frances—her precise location, size, intensity, and internal barometric pressure. We'd fly directly into the eye of the hurricane.

"We're accident-free and fatality-free," a lieutenant colonel said. "Fortunately, we've had a precisely equal number of takeoffs and landings."

"But what about this Frances?" I asked. "You think she could be a killer?"

"That's what we're going out there to find out."

Every year between June and November an average of one to three hurricanes hit the United States. They spawn over warm tropical water in the Atlantic, sometimes as far east as the Cape Verde Islands off the coast of Africa. Photos from the satellites GOES 1 and 2 initially show a central dense overcast. This is an area of intense low pressure, and it pulls the surrounding air to it the way gravity pulls water down a hill. But because of the spinning of the earth, the Coriolis effect, the inward-rushing air begins hooking in a counterclockwise direction. (Take a globe and set it spinning. Now, using a marker, try drawing straight lines on it, north to south and south to north. The curvature of the lines is the result of the spinning of the globe, and it is more pronounced at the equator, over those warm waters where hurricanes are born.)

The winds want to fall into that low-pressure hole and fill it up, but because of the Coriolis effect, they end up veering off to one side and spinning around the most intense area of low pressure, like a satellite around the earth. As the system becomes closed, circular, the spinning wall of wind can reach speeds in excess of two hundred miles an hour. And this "eyewall" is, in effect, a solid bank of thunderstorm cells several miles thick. The area of utter calm inside the eyewall is the eye of the hurricane, an area of such intense low pressure that it draws the eyewall to it, tighter and tighter, making it move faster and faster. (For example, a whirling ice skater: With arms outstretched he moves slowly, but with arms pulled in, he is a spinning blur.)

Full-blown hurricanes look exactly like a child's pinwheel in photos transmitted from the satellites. But scientists working with the photos can only compute the storm's position to within forty or fifty miles, not well enough to provide adequate warning to residents of an area where the hurricane may come ashore. And that is where the Stormtrackers come in. Their job is to provide the information scientists need to predict accurately what the hurricane will do. They must penetrate the eyewall and take the barometric pressure within the eye; the lower it is, of course, the more intense the hurricane is likely to be. They pinpoint the exact location of the beast and measure its intensity. As one lieutenant colonel said, "It's like they told you there's a big mean bear in a cave; then they give you a thermometer and say, 'Here, go take its temperature.'"

The bear's temperature is the information that allows scientists to predict, within about a hundred miles, where the hurricane will hit, giving residents twenty-four hours to evacuate. A real killer hurricane can drive a fifty-mile-long dome of water twenty to twenty-five feet high before it. At the turn of the century—long before the Stormtrackers got into the business of taking the bear's temperature—a storm surge estimated to be in excess of twenty feet hit Galveston and killed more than six thousand people. By contrast, a surge from Camille, which hit the Gulf Coast in 1969, killed only three hundred, many of whom had simply ignored the order to evacuate.

Now Frances was forming and becoming more intense out in the Atlantic, and we were preparing for the first fix. The plane was a weather-modified WC-130H, a turboprop cargo carrier with a reputation for near-indestructibility. We took off at 3:30 A.M., threading our way between twenty-thousand-foot-high pillars of stratocumulus clouds. By 5:30 the sun was beginning to rise above Frances: We could see the curve of the earth below, but half the horizon was a raging, churning black cloud, its top fringed with pink.

The plane dropped to ten thousand feet, the altitude at which we'd make the penetration. Now we were making our way through the feeder bands, the outer arms of the pinwheel: great curving lines of thunderstorm cells. The sky was blue in the spaces between the bands, but occasionally we had to break through one of them. At those points the pilot asked the navigator to find him a "soft spot." The thunderstorm cells were composed of updrafts and downdrafts that could lift or drop a plane seven hundred feet in seconds, that could sheer off a wing or crumple the plane. The navigator read his radar, looking for a cell less bright than those around it. A soft spot.

We burst through the soft spot with a terrific jolt, and lightning crashed all about us. The wall cloud, that spinning mass of thundercloud cells several miles deep, was only twenty miles ahead. Just for a moment I could see the ocean below, and it was webbed with long, thin streamers of bright green. The weather officer estimated—by the condition of the water—that the winds down there were blowing at a hundred miles an hour.

We hit the eyewall at 183 miles an hour, the exact speed needed for penetration, given the current weight of the plane. The pilot wanted to keep the left wing of the plane pointed directly into the wind. To get twisted about and to fly nose-first into the wind would cause a stall, and a stall would be fatal.

Sometimes the eyewall will simply spit the plane out, like a penny dropped on a spinning 75-rpm record. But we hit the wall right at 183 miles an hour, our left wing into the wind. And then there was no way the pilot could read his instruments, because we were all being hurled in every direction at once. The bite of the seatbelts against our shoulders and waists was painful. There was a deafening clatter, like the sound of an ice cube dropped into a blender. Outside, a ghostly light, St. Elmo's fire on the wing, glittered obscenely in the darkness. Lightning exploded, freezing us all in a single stroboscopic burst. Our faces were wide-eyed, contorted, and white as death.

And then we were through the eyewall, into the eye, and there was no more turbulence, none at all, but I heard several seconds of heavy breathing in my earphones before the pilot could make himself sound professional and unconcerned. "Piece of cake," he said.

There was blue sky above, blue mirror-calm below, and a single pink cloud floating peacefully at about four thousand feet. The sun, still low in the east, lit the west eyewall, a terrifying, churning mass of darkness showing tinges of pink and crimson and gold. The eye itself was elliptical in shape, ten miles by fifteen, and some of the southern wall had sheared off. Not at all a tight or classic formation. An instrument dropped into the eye on a parachute showed the barometric pressure to be 960, nowhere near the 911 of Allen. The winds in the wall had not exceeded 140 miles an hour. Though she was no lady, Frances wasn't shaping up as a killer, either.

Several days later a high pressure dome north of Frances dissolved. The hurricane made an abrupt right turn and blew itself out over the cold waters of the North Atlantic.

Over My Head

No Laughs in Satan's Silt Hole

In a recent edition of the magazine *Underwater Speleology*, there is a cartoon by H. V. Grey labeled "Open Water Certification." It shows five scuba divers, just the tops of their heads and their snorkels protruding from the water. Four of the divers, apparently, have just completed the necessary classroom and pool work and are about to make their first dive. The instructor, who has chosen a submerged cave for the certification dive, is saying, "Okay, here's the dive plan: You guys go in first, then I'll follow and tie the ski rope to the big warning sign. Then we'll leave when the last person reaches the reserve on his J valve. Is there at least one light for every three people? Good, then let's all see Satan's Silt Hole."

Now, I like to think I have a good sense of scuba humor, and it bothers me when jokes swim right by without so much as a friendly wave. So I asked a certified cave diver named Steve Hudson to explain H. V. Grey's joke. Hudson, a Georgia executive who is active in underwater cave rescue, said, "Well, it's sort of a sick joke, one of those things you laugh at because it's too true."

All the divers in the cartoon, he said, are about to die. They are going to have an inevitable and exceedingly dumb accident, some-

thing along the lines of stepping into an open elevator shaft or
backing the station wagon over the lip of the Grand Canyon. A
laughable death.

I still didn't get it, and Hudson offered to take me cave diving.
Half an hour inside a water-filled cave, Hudson said, and I'd be able
to appreciate the deadly serious nature of H. V. Grey's humor.

In the two decades between 1960 and 1980, ??4 people have died
diving the dark waters of Florida's caves. That's a little more than
eleven deaths a year, making cave diving the most dangerous risk
sport in America. Of the 156,000 people who dived Florida caves in
1979, there were five fatalities, a bit under average, but still one
death for every 31,000 divers. Deaths have been reported in other
areas—in Texas, California, and elsewhere—but the situation has
gotten so bad in northern Florida that several counties, tired of the
waste of lives and the risk inherent in recovering the bodies, have
contemplated closing the caves to divers.

Among certified cave divers, those who have completed a
National Speleological Society (NSS) course, there has been only a
single fatality. But many certified cave divers—Steve Hudson
estimates there are no more than a thousand of them in the
country—have been called upon to recover bodies from the
underwater caves. This is grim work, and the NSS Rescue Recovery
Team has installed warning signs at the mouths of certain underwater caves: PREVENT YOUR DEATH, BE TRAINED IN CAVE DIVING or
DON'T GO FURTHER. MANY CERTIFIED DIVERS—EVEN INSTRUC-
TORS—HAVE DIED HERE DUE TO IGNORANCE OF CAVE-DIVING
PROCEDURES. PLEASE LISTEN.

The instructor and the students in Grey's cartoon plan to ignore
what seems to be a persuasive warning.

We arrived around dusk. The 'Bama Blue Hole was little more than
a limestone pond: a depression sunk deep into the wooded Alabama
countryside. The water was green with midsummer algae. At the far
end of the pond was a limestone cliff with a bit of an arch rising
above the scummy surface of the pond. I could see where the water
disappeared into what looked like a deep, wide passage in the
limestone wall. Beyond that, darkness.

Steve Hudson helped me suit up for the dive. I wore a hooded wet suit, weights, a forearm knife, a buoyancy compensator, mask, fins, a pressure gauge, a depth gauge, a diving watch, three separate powerful underwater lights in waterproof housings, and an outsized steel hundred-cubic-inch tank with a dual valve and two complete regulator systems, one of which had a five-foot hose. The whole rig weighed well over 100 pounds. Steve Hudson wore two steel tanks— double 100s—and carried a plexiglass reel that contained several hundred feet of nylon line. His outfit weighed in excess of 150 pounds. We waddled to the warm water like a pair of extraterrestrials crushed by the curse of unfamiliar gravity.

Hudson briefed me on certain signals new to open-water divers: I was to make a circle with my light to catch his attention, for instance. I was breathing from the regulator on the long hose. The short one hung from a loop around my neck. If Steve signaled that he was out of air, I was to give him the long hose and breathe from the short one. He'd do the same if I signaled. "You want to prevent panic," Hudson said. "The short hose might have silt or weeds in it, but you know the long hose works. If an out-of-air diver doesn't get a functioning regulator right away, he can easily panic." We practiced buddy breathing in this way, then set out for the arch in the limestone.

There was a submerged tree at the entrance to the cave. At about thirty feet, we saw a length of 180-pound test nylon line tied to a stout branch. It led into the absolute darkness of the cave. Following Hudson, I drained the air from my buoyancy compensator and descended to the line.

Unfortunately, I had calculated my weights for the superior buoyancy of salt water, and I sank like a stone into the darkness. In open water this is no problem. You just blow a little more air into the buoyancy compensator and float up to the level you want. Or kick a little if you like.

Ten feet inside the entrance to the hole, I kicked a bit and my right fin hit bottom. Silt, like an underwater dust storm, rose around my feet. I ascended to the line, and Hudson motioned urgently. He wanted me to "Okay the nylon." I circled my thumb and forefinger around the line—okayed the nylon—as silt blossomed below us. Our lights broke and scattered against the suspended particles. We waited, ready to call the dive, but the cloud didn't rise as high as the line.

The silt, composed of fine particles of clay, fine as talc, is marbled throughout the limestone, and it covers the floor of every passage. Hudson had told me of three divers who'd died in a Florida cave. "There were fin marks four inches deep on the floor of the cave," he said. The three men, all veteran military divers with little cave-diving experience, must have panicked and lost the line in a zero-visibility silt-out. (The NSS *Cave Diving Manual* suggests that a prospective diver simulate the view in a silt-out as follows: Splash through a mud puddle, then put on a face mask and look into the water.)

Hudson and I okayed the line and moved out of the rising silt, farther into the depth of the cave. The green water of the pond suddenly turned cold, and visibility expanded to seventy feet; in our lights, the water was crystal blue. We swam along the line, against the wall of the passage. There were no formations: The stalagmites and stalactites had been dissolved by the naturally acidic surface water. The passage seemed friendly, enclosing, womblike. It curved around to the right and opened out into a huge underwater cavern. Hudson clipped the line from his reel onto the nylon lifeline, and we moved out into the center of the room, unreeling line as we went, exploring what may have been a virgin cave and staying high to avoid silting the room.

We swam with our knees bent, so that the turbulence from our fins was directed backward and not down. We might have used another silt-avoidance technique called the "fly walk." This involves swimming upside down and moving hand over hand along the ceiling, which in our case was right there, four or five feet above us. With the ceiling so close, I assumed that we couldn't be very deep. The depth gauge showed we were already at ninety feet.

Such deception is a big killer in Florida's caves. Rapture of the deep, or nitrogen narcosis—the effects of concentrated nitrogen accumulating in the fatty tissue—can be roughly calculated by depth: Every thirty-three feet is equal to one martini on an empty stomach. We were down around three martinis. Some divers die at the ten-martini level: Unwittingly dropping to that dangerous depth, they become confused or panicky in their narcosis, lose the lifeline in a silt-out, and drown.

I checked my pressure gauge and found I had 1,400 pounds per square inch left. According to the "rule of thirds," this was our turn-back point. I had started with 2,100 pounds. The first 700 pounds were used for penetration, and the next 1,400 pounds—two-thirds of my air—would remain for the trip out.

The divers in Grey's cartoon will depend entirely on the reserve air in their J valves: a couple of hundred pounds of air, which lasts only a few minutes at ninety feet. In open water, the J valve reserve is enough for an easy ascent, but someone who has used 2,000 pounds of air to penetrate a cave is not going to make it back out on a mere 400.

Hudson and I followed the line back to the point at which it joined the main length of nylon. At the junction of the lines, Steve had placed a small arrow, pointing out. In case of silt-out, or disorientation, or the improbable failure of all six of our lights, we'd be able to feel the line and the arrow pointing to the nearest exit. Steve reeled in his line behind me, and we swam slowly out of the cavern and back into the passage.

Swimming along the rot-proof nylon, I inadvertently let myself go negative and dropped below the line. No problem. Don't kick, though: Don't silt-out the passage. Just put some air into the compensator and rise . . . directly into the nylon line, which got tangled with the valve on my tank. Turning to extricate myself, I got my reserve lights caught up.

It took the two of us perhaps thirty seconds to get everything unwound. There was a moment then of, well, call it intense anxiety. Hudson had warned me not to get below the line. "Every time you come up, you tend to get tangled," he said. I wondered how the fictional divers in Grey's cartoon could possibly avoid getting entangled in a ski rope: a floating line that, unlike slowly sinking nylon, would rise above them at the slightest slack.

I could envision them—the doomed cartoon divers—running out of air deep in the cave. After kicking silt-outs at every turn on the way in, one of the new divers becomes disoriented: He has no light, and he swims deep into the cave, looking for an exit, the narcosis spinning in his brain. The instructor can't follow: He is perilously low on air, and the maze of passages looks entirely different now, coming back. Where's the line? In the inevitable silt-out, no one has bothered to okay the ski rope, and it is floating on the ceiling, unseen and useless. One of the students, in a typical panic reaction, tries to grab a light from another, and there is an underwater fight. The effort involved causes both to run out of air. Soon the third student runs out of air. The instructor attempts to buddy breathe with three students, but there is a terror in the silt-stained darkness: a fight for the only functioning regulator. All three of the students and the instructor pass out there, in the darkness, fighting for air, dying of stupidity. Rescue workers find the last, lost student, tanks empty, at 280 feet.

Typical fatalities: An analysis of cave-diving accidents by the NSS Cave Diving Section shows that almost all deaths can be traced to one of three causes: The diver didn't have a line, didn't follow the rule of thirds, or went too deep. Often the accidents involve a combination of these errors.

Hudson and I swam through the suspended silt I had kicked up at the mouth of the cave. We hung off, decompressing at twenty feet for a few minutes, then surfaced into an Alabama summer night and the sound of crickets. There were fireflies in the trees.

Steve Hudson wanted to know if I understood H. V. Grey's cartoon now. Well, sure, I said, but like any real knee-slapper, it seemed to lose a few laughs in the explanation.

Caving in Kentucky

Anyone who has ever tried to crowbar a little subterranean information out of people who habitually stumble around in caves—cavers—knows that these people are, by and large, a closed-mouthed, introverted, even slightly hostile group. I was thinking about this late one Sunday evening recently while I was standing waist-deep in a slate-green body of water called Dread Pool, which is two hours deep into a twenty-three-mile-long cave network in central Kentucky. The waters were thick, glassy, ghostly, and cold. To get to some interesting caverns deeper down, one must wade through Dread Pool, and, in certain seasons, the water may reach up to one's chest. About an hour into the cave you start thinking about how cold the water is going to be and you spend the following sixty minutes dreading the pool. Hence the name.

Bad enough to wade through the pool. Worse to stand there, motionless. Posing for a photograph.

Some months previous, a set of remarkable photographs had come into the office. Taken in the same Kentucky cave by a young Ohio businessman and commercial photographer named Jeff Thompson, they were unlike anything I had ever seen. The images were weirdly striking, contorted, vast. They looked the way the Viking's photos of Mars *should* have looked.

I called Jeff, and we made arrangements to see the cave. Thompson described himself as a "soft-core, weekend caver," then launched into a series of relatively hard-core conditions. According to Jeff's instructions, I spent three days at Yosemite sharpening my rock-climbing skills, and a day practicing rappels—a method of descent using a rope with mechanical aids.

I read the books he recommended. I figured I knew every esoteric cave danger encountered by man from time immemorial. Lightning, for instance, can strike deep into a cave, and when such a bolt hits an accumulation of bat excrement—guano—an enormous explosion can result.

Exploding bat shit I was prepared for. Cave photography was another thing altogether. It is, of course, totally dark inside a cave. This means you can leave the shutter open on a camera, then strobe-light dozens of different specific areas around your central subject. It takes time to effect such stygian chiaroscuro. The human subject in such a photo must stand stock still. When the human subject is waist deep in the frigid waters of Dread Pool, he tends to become cranky. He wonders why cavers, as a whole, treasure these experiences, and why they are so secretive. Jeff, for instance, didn't want me to mention the name of the cave in my article. Did he really expect one day to crawl, creepy-damp, through this cave, and find seventy or eighty people lolling around in Dread Pool?

They breathe, caves do, and, depending on the barometric pressure, they inhale or exhale. When we approached Minton Hollow—one of sixteen entrances to this cave, which is one of the twenty longest in the world—I could feel that cold, dark breath on me at fifty yards. The entrance, positioned on the side of a knoll, was surrounded by ferns and looked like a huge, baronial limestone hearth.

We walked, for the first few minutes, through spacious passages, well lit by the miners' lamps we wore. There were five of us: Jeff; myself; Jeff's business associate, Chip Northrup; Mike Davis, a media specialist; and Jon Luzio, a dog warden. Jon, with distressing regularity, kept pointing out wet green leaves stuck in the overhangs at the top of the cave. The cave had been completely flooded, recently, and Jon had read that this low section near Minton Hollow could fill within forty-five minutes.

Twenty yards into the cave, there was no way to know what was going on outside, whether, in fact, a freak rainstorm had burst out of a clear blue sky. If the water began to rise around our feet, we would have to go back the way we came, likely bucking a stream growing geometrically in power. If the water began to rise when we were several hours in, we'd have to look for a high, dry dome—some rise one hundred feet, and more—and climb to a safe spot. If the walls could not be scaled, we'd have to wait in a high room and tread water until it rose to a climbable section of wall.

Experienced cavers have died during unexpected floods. They retreated to the highest rooms, and the water simply continued to rise: to their waists, to their chests, to their necks. In the end—the idea is horrifying—they must have lain back in the water, lips against the cold rock ceiling, and taken one last breath before the room filled completely.

Because of the danger of flooding, Jeff marked the location of the highest dry domes on his map.

Twenty minutes or so in from the entrance, the ceilings began to drop and we adapted a variety of stoop walks. In a passage five feet seven inches high, a six-footer like myself can walk with slightly bended knees. But this is very tiring. Better to tilt the head so that the ear rests very nearly on one's shoulder. A person walking rapidly in this position tends to look slightly psychotic, like Terence Stamp in *The Collector*.

In shallower passages, cavers are obliged to double over, bowing from the waist. One cannot, however, stare only at the passing floor because a slight irregularity in the ceiling can cause a concussion. So one tilts the head up in a comical, neck-straining posture. Technically, such passages are referred to as "Groucho walks."

Passages can get considerably tighter, but only once in twenty hours of heavy caving did I get seriously stuck. There was a narrow hole in the ceiling of a passage leading to a higher room. A slick pile of mud with a single foothold led to the hole. My arms went through first, like a diver's, but just as I pushed my triceps through, I lost the foothold and hung there, absurdly, with my feet dangling below and my arms pinned over my head.

I tried to deal with the panic in a rational manner. I am not, ordinarily, a claustrophobic person, but it seemed to me that I would remain stuck for, oh, ten days at the most, by which time I'd have lost enough weight to slide out of the hole. Of course, there was always the danger of flood during those ten days. The idea of an earthquake—shit, even a minor settling of the stone—was terrifying. I'd end up all bulgy-eyed with my swollen tongue sticking out of my mouth, looking like a gruesome photo in some sleazy tabloid captioned: "Garbage Man Crushed to Death in Own Truck!"

Mike pointed out, in an excessively calm voice, that there was a handhold to my immediate right and that, if I so desired, perhaps I could reach over and pull myself up. Unless, of course, I wanted to rest some more. There was no hurry. This process is called "talking through," and even veteran cavers sometimes catch the fear and have to be talked through tough spots.

For every tight spot, there are dozens of crawlways: nearly oval tubes with fluted walls and ceilings. It was Jon's contention that certain crawls resembled birth canals. Sometimes, so Jon says, the Earth Mother is good, and the floor is sandy. Sometimes she is a bitch, and the floor is covered with sharp baseball-sized rocks that bite right through your mandatory basketball kneepads.

For some reason, the birth-canal analogy offends me, but even more repulsive is the phrase "bowels of the earth." If you consider a certain passage to be a section of bowel, and carry the metaphor to its unfortunate conclusion, then cavers, moving as they do through the bowels, become . . .

Enough.

Jeff says caving scratches his explorer's itch. Where he lives, the land has been given over to farms for more than a century. But precious few people have ever set foot deep into the caverns he loves; and, amazingly, new, virgin caves are being discovered every year.

While Jeff is pragmatic about his romanticism—Stanley and Livingstone in the netherworld—I prefer to let my imagination take control. We had, for instance, been following the sound of falling water for some time when we came to an unnamed waterfall. The dark green river erupted out of an upper passage and tumbled down a twenty-foot pit. It shone green, then silver in our lights. The walls of the pit were striated in browns and greens and ghostly whites. Two smaller streams poured out of a lower passage through formations that looked like nothing so much as balcony windows. On either side of the windows strange, twisted gargoyle shapes stood patient guard. Opposite the falls there was a gnarled, pulpitlike affair, and one could imagine foul rituals, and obscene sermons shrieked through the silent canyons.

The formations had the look of something otherworldly, yet man-made, elegant relics of some twisted culture predating the Ice Age: a culture that had flourished, and decayed. I wanted to imagine a people given to the worship of dark things: cruel dwarf gods and evil warlocks could be seen in the flawed and contorted sculptures before us.

Sitting in front of that waterfall, I got as goofy as I've ever been, dead sober. I had just run through a fantasy about ebony and albino warriors and their revolt against the evil king and his necromaniac rituals, and was working on the one about the torchlit masked ball in the Thunder Room; sautéed eyeless fish, batwing soup, a weird, discordant melody echoing off cold stone, when it occurred to me that this was a very vulnerable fantasy. None of it would be any good if there were some old candy-bar wrappers and a broken RC Cola bottle on the floor.

And I got my first dim glimmering of why cavers are not evangelistic about their sport.

Millions of years ago this area of Kentucky lay submerged beneath a shallow sea. Uncounted billions of marine plants and animals lived, absorbed calcium compounds from the sea, died, sank to the bottom, and formed thick beds of limestone. The sea retreated and, to the east, the Appalachian Mountains punched up out of the earth, wrinkling the landscape of Kentucky, forming ridges and low, rolling hills. Many of the valleys here have no surface drainage system: no rivers or creeks.

The water goes underground, and, in so doing, it carves out caves. Rainwater percolating through topsoil absorbs carbon dioxide and becomes carbonic acid. Limestone is soluble in carbonic acid. The weakly acidic water finds cracks and fissures in the stone. Sometimes it carves out huge vertical shafts, pits, and chimneys. Then again, the water may flow horizontally, hollowing out oval tubes, some the size of a straw, some eighty feet in diameter.

As the water table sinks—because of drought, or the shifting of the earth's crust, or simply because the nearby river has carved itself a deeper valley—the tubes and pits are left relatively dry. In the rainy season, water, seeking its own level, roars abrasively through the tubes, carving out canyons. Eventually, most of the water makes it way through the maze of underground caverns and empties into a major surface lake or river.

Meanwhile, especially in the big rooms, water is still seeping through small fissures. It may enter the room through a drop-sized crack in the ceiling. Because cave air is almost devoid of carbon dioxide, the acidic water wants to reach chemical equilibrium by giving off CO_2. The water loses its carbonic acid and the dissolved limestone it carries will solidify. Over hundreds of years, limestone deposits, released from a single-drop fissure, can form a spectacular stalactite (these icicle-shaped formations hang *tight* to the ceiling). Water dropping from the tip of a stalactite may form a corresponding formation on the floor (you *might* walk into a stalagmite).

When water runs down the side wall of a big room, it can form fantastic draperies; and when a thin sheet of water runs along the floor of a cave, it forms flowstone, which looks very much like a river frozen into stone. Permanent pools often contain thin stone "lilypads" held on the surface by water tension.

Sometimes passage containing no formations at all have a special beauty. The ceiling may often be covered with closely spaced hanging water drops that, in miners' lights, look like molten silver studs. A bat, hanging upside down in sleep there, may be covered with drops, shining silver in your light.

In certain rooms, bats congregate by the thousands, and they hang there in one vast furry silver gray colony. At dusk, they leave the cave to feed outside, belching up out of the earth like a mass of swooping, swirling refugees from some Baptist preacher's hellfire sermon.

Chip and Mike and Jeff like to tell a bat story on Jon, who was a biology major in college. It seems they were making their way through a narrow passage when a number of bats in exit swooped by. Jon told everyone to remain still. Bats, he explained, send out high-pitched squeaks—inaudible to the human ear—receive the echoes, and fly by an amazingly accurate sonar system. No way could one hit you. At this point, a bat flew directly into Jon's neck and fluttered there, frantically. The bat screeched, audibly. So did Jon. It was hard to tell which was which.

Bats, Jon found out later, switch off most of their sonar in the familiar confines of their home cave and fly by memory. Unfamiliar objects, like cavers, confuse them. The audible sound the bat made, like the audible sound Jon made, was an expression of surprise and horror.

Bats have precious little company in caves. Near the entrances you may find common spiders and salamanders and some nesting birds. In the deeper caverns, far from the twilight world of the entrances, we saw white, eyeless crickets. They had antennae longer than their bodies and they moved surely, in braille. A number of pools contained eyeless, albino crayfish. There are also albino fish in some of the lakes, and where the eyes would be on these fish, there is only smooth, white flesh.

On the whole, however, nothing much lived deep in the limestone caverns we explored, and the air there was cool, sterile. It was without the scent and stench of life and death. There was no mustiness, no dankness. It was unexpectedly fresh and pleasant and primitive, and it tasted, I imagined, much the way the atmosphere of the earth must have when it was newly formed.

The saga of the West Virginia Death Cave is not something Jeff Thompson likes to talk about, but the tale does have its cautionary aspects. "It was about four years ago," Jeff told me. "We were beginners—a real buncha nerds." In a retarded-sounding drawl he added, "Well, shit-fire buddy, we read two whole books. We figured we knew it all."

Jeff and Jon and Jon's wife, Ronnie—who wrote up an account of the ordeal for me—had entered the cave about noon on a Saturday. The only smart thing they did that day was to tell some fellow cavers they would see them for a party that night around eight.

The first few hours were pretty routine: Groucho walks, crawls, careful climbs over breakdowns, where the ceiling of a big room had caved in. No one thing was very difficult in itself; but, in total, it was exhausting work, especially when done with little rest and at the impatient pace Jeff and Jon cultivated in those days. Fatigue colored their judgment and they began to make mistakes, deadly mistakes.

Five hours in, at the point they should have turned back, they met another group of cavers, coming the other way. That meant there was a connection to be made from where they were, a way out without retracing their steps. They didn't carry maps or compasses at that time, so they listened to a complicated series of instructions, then started off to make the connection. "We thought we had come through the worst of it," Ronnie wrote, "and that it would only get easier. We didn't recognize that the other cavers were very tired."

They stepped up the pace a bit. The party was scheduled for eight. A low, two-foot crawl dropped to one foot. They had to remove their helmets and push them along ahead. Feet wouldn't fit unless they were splayed out sideways. It was a real nose-to-the-limestone, three-hundred-foot squashed bellycrawl over sharp rocks. And now they were lost.

There was a hands-and-knees grotto at the end and two passages leading off from that. "One was an easy crawl over a soft mud floor," Jon said, "and the other was much lower. That easy passage just sucked us in." Jeff tried the passage to see if it would go, returned, and then Jon pushed it for forty-five minutes, while Jeff and Ronnie knelt in the windy grotto. Jon returned and said that he had taken the passage to a series of short climbs that would probably take them to the surface. Ronnie noticed that Jon was very wet. She remembered the other cavers being dry.

Jeff led the wet, muddy crawl, then pushed over the short climbs through a small hole that should have led to the surface. "Oh no," Ronnie heard him moan. Her heart sank. She emerged into a pit surrounded by unclimbable twenty-foot walls.

It was now 6:30. They were scared, lost, exhausted, and freezing to death. The temperature in the cave was perhaps fifty-two degrees, and there was a slight breeze, say five miles per hour, which put the wind-chill factor at about twenty degrees. Worse, they were wet, and water chill is an even more efficient killer than wind chill. Jeff, who had been a medic in the army, diagnosed hypothermia, that deadly dropping of the body's core temperature, sometimes called exposure. In its first stages symptoms of hypothermia include controlled shivering and goose bumps. Then comes uncontrolled shivering, followed by acute confusion and a lowered pulse and heart rate. When the body's core temperature drops below seventy-eight degrees, death comes quickly.

There was no good rest in that pit. Lying on the rocks was suicide: the cold wetness of the stone sucked the heat from their bodies. So they formed a standing tripod. "I never believed I could sleep on my feet," Jon said. But he did and almost instantly rescuers were there and he was whisked out of the cave and into a grassy West Virginia field under the warm West Virginia sun, drinking a nice warm cup of soup. Suddenly his knees buckled and he woke from his dream into a cold, dark, living nightmare. Jon was shivering uncontrollably; shivering so badly, in fact, that he pulled a muscle in his stomach.

Jon and Jeff, who had twice tried to make connections by crawling through half a foot of water, were the worst off. Jeff figured the two of them had about thirty hours to live. Ronnie, who was drier, might go forty-eight. Maybe the cavers they had talked to would notice that they hadn't turned up for the party. Maybe. But more likely their absence wouldn't be noted until they didn't show up for work on Monday, thirty-six hours in the future.

At half-hour intervals they did five minutes of jumping jacks in order to maintain their temperature. Jon's pulse never rose above an ominous sixty-two. They were dead. It was absurd. Here they were, young and in the best of shape, and they could expect death in a day and a half.

Jon switched on his miner's lamp, the only functioning light they had left, and Jeff saw a sad, bitter thing in the sudden brilliance. The cave was sucking away the heat he built up exercising. Steam rose from his hand; rose in five straight shafts from the tips of his fingers. "I'm watching myself die," he said.

They had been hearing the sounds of running water all night, but now it seemed there was something more than water. If you held your breath and listened hard . . . yes, it was the muffled sounds of voices. They called out. They shouted themselves hoarse, and waited for a reply; but the only sound was the distant mumble of running water.

They slept, woke from pleasant wishful dreams of sunlight into their nightmare of frigid darkness. Again they exercised, and watched the cave suck the life out of them. Jeff found his bank book in one pocket, and that was pretty funny. Pretty goddamn funny. They talked about their values and their lives, and the things they had left undone. They resigned themselves to death.

Ronnie had a Timex watch, and as sunrise approached their spirits lifted. It had been no use looking for an exit in the dark. In the daytime they could switch off Jon's lamp and look for a shaft of light from above. At dawn, they started back down the agonizing series of crawls that had trapped them. They dead-ended, backtracked, and finally found a series of climbs that brought them to a big ledge.

Jon spotted a daddy-longlegs spider, an entrance dweller. And they could smell air: real living air, humid and heavy with the scent of wildflowers. There had to be an exit nearby, but when Jon snapped off his lamp it was, as before, absolutely black. The final desperate crawl had sapped the last of their strength. They sat down on the cold rocks and waited to die.

Which is when the members of the Monongahela and Pittsburgh grottos (chapters) of the National Speleological Society found them. They were fifty feet from a rabbit-hole exit; but, in their exhaustion, they might never have made the necessary traverse of a thirty-foot pit to find the exit that was hidden behind a large pile of breakdown.

The rescue operation had been launched at midnight after Jeff and Jon and Ronnie failed to show for the party. "They spent eight hours searching for us," Ronnie wrote, "and I want to thank them publicly."

"We were," Jeff said, "literally born again. When they found us and discovered that no one was seriously hurt, we had to listen to a lot of lectures about what a bunch of nerds we were. Well, we were. I mean, that had been proven. But it didn't matter. I was as happy as I've ever been in my life and the feeling lasted for days. I was a nerd, all right, but I was a *living* nerd."

Early one afternoon we rappelled down a narrow twenty-five-foot-deep hole called the Post Office entrance. What happened that day is a good example of how decisions are made in caves.

We pushed through a tight, muddy, painful crawl to a ten-foot drop into a muddy lower level, then walked for some time through a shallow, flowing stream. We climbed some breakdown before coming to a tight hole Jeff persisted in calling a "whoop-de-do." Imagine a vertical "S" curve of basketball hoops eight feet long. Now imagine squeezing through it feet first. I would estimate that it took me a three-mile jog's worth of energy to squeeze my 210 pounds through Jeff's whoop-de-do.

We crawled to a waterfall so high we could see it from both an upper and a lower passage. The water fell in a silver circle around a perfectly symmetrical stone column the width of an old redwood tree. The circular waterfall emptied into a placid pool whose edges glittered like a pane of opaque green glass.

After a short rest, we pushed on. Our goal was to connect with either Screamin' Willy's entrance or Scowlin' Tom's. According to the map, we would pass through a big room, a lake room, a massive meeting of passageways called Echo Junction, and finally, Grand Central Spaghetti, a bewildering maze of interconnecting passages on several different levels.

An upward-sloping, tube-type crawl ended at a porthole overlooking the Big Room. We were thirty feet up a sixty-foot wall. There was a rope ladder at the end of the tube, but the rope looked old and there were some awful nasty-looking rocks below, not to mention a dull green lake, and no one was willing to bet his life on the ladder. Jeff drove a new expansion bolt into the rock and we rigged a rappel to a ledge twelve feet below. We pulled our doubled rope down after us and followed the ledge to a pile of breakdown, then climbed over into the main section of the Big Room. We found ourselves facing a flooded passage. A heavy rock tossed into the lake confirmed what we already knew. Deep water.

We were only three hours into the cave. I wanted to see Echo Junction and Grand Central Spaghetti: I had connection fever. It seemed to me that doubling back the way we came would be an admission of defeat.

I proposed a plan: at its narrowest point, the lake was fifty yards across; we had that much rope. Since I was relatively certain that there was nothing in the lake that bit or leeched blood, and since I had spent a dozen years of my life engaged in serious competitive swimming, I offered to swim the rope across. I'd tie it off on my end, they'd tie it off on theirs, and they could hand-over-hand to my side of the drink.

A beautiful plan. Mike and Chip and Jeff and Jon were very patient. They never once called me a nerd. They simply pointed out, quite logically, why it would be dangerous and stupid to push on.

Point on. the map showed that parts of Grand Central Spaghetti wer, at the same elevation as the Big Room. That meant that essentia¹ connecting tubes and crawlways were likely to be completely flooded, top to bottom, and totally impassable without scuba gear.

Point two: inevitably, we'd get lost. If we got seriously lost, it could be deadly. We'd left word on the outside, but would rescuers assume that we swam the lake? There we'd be, soaked to the skin in some windy passage, dying of hypothermia and every few minutes I'd find myself saying, "Gosh, you know I'm really sorry about this, guys."

Point three: our lights and batteries were good for twelve hours. We could, conceivably, push on for three more hours. But then, if we didn't make the connection, we could double back and hit the Post Office entrance in twelve hours even. That left no margin for rest or error.

Point four: we'd already made a minor error. (Most cave accidents seem to be built on a foundation of minor errors.) We had brought the rope down after us. We should have left the rope, climbed the breakdown, and examined the Big Room first. Now we'd have to climb from the ledge to the overlook without the aid of the rope.

Luckily, Mike had fastened his etrier to the expansion bolt and left it hanging from the overlook. An etrier is a long, strong piece of nylon webbing tied into two stirrups, one above the other. Like the rest of us, Mike had figured that we'd make the connection. He left the etrier, a sacrifice to an imaginary emergency that had just developed.

We trekked back over the ledge to the point just below the overlook. Mike tied into the rope and Chip put him on belay. If Mike fell, Chip could hold him easily. But say he fell from the mouth of the tube: he'd plummet twelve feet to the ledge, then probably twelve more feet to the end of the rope. A total of twenty-four feet. A fall like that means nasty cuts and abrasions, perhaps even a broken bone, and would leave poor Mike dangling there in agony. We'd have to hoist him up to the ledge where Jeff could put a splint on him. Someone else would have to climb the etrier. Then we'd have to pull Mike up to the overlook, get him down the tube, through the crawls, up the whoop-de-do, and finally pull him twenty-five feet up to the Post Office entrance.

So it was with some trepidation that we watched Mike make the first move around a large boulder on the ledge. There was room for more than half your foot, and the handholds were good. It's just that the concave shape of the boulder forced one's ass into the abyss and, at this point, the heart refused to beat in a regular fashion. On the second move Mike got hold of the etrier, and on the third he placed his left foot in the lower stirrup. He searched for a high handhold, found one, put his right foot into the upper stirrup and did a pushup into the safety of the tube.

Mike belayed the rest of us from above, and this arrangement limited any potential fall to three or four feet. We each accomplished the climb with relative degrees of ease, and started the three-hour hike, climb, squeeze, crawl back.

In the tight crawl between the whoop-de-do and the entrance, we heared the muffled sounds of what seemed to be a child screaming in terror and agony. The screams came from the entrance, the twenty-five-foot drop we had made on rappel. From below, we saw a five-year-old boy halfway up the drop. He was hanging there on a rope which was wrapped painfully around his chest and tied, dangerously, with an ordinary square knot. The rope itself was a wonder: frayed black plastic clothesline. The kid was being hauled out of the pit by an unseen force above and he was thumping against ledges and outcropping with painful regularity.

On the surface, we met the unseen force, who turned out to be the boy's father, a pleasant, sandy-haired thirty-year-old I'll call Bob. It turned out that Bob had done some backpacking and river running, and now he was interested in learning a bit about caving. Clearly, he wasn't the sort of pimple who'd snap off a hundred-year-old stalactite for a souvenir, or go around spray painting his name on walls, or leaving empty tins of Vienna sausage in some pristine grotto. But he was dangerously unprepared, and Jeff had no idea what to say to him.

Bob obviously had no technical rock-climbing experience. Swinging the kid around on that idiot rope was likely to put a permanent end to father-and-son outings. Between the two of them, the boy and the man, they had one source of light, a number that fell five short of minimum safety standards. The kid had no helmet, and since there were rockfalls inside, and because *everybody* cracks his head in a cave, he was risking serious concussion. Bob had no map, no compass. The kid had no coveralls. He'd have to crawl through flowing streams in a thin cotton T-shirt, then stand around in a twenty-degree wind chill while Bob tried to figure out where they were.

Bob chatted pleasantly. Jeff didn't say much. He was thinking: Should I tell them about the West Virginia Death Cave? Can I really give this guy a stiff safety lecture in front of his kid? If he did, Bob would think he was an arrogant, condescending turd.

"What you ought to do," Jeff said, "is join the National Speleological Society. They have a grotto here. . . ."

"I heard about them," Bob said, "but first I want to see if I really like caving. Isn't there an easier entrance around here?"

Chip and Mike and Jon faded away from the conversation and got real busy coiling muddy rope. Jeff hesitated way too long and the fellow looked at him strangely. Someday Bob would tell his friends that cavers are, by and large, closed-mouthed, introverted, even vaguely hostile people.

"My boy really wants to see the cave," Bob prodded.

Jeff worked hard on a smile and gave the two of them directions to a distant, empty, caveless field.

Shark Dive

"This," Jack McKenney said, "is your shark club." It was a broom handle with a nail in the end and I was supposed to use it underwater, while scuba diving, to whap the menacing sharks we hoped to attract and thus convince them, Jack explained, that we weren't to be considered appetizers. I said that a broom handle seemed somewhat fragile for the task at hand.

"Well," Jack said reasonably, "you won't have to use it if you don't get out of the cage."

We were standing on the stern of a dive boat called the *Atlantis*, which was drifting out in the channel between San Pedro Harbor and Catalina, near a place called 14 Mile Bank. The water was glassy blue, under blue skies on a nearly windless day. Off half a mile in the distance, dense clouds of sea birds were whirling and diving above several city blocks' worth of ocean that seemed to be in full boil. Tony, the captain of the *Atlantis*, figured that bait fish were being driven to the surface by marauding sharks. I was looking at an acre or so of pure terror.

The shark cage sat on the deck. It was tied to a boom that would lower it ten feet into the water. I had always supposed that such a cage would be constructed of heavy metal, that it would be made of wrist-thick prison-type bars. The contraption in question, however, was constructed, for the most part, from wire, the kind of stuff used as bedsprings in cots.

"How many sharks will we get?" I asked Jack.

"Hard to tell," he said. "I don't think we'll be skunked. If we're lucky, we could have as many as twenty."

"Oh boy," I said with a singular lack of enthusiasm that seemed lost on Jack McKenney.

"Yeah," he said, "it could be a good one. Problem is: it's too nice a day."

"Just our rotten luck, all right."

"If we only had some wind," Jack said. We had been adrift for a little less than an hour and hadn't seen any sharks yet. We were chumming for them, sending out little invitations: come to the feeding frenzy. Sitting on the deck, near the shark cage, were several boxes of mackerel: about four hundred pounds of foot-long frozen fish. As soon as Tony cut the engines, Jack and his son John put fifteen pounds of the fish into one of those plastic mesh boxes designed to carry milk cartons. They wired a second such box onto the first—open end to open end—and dropped it over the side on a rope so that the box was half in and half out of the water. The rocking of the boat maserated the defrosting fish, and I could see oil and blood and bits of mackerel floating away from the boat in a snaking line.

A cruising shark that crossed the chum line would turn and follow it to the boat. To attract the maximum number of sharks, we wanted to spread that line out across a mile or so of sea. With the boat dead in the water, the chum tended to sink to the bottom. We couldn't motor, though: engine noise and fumes would confuse the sharks. We needed a stiff wind to push the boat along and spread out the chum line.

I was going through a final check of my dive gear when Tony mentioned, rather cavalierly I thought, that "we got one." It was a six-foot-long blue shark, and it had rolled over onto its back and was chewing, half-heartedly, on the milk boxes full of chum. It rolled slightly and one flat black eye looked up at the faces peering at it over the side of the boat. The shark rolled again, like a jet fighter doing a barrel roll, and disappeared under the boat.

In the distance, about a hundred yards off, I could see another fin, gliding along the snaking path of chum toward the boat. Beyond that was still another fin coming in our direction along the same meandering path. It was early in the morning, and the sun was low in the sky, so that the water seemed cobalt blue, but the wake behind the shark fins was an odd emerald color that glittered on the surface of the glassy sea. There was a muffled thump as the first shark hit the chum box a second time.

Jack McKenney said, "Let's get the cage in the water and go diving."

Canadian-born Jack McKenney, who lives in Los Angeles, is a legend in the diving industry; a filmmaker, photographer, and adventurer. He has filmed whale sharks and ridden manta rays in the Sea of Cortez; he has made more dives on the *Andrea Doria* than any other person. Hollywood has paid him to learn a lot about different kinds of sharks. He was a stunt double in both *The Deep* and *Shark's Treasure*, two movies in which he also filmed some of the underwater sequences.

Jack and his twenty-six-year-old son, John, were making their first video production for the home market: it would be a documentary about shark diving, which they hoped to sell in the scuba magazines. The production would show that a shark dive can be "a safe and enjoyable" experience . . . when done properly.

On hand to coordinate the dives were Bud Riker and Susan Speck, co-owners of Divers West, a dive shop in Pasadena. For the past two years, Bud and Susan have been sponsoring four or five shark dives a year. The trips are open to advanced open-water divers with "a lot" of open-water experience. Previous shark-diving experience is not necessary.

The video documentary would concentrate on three novice shark divers: Paul Bahn, a musician; Laine "Buck" Scheliga, a bartender; and Pam McKenney, a flight attendant. These were the people who were going to experience "safe and enjoyable" diving in the midst of a feeding frenzy.

Also on hand for the experience were Bonnie Cardone, the

executive editor for *Skin Diver* magazine—it would be her second planned shark dive—and Chip Matheson, a stunt man "trainee" whose work you may have seen on *Riptide*. Chip has been diving with sharks for seven years.

I have been diving and writing for various scuba magazines for a decade, and in that time have found myself in the water with tiger sharks on the Great Barrier Reef, with hammerheads off Central America, with Caribbean nurse sharks, with black tip and white tip reef sharks, with carpet sharks, sand sharks, and lemon sharks. None of this was intentional. These sharks just appeared, entirely unwanted, like ants at a picnic. The idea of purposely getting into the water with a dozen or so man-eaters seemed silly, suicidal, dumb as rocks. Still, Jack McKenney had asked me to participate, and Jack knows what he's doing. It was Jack McKenney, doubling for Nick Nolte, who made a free ascent through that shark feeding frenzy in *The Deep*. No longtime diver would pass up an opportunity to dive with Jack McKenney, just as no pilot would turn down an invitation to fly with Chuck Yeager.

McKenney had also invited Marty Snyderman to appear in the video. Marty is a well-known underwater photographer from San Diego. About ten years ago, it occurred to him that people weren't paying proper attention to his photos: all those shots of corals and "scenic" fish, of sponges and nudibranchs in blazing color. It was the time of *Jaws*, and the public was interested in sharks. "So I became good at shark diving and shark photography," Marty told me, "and, when people know that, somehow they seem to find my other photos infinitely more interesting and beautiful."

Since Snyderman spends so much time in the water with sharks, shooting stills and filming television documentaries, he has also seen fit to spend $5200 on a custom-made Kevlar and chain mail shark suit. In this suit, he told me, he has been "nipped" by sharks "literally hundreds of times." McKenney hoped to get some good footage of sharks nibbling away on Marty Snyderman.

The real stars of McKenney's video promised to be the sharks themselves. There are 250 or more species of sharks—research is still being done on the matter—and not all of them are dangerous to man. In Australia, for instance, I have been diving with a small, sleek, pretty little fish known as an epaulette shark because of the white-rimmed spots it carries above its pectoral fins. It is a timid beast, the epaulette shark, and it flees the approaching diver in what appears to be a frantic subaquatic panic. Like the ostrich, the epaulette shark considers itself hidden if it can't see you, and the fish can often be found with its head wedged into some small coral cave while the rest of its body is completely and ludicrously visible. This shark, incidentally, has no teeth at all, and Australian divers refer to it as a "gummie." Dangerous sharks, man-eaters like tigers and great whites, are called "munchies."

Some fishermen and boating enthusiasts believe that blues are not munchies, that they are virtually harmless, but there are documented cases of blues attacking human beings. Don Wilkie, Director of the Scripps Institution of Oceanography at UCSD, says flatly that "blues are potentially dangerous, but it is unusual for them to be involved in an unprovoked attack." Setting out a chum line, Wilkie said, "is a clear provocation."

Blues are common in the deep waters between Los Angeles and Catalina: they are fast, slim-bodied sharks with pointed snouts and saw-edged teeth. They can grow to twelve feet in length—man-eaters become dangerous at three or four feet—and often follow boats, feeding off of discarded garbage. Sometimes called blue whalers, these sharks are noted for the speed with which they materialize around slaughtered whales and for their piranhalike feeding frenzies.

"If there's only six or seven down there," McKenney told me, "it'll be pretty calm. If we get twenty or more, they can get a little aggressive. I suppose it's competition: when there's a lot of them, they have to move fast to get their share. Also, when there's more than two or three, it's hard to keep track of them. They can come up behind and nip you."

Which, I imagined, would be like getting "nipped" by a Bengal tiger, only underwater.

We had fifty feet of underwater visibility and everything down and up and all around was blue, including the sharks milling around the cage and chum bucket. Their bodies were brighter than the sea water and their bellies were a contrasting white. The cage was positioned ten feet below the chum bucket. Little white bits of mackerel were dropping down through the bed springs. The divers brushed the stuff off their shoulders, like dandruff. I could see five blue sharks outside the cage. There were swooping lazily through the water like eagles soaring over the prairie on a blue summer afternoon.

Just getting into the shark cage had been an adventure. You don't get to go down with it on the boom. Bed springs won't hold the weight of several divers. No, you have to swim to the cage.

"Go now," Bud Rilker had told me, as I sat with my legs just out of the water. The command meant that there weren't any sharks in my immediate presence, and I reluctantly slipped into the water beside the chum bucket. In a shark dive, you don't want to roll or jump off the boat because the bubbles you create obscure the view for ten or fifteen seconds, during which time a guy could get "nipped." Not incidentally, the bubbles also attract curious sharks.

So I sat on the swim step, edged into the sea, broom handle in hand, and rocketed through the blue water and blue sharks to the open cage door in ten seconds flat. Paul was already in there, along with Buck. Bonnie hovered just above the door, taking photos. Above, the boat was rocking in some gentle swells that had just come up, and the cage, which hung from the boom by a ten-foot line, echoed that rocking. I kept banging my head or knees on the wire and the temptation was very great to hold on to the side of the cage, but that meant that part of my hand would be outside, in the open sea, where the sharks were, and Jack had warned us that holding on to the cage in this manner was "a good way to get nipped."

The five sharks were milling around, aimlessly cutting sine curves in the sea. Occasionally, one would swim up to the chum bucket and nudge it with its snout. Then, with a figurative shrug of the shoulders, it would drop down to join the other sharks. They seemed curious and a little confused, these milling blues.

Above, along the chum line, I could see another shark accepting our invitation. The new guy was big, ten feet long at a guess, and he was moving purposefully toward the chum bucket, which he hit without hesitation. Nothing for him there but a mouthful of mackerel-flavored plastic. He dropped down to join the other sharks and they all made several passes by one another just outside the cage door.

If sharks can be thought of as having a conversation—which of course they can't but never mind—the newcomer looked as if he were saying: "What's going on here?"

"Dunno," another replies. "It's weird."

"What are those funny-looking things there?" The big blue was twenty feet off, looking at us.

"Potential breakfast."

He came at us then, this new shark just off the chum line, but he was swimming slower now, and moving toward the cage at an oblique angle. I revised my estimate: up close this shark was a good twelve feet long. It coasted slowly by the cage, apparently staring off into the distance and not interested in us at all, but it passed within inches of the wire and I could see its near eye—perfectly round and flat black with a small circle of white all around the pupil—and that eye swiveled back as the shark passed.

I've done pretty much the same thing: you're walking along a city street and see a cop handcuffing some guy who's shouting obscenities. A crowd of street folk has gathered, and you walk right on by, staring straight ahead but glancing surreptitiously at the scene out of the corner of your eye. You're curious but you sure don't want to get involved in any trouble.

That was something of the message I got from the sharks cruising by the cage: If you're weak and bleeding and helpless, they seemed to be saying, we'd be happy to rip you to shreds. But, hey, we just came here for breakfast. We don't want no trouble.

In two days I logged over seven hours in the water with sharks. We took goodie bags full of mackerel down with us and hand-fed the sharks as they cruised by little gunsight windows in the cage. (Hold the fish by the tail and shake it outside the cage. Keep your hand inside, of course.) The sharks do not roll over onto their backs when feeding, as one myth has it. They'll eat in any attitude at all.

As the shark's mouth opens, a kind of lower eyelid—a white, nictitating membrane—covers the eye so that, at the moment of munch, the animal is effectively blind. This protects the shark's eyes from its prey. Several times, out of curiosity, I offered the fish, then yanked it away while the fish was blind. Ha-ha, shark. Neener neener neener. The phrase "open your mouth and close your eyes" kept running through my head. Presently, I began feeling a little guilty about teasing the man-eaters. They had these large, sadly surprised-looking eyes that never blinked . . . except at the moment of the kill.

On my second dive, I began to find the cage confining, and decided to go outside where Jack and John and Marty were filming. I had had, in my mind's eye, a vision of sharks as swift predators, torpedoes rocketing in for the kill, and that is the way they came up the chum line. But once they hit the chum box and began milling around as if confused, you could track them as they came toward you, as they made their studied, nonchalant passes.

Off forty yards in the distance, Jack McKenney was shooting a sequence in which his son John swam alongside a shark and pushed it around with a broom handle. The shark, a six-foot-long male, seemed mildly annoyed. It put on a slight burst of speed and came gliding in my direction. I had a full ten seconds to get my own broom handle in position, and when the shark was within a foot of me, I whapped it a good one on the snout. Its body twisted away from me—a snakelike gesture of avoidance—and the shark dived at a gentle angle, disappearing into a cobalt blue that purpled down into the blackness of abysmal depths.

I turned and saw another shark approaching from the rear and I beaned him as he made his pass. It seemed clear that the mildest show of aggression put these fellows off their feed. The broom handle was handy when a shark was coming at you with its mouth open and eyes closed, but, in general, you could send them skittering off into the distance with a casual backhanded gesture, the sort of motion you'd use to shoo a pigeon off some picnic table in the park.

Conversely, the sharks hit anything that didn't move. Marty Snyderman, in his chain mail shark suit, was shooting stills of the divers in the cage watching half a dozen sharks swooping by. He was kicking slightly, but his upper body was motionless and the camera was steady. A shark came up behind him: the mouth opened, revealing saw-edged teeth, and the eyes closed. The shark hit Marty in the upper left arm. He elbowed it in the snout, the shark swam away, and Marty never even looked at it. He was busy shooting pictures and getting nipped was an annoyance. Marty's shark suit cost more than my car and I wanted one.

Jack McKenney didn't have a shark suit, and either Chip or John swam above him: safety divers who swung their shark clubs over the filmmaker's motionless upper body. Jack wanted to get lots of sharks in the same frame, and he tended to hang around the chum line, where they were the most dangerous. On the second day, late in the afternoon when the night-feeding blues were getting aggressive, one came up from below and hit Jack in the finger. He was not wearing gloves, not when he had to constantly adjust focus. The bite, truth to tell, had been really just an experimental "nip," and the wound was a small jagged tear, less than an inch long: the sort of thing that might happen to you if you brushed your hand over some barbed wire. A small bit of blood rose from the cut and floated toward the surface. The blood, in this blue water, looked green. (I know. Blue and red don't make green, but that's the way it looked.)

The sharks did not go into a feeding frenzy. Everything was as it was before, and Jack kept on filming.

These little nipping incidents I saw tended to make me extremely alert when I chose to be out of the cage. It wasn't that you had to watch just your backside: the sharks could come at you from every point of the sphere. You lost them at about fifty feet and they would circle around and come at you from another angle. When there were more than three around, you could never keep track of them all. Bonnie told me that she got a picture of me concentrating on a shark that was coming at my chest. "Did you know there was another one just behind your head?" she asked.

"Of course," I lied.

After that, whenever I was out of the cage, and there were no sharks in sight, I swung the broom handle over my head, just in case. In general, a diver's arms and legs are moving, but he tends to be motionless from the shoulders up and that is where he is likely to be hit: right in the back of the head.

It took a tremendous amount of concentration to swim around outside the cage, and I found that fifteen minutes was about all I could take before a kind of numbing fatigue sent me shooting back to the safety of the bed springs. Jack, John, Marty, and Chip never got in the cage. They were pros and their discipline amazed me.

Marty Snyderman and I were sitting in the galley, drinking coffee and discussing what is likely to be the most talked-about sequence in McKenney's video. Jack had been shooting Marty hand-feeding several large sharks. One six-footer rose to the bait, and when it closed its eyes, Marty thrust his whole forearm in the animal's mouth. The shark ragged at his arm for a full sixty seconds. Marty was jerking the man-eater around in the way that you'd play with a dog.

"What about the jaw pressure?" I asked. "Doesn't it bruise you?"

Marty showed me his arm. There was no bruise: only a slight redness there. "They calculate jaw pressure from the point of one tooth," Marty said, "but I had my whole arm in the mouth and that spread the pressure out. And then the chain mail tends to distribute the pressure over a larger area."

The Neptunic Shark Suit is custom-made for each diver by Neptunic, Inc., a San Diego company headed up by the inventor of the suit, Jeremiah Sullivan. The underlayer is a Velcro-covered wet suit. Twenty-three Kevlar pads—they look like shoulder-pad material—fasten onto the Velcro. The chain mail forms the outer layer. It is made of 400,000 stainless steel links and weighs twenty pounds.

"I put my arm in a shark's mouth the first day I had the suit," Marty told me. "I needed to know if it would work."

"You're right-handed."

"Yeah."

"You put your left arm in the shark's mouth, then?"

"Well, I didn't know if it would really work."

"What does it feel like?" I asked.

Marty grabbed my forearm and squeezed, careful not to dig his fingernails into my flesh. I calculated that he was squeezing at about three quarters of his full strength. "It feels like that," he said.

Out on the deck, John McKenney shouted, "Hey, shark wranglers, we got four or five more blues coming up the chum line."

We were, all of us, suited up in less than ten minutes: eight fools in dorky-looking rubber suits, one fool in a dorky-looking chain mail suit, each of us ridiculously eager to get in the water and battle man-eating sharks with broom handles. An outsider, someone who hadn't been down there with us, would have to think we were brave as hell. Or dumb as rocks.

A twelve-footer was gnawing away at the chum box. I could see at least a dozen sharks milling around the cage. "Let's go diving," Jack McKenney said.

Kayaking Among

the Ice Children

In the unlikely event that I am commissioned to produce a horror film designed to frighten harbor seals, I'll construct the sound-track around the awful breathing I once heard while I was kayaking in Alaska's Glacier Bay National Monument.

It was late in the afternoon. Photographer Paul Dix and I were paddling across the icy waters of Muir Inlet on our way from Muir Glacier to a place called Wolf Point. The east arm of Glacier Bay is a fjord about two miles across, and we were out in the middle of it. Bare stone ridges stand on either side of the inlet so that echoes ping-pong back and forth across the water, which is still and milky-green in the shadows cast by the rock walls. In the center of the inlet, out of the shadows, the water takes on the blue of the southeastern Alaska sky. The land that projects above the ridges is reflected on the surface of the sea.

Our kayaks were slicing through the strangely shimmering image of ice-capped Mount Wright, which was a few miles to the south: a mountain that rises virtually out of the sea to a height of 5,138 feet. It was as if we were paddling across the face of the mountain, working our kayaks across a snow field. And there were small icebergs—bergy-bits, we called them—floating on the frigid waters. The sun was burning down from the ice-blue skies and the temperature stood at fifty-five degrees, so the paddle work and our long-john shirts were enough to keep us warm.

Then we heard it: breathing that sounded like that of a man surfacing after minutes underwater. But it was much louder than that, and some instinct told me that it came from a distance. Paul and I both looked south to the place where Muir Inlet empties into Glacier Bay proper. About three miles away we saw a plume of steam and spray shoot perhaps twenty feet into the air. Then, a second or so later, I heard a great exhalation of air that bounced like a fat aural balloon against the rock and rumbled up the inlet.

"Whales," I said, needlessly.

"Orcas," Paul answered.

There were eight of them, a hunting pod, and they were coming up the inlet—killer whales swimming eight abreast, so that there was no place we could go to avoid them. They were moving fast, coming directly toward us at about thirty miles an hour. Whales twenty to thirty feet long were rolling to the surface to breathe and then covering a quarter-mile or more underwater. Their six-foot-high, triangular dorsal fins cut the water on each roll so they looked, for a moment, like marauding sharks.

Glacier Bay regulations require kayakers to give any whale—humpback or killer—a quarter of a mile of respect. Paul and I decided to stay put, paddles across our laps, and let the whales break the rules. Neither of us had ever seen an orca in the wild, and now there were eight of them racing toward us, splashing through the snowy, blue reflection of Mount Wright. In that moment I felt a sense of wondrous privilege expand inside my chest, a sensation that I will forever associate with a warm spring afternoon outside junior high, when a girl named Jackie B. said she liked me, too.

The largest of the orcas was headed directly for my stationary kayak. Paul was snapping pictures, changing from the telephoto to the wide-angle lens, and he said, "Oh my God, I'm going to get you and the big one in the same frame."

The whale surfaced one hundred yards in front of me. Its dorsal fin was broken and askew; its back was shiny black against the impossible blue of the sky, and I could see a pair of white oblong markings just above and behind the eyes. The orca's great head rose completely out of the water. Its underside was snowy white. Then the whale was down again, the bent, black dorsal fin cutting in my direction.

The expansive feeling inside my chest vanished in an instant, and I felt as if my lungs had suddenly collapsed.

"Paul," I said, my voice cool and steady as only intense apprehension can make it, "why do you think they call them, uh, killer whales?"

I knew, of course. Most whales lack real teeth; they feed by straining the sea for plankton. But orcas are actually large dolphins: they have teeth and bite things like sea lions, seals, porpoises, sharks, squid, and even other whales. They have been known to kill and eat one-hundred-ton blue whales. In Glacier Bay these highly intelligent "wolves of the sea" hunt in packs. There has never been a substantiated case of an orca killing a man, despite the 1977 movie *Orca*, in which a killer whale seeks revenge on Richard Harris by eating all his costars. The movie was so silly, unscientific, and unbelievable that one critic suggested Harris fight a duel to the death with his agent for getting him the role.

Silly, silly movies tend to weigh on the mind when it's a virtual certainty that at this very moment there is a huge, toothy carnivore only a few feet under your kayak—a craft so light that you can carry it on your shoulders for miles.

"They're going for the seals," Paul shouted.

Twelve miles to the north at the head of the bay, the harbor seals live and sun themselves on the icebergs in large, gregarious colonies. Occasionally a seal slips off a berg to dive for fish or shrimp. The waters are rich in food, the climate's pleasant—by arctic standards—and the harbor seals grow fat and complacent. At the head of Muir Glacier, they have but one natural predator: the killer whale.

The guidebooks say that orcas avoid the glacier, and rangers say that killer whales don't like to navigate among icebergs at thirty miles an hour. But this pod of eight was steaming toward Muir Glacier, taking what can only be described as a quick trip to seal McDonald's. Fast food on ice.

Several orcas, acting in concert, have been known to come up under one side of an iceberg in a heaving mass. The seals sunning on the berg slide willy-nilly into the open mouths of other killer whales cleverly waiting on the downside of the suddenly treacherous ice.

The orcas were after seals. So there was nothing for me to worry about out in the middle of the Muir Inlet, where the water is only a few degrees above freezing and prolonged immersion would be fatal.

Morbidly, I began calculating my resemblance to a harbor seal. The males can be six feet long; I am a little over six feet long. They carry an insulating layer of blubber and weigh as much as 290 pounds; I can't get rid of this roll around my waist and I weigh 195. Harbor seals sun themselves on icebergs; I was sitting in what might appear, from below, to be a long sliver of floating ice.

It occurred to me that the killer whales could make a completely understandable gastronomic error. I suddenly felt like an appetizer.

An orca rolled no more than fifty yards to my right and I heard, in the harsh gasp of its breath, the glottal pop of some fleshy mechanism opening and closing. Another one surfaced, spouting, to my left, and then the big fellow with the slightly bent dorsal fin, the one who'd torpedoed under my kayak, rose and rolled beyond me, to the north.

They were rising regularly, rhythmically, first one . . . then another . . . and another . . . so that altogether, over the space of minutes, their sound resembled the awful, amplified breathing of some masked ax murderer in a slash-em-up drive-in horror film.

The orcas disappeared into the distance, but I could still faintly hear them and see their spray when they were four miles away and going around a bend. They'd cover the eight miles to the head of Muir Glacier in a quarter of an hour, but the seals would sense them long before that. They'd hear that homicidal breathing coming at them at thirty miles an hour and there'd be terror on the ice.

"Some of our pals are going to buy it today," I said.

"Yeah," Paul agreed, "blood on the ice before sunset."

We were being tough about it because we'd just spent several days camping and kayaking at Muir Glacier, where we'd come to think of the seals as our own personal pets.

Glacier Bay, a 4,375-square-mile national monument located about 70 miles northwest of Juneau, is like an immense amphitheater beside the Pacific Ocean. The bay is sheltered from coastal storms by a range of mountains that's noted for its foul weather and absurd name. Mount Fairweather, at 15,300 feet, is the world's highest coastal mountain, and the Fairweather range catches the brunt of hundreds of Pacific storms yearly. The moisture falls as snow, and it's there, high in the Fairweathers, that the glaciers are born. Over the millennia, the ceaselessly falling snow—each year's accumulation atop the previous one's—crushes lower layers into a kind of elastic, flowing ice that pours down the slopes of the mountains and smothers the land.

Four thousand years ago, Glacier Bay was a massive icefield. The bay and the land that surrounds it are new—brand new. As little as two hundred years ago, they simply didn't exist. In 1741 a Russian packet boat sailed by what is now Glacier Bay, and Captain Alexis Tchirikov noted no inland passage, only a sheet of ice that was nearly a mile high. Fifty years later Captain George Vancouver found a small inlet that became known as Icy Strait. Sailing east through the ice-choked waters, Vancouver found, to the north, a cliff of ice that was four thousand feet high.

Then the ice retreated even more; it grumbled back toward the mountains in what amounted to a single geological heartbeat. In 1879 naturalist John Muir found the wall of ice forty-eight miles farther north. Where the glaciers once reigned, Muir found a seawater bay that was miles across. The northeast arm of the bay, Muir Inlet, didn't exist in 1860. Today it is an awesome fjord over twenty-five miles long, seventeen hundred feet deep, and two miles wide. Muir Glacier stands at the end of the inlet, still in retreat, groaning, rumbling, roaring in the agony of its defeat. The glacier is being driven back into the mountains at a rate of at least a quarter-mile a year.

Glacier Bay is surrounded on three sides by a horseshoe-shaped rim of high mountains: the Fairweather, Saint Elias, Alsek, Takhinsha, and Chilkat ranges. Glaciers still form on these mountains and flow slowly down to the new sea. Nowhere else in the world are there so many tidewater glaciers. Nowhere else are the glaciers in such rapid retreat. A warming trend that started at the beginning of this century has made Glacier Bay a master of the ice.

The Tlingit Indians are native to the bay, and their legends encapsulate this geological history in myth. They tell a story of the ancient ones, the Hoonah Kwan, who lived in the time of the ice. They speak of a young girl, Kahsteen, who was kept in seclusion until her marriage. Unbearably lonely, Kahsteen called down the ice to punish her people. The glacier drove the Hoonah Kwan all the way back to Icy Straits. Kahsteen was sentenced to be left behind as a sacrifice to the ice, but an old woman, Shaw-whad-seet, who was past childbearing years, gave herself up to the ice so that the girl could strengthen the tribe with children.

It is Shaw-whad-seet who is said to cause the tidewater glaciers to retreat so rapidly, over so short a time. The old woman in the ice gives birth to her children—the great slabs of ice that calve off the tidewater glaciers and thunder into the sea.

Bartlett Cove, at the mouth of Glacier Bay, lay crushed under a mile of ice just two hundred years ago. Today it is a dense rain forest, a jungle of Sitka spruce so thick that little light reaches the forest floor, which is carpeted in luxuriant moss that holds the imprint of a boot for days.

Paul and I began by loading our kayaks aboard a tour boat at the edge of the dark forest. As we sailed north toward Muir Glacier, we were able to leisurely view the bay's spectacular wildlife and geologic scrapbook. There are golden beaches where you can see fifteen-hundred-pound Alaskan brown bears plodding across the sand.

Out ahead, a kayaker is crossing an inlet. But no, closer now, you can see that it's a moose swimming across the water with its antlers swaying side to side like a kayaker's paddle. Toward the center of the bay a humpback whale bursts forth, all fifty feet of it arching up over the surface before it crashes back into the sea.

As you approach Muir Inlet, the scars left by the ice are still apparent on the land. There is nothing like the rain forest of Bartlett Cove here. Dense thickets of interlocking alder willows that are no more than ten feet high—a backpacker's nightmare—have covered this land that emerged from under the ice less than fifty years ago.

Near Muir Glacier, the alder stands give way to small meadows of dryas, palm-sized leafy plants that bear a single bell-like flower. This is land the glacier relinquished only in the last two decades.

The tour boat pulled into a small cove that's set amid the rock and talus of ice-scoured land. Not a plant grows on this new earth. It's all hard planes and sharp angles, less than ten years old. The trip from Bartlett Cove was a lesson in how the earth clothes herself in foliage over the years. Now we saw her naked and newly born.

We lowered our kayaks into the water, where they sat precariously amid floating chunks of ice. Paul and I wanted to paddle to the glacier, alone.

Rain, constant and unremitting. The sky, the water, the land: everything's the color of lead. The fog's driven over the sea in wind-whipped shards. There is a silence here so immense that the whisper of the wind and the patter of the rain are swallowed up inside it, as the beam of a flashlight is engulfed in the darkness of a bottomless pit. And then—an explosion sharper than the crash of thunder, a sound that rumbles on for two, three, four seconds and is felt inside the chest like the boom of a bass drum at a parade. Shaw-whad-seet, the old woman in the ice, has given birth.

Paul and I were still a mile from the wall of ice, dimly seen ahead, but a small tidal wave that was spawned by the calving glacier lifted our kayaks and the icebergs we'd been navigating through.

We camped that first night at the base of a bare rock mountain in a gravelly cleft formed by a river that had changed its course. There were no flies, birds, bears, bees, wolves, or moose. We were camped on the new, still-lifeless land. The eerie silence of the night was broken now and again by the groaning of the glacier and the roar of the ice children as they crashed into the sea.

John Muir called Glacier Bay "dim, dreary, and mysterious," by which he meant to indicate that it rains every single day, four hundred days a year, there in the shadows of the glaciers. Somehow Paul and I didn't feel at all cheated when the next day dawned clear and bright.

In the distance, Muir Glacier spilled off the mountains behind it. The snow and ice flow down into the sea where they form a vertical wall of groaning glacial ice, 250 feet high and a mile wide. As rising and falling tides eat away at the base of the glacier, great slabs of ice come crashing into the water with a roar beyond rage or fury. From our campsite we could see the strange towers and gothic spires that stand together in bizarre profusion atop the glacier. The frozen cliff face took on the colors of the rising sun, so that there were crystalline pinks and golds glinting for a moment before the entire wall began to glow, as if from within, with a crimson that suggested a great heart pumping inside the ice.

As I paddled out in the kayak, moving closer to the wall, I lost sight of the spires above, and the ice seemed to loom over me. There were icebergs everywhere—white ones containing bubbles of trapped air, dense blue ones, and black ones with the mud of another era frozen inside—floating past me on the outgoing tide, as I paddled toward the glacier. There was a cracking sound and I looked to the wall, where ice fell in tumbling slabs against the frozen face of the cliff and bounced into the sea with a booming thunder.

The sound rumbled down the inlet, and there was silence again. To my right a towering iceberg was melting under the unfamiliar sun. Water dripped rapidly from various craggy points, and a small waterfall that had formed near the top spilled into the sea. Slowly the iceberg lurched over onto one side. All at once the whole affair tipped over, and the bottom side bobbed to the surface.

Harbor seals by the hundreds, sunning on flatter icebergs, watched curiously as I paddled by. One surfaced just behind me, with only its head, like a periscope, projecting above the surface of the water. Its face was very much like that of a dog—a golden retriever, say—with the mouth turned up, as if in a smile. As long as I didn't look directly at them, the seals might stare and smile in this way for a minute or more.

The sun was warm on my back, and I stripped off my shirt. Harbor porpoises rolled among the icebergs, and arctic terns and gulls wheeled above. Everyone was out having a fine time on a bright sunny day.

It seemed then that I was perhaps *too* close to the wall. All around me the icebergs were cracking in the manner of an ice cube dropped into a drink. It sounded like electricity. I looked at the wall. The Park Service recommends that kayakers give the glacier half a mile, but it was difficult to judge distances. Something about the ice, glowing aquamarine in the early-morning sun, drew me closer.

"I'm going in," I called to Paul, and paddled fast until I could clearly see the terns circling against the wall, waiting for the falling slabs of ice that would bring shrimp and stunned fish to the surface. Closer. Crackling electricity all around. There was an indentation at the base of the glacier where the tides had eaten the ice and undermined the wall. I moved closer still, until I could feel my hands tremble.

A great pillar of ice perhaps two hundred feet high, the size of an office building, separated from the main body of the glacier and fell in slow motion. The pillar cracked down on the ice that was floating at the base of the glacier, and spray exploded in an upward blast that obscured almost a quarter of the wall. At the base of the glacier, a wave of about twenty feet high rose and rolled rapidly toward me. The wave was white with glacial till, dark with ancient dirt, and it crested like high surf, tossing barge-sized icebergs before it.

That is what Paul and I did for two more days: we played chicken with the glacier while our pals, the seals, urged us on with silly smiles and blubbery good humor.

Dusk. The last night, camped at Wolf Point. I sat out on a high promontory, overlooking the sea on one side and a valley that extends back into the Fairweathers on another. Above, the sky was pulsing with pale green arcs and shimmering curtains. The Innuit people call the aurora borealis the "spirit lights." They dance over the new land and the living sea, these spirit lights, glowing with the vast, pale mysteries of life and death. In the valley below, a moose called; she sounded like a cow, lost and lowing. Nearby, wolves yipped and howled, planning the hunt.

To my left, out in the inlet, I heard the breathing of the killer whales as they moved back down the inlet. Some seals had surely died, just as the moose might die that night. In the far distance, there was the faint thunder of Shaw-whad-seet's children, of the new land being born.

Manifest Destiny

The New Desert,
an Old Woman

I n the soft, cool light of the desert's false dawn, before the sun
rises high enough in the sky to batter the land and stun all
sentient life into silence, unseen coyotes, separated by half a
mile of sage and sand, celebrate the night's hunt. It is a harmony as
joyous as birdsong.

Listen:

A series of high-pitched yips from the foothills to the east: This
one is saying he's eaten his fill of gecko lizard.

In the distance to the west, near the dry expanse of what was
once Owens Lake, an answering call: I've dug successfully for the
kangaroo rat.

To the north now, and the south, other coyotes join in the
symphony, and the yips build into howls and answering howls so
that, just for the moment of false dawn, when there is light without
merciless heat, the desert is alive with the music of the hunt.

A gray fox moves through the night-cooled gravel and sand,
stalking one last living tidbit. The top branches of the sage shine
silver, as under a full moon, and the fox pounces, agile as a domestic

cat. It has, perhaps, caught one of those lizards we call horned toads: ancient dinosaurs with small, slowly blinking black eyes that make them seem indifferent to the sun and the passage of millennia. The back-slanting horns behind the animal's neck, the unicorn scale on its head, all make the horned toad a difficult meal for the Panamint rattler, a nocturnal hunter in the heat of summer. The lizard's horns, however, are no defense against the jaws of a fox.

The sun, like a silent eruption, sets fire to the sky. In the still prism of desert air, slanting light is broken so that it scatters over the land: Sage and sand stand red and orange under the dawn. Liquid crimson, bright as rose petals, spills down over the wrinkled brown skin of nearby mountains, defining tortured ridges and filling high canyons with blood.

To the west, rising in baroque granite spires ten thousand feet above the valley floor, are the peaks of the Sierra Nevada. To the east, and soaring nearly as high, are the less celebrated Inyo and White ranges. The mountains catch the dawn and throw it down onto the floor of the desert that lies below them.

All these mountains should surely drain into the valley, but there is no water in this desert, only the baking mineral residue of what was once Owens Lake. It covers one hundred square miles, this great salt flat that has been stolen by the sun and drained by man. In the central depth of the flats, there is a hint of green—false water—rimmed with the chemical red that will, over the next few months, eat the green and fill the lake. Then, later still, the dry lake bed will revert to salt white. Whirling gusts of wind, dust devils, will lift a thin layer of sodium carbonate off the flats and take it dancing over the lake bed, take it spinning and whirling out into the world of sage and sand. But there is no wind in the desert dawn this day, and the lake lies red-rimmed, green and white under brown, bleeding hills.

There is a sense, at dawn, of a time and place without man, like an unexplored planet under a strange red star.

I was walking down out of a canyon to the east, stepping over narrow gullies and dipping down into flash-flood-carved washes on the desert floor. It was still cool, and I was making good time over sand

and gravel as the dawn passed over a sea of sage in waves of pastel light. I was racing the heat of day, hurrying toward shelter at the shore of Owens Lake, where there is a town called Keeler.

Keeler was still two hours away, a dark semicircle on the shore of the salt flat. It was built in the late 1870s, when the mine called Cerro Gordo—Fat Hill—yielded a bonanza of silver and Owens Lake was thirty feet deep with water. The mine, five thousand feet above Keeler, on Buena Vista mountain, drew men and women from the depleted gold fields of Northern California and Montana.

In those days, more than a century ago, the silver bullion was loaded onto steamships that crossed Owens Lake and freighted, by mule team, to Los Angeles. Cerro Gordo produced so much silver in its first years of production that millions of dollars worth of it was stacked in bars on the docks of Owens Lake, awaiting shipment. Men, seeking shelter from the sun, built walls of silver and draped canvas over them: men, on the docks of a mineral lake, living in mazes of silver.

It was the incredible wealth dug out of the hills above the Owens Valley that built Los Angeles, just as ore from the Comstock Lode had built San Francisco.

The mine was played out in less than a decade, but then zinc was discovered in 1879, and Keeler was founded on the shore of the lake, at the base of the mountain, to serve the new influx of miners. In 1907, an aerial tramway was built to haul ore down the hill in buckets. It is said that drunken miners, down in Keeler on a toot, hitched rides back up to Cerro Gordo in ore buckets. According to legend, some of them stood up to measure their progress and had their heads lopped off at the tramway towers. There are skulls, say the old-timers, to be found on the hillside along the path of the old tramway.

Cerro Gordo was the world's major source of high-grade zinc, and Los Angeles, booming with wealth from silver and zinc, found itself unable to provide water for a growing population. It was then, just after the turn of the century, that civic leaders in the City of Angels hatched a plan to divert water from the Owens Valley to the Southern California coast. Land and riparian rights were bought and paid for, often under shady circumstances, and an aqueduct was constructed. Three-quarters of a century later, orbiting astronauts would say that the California aqueduct was the only man-made object visible on the face of the earth.

Los Angeles assured the ranchers of Owens Valley that it wanted only enough water to quench its thirst, but the thirst was insatiable. By 1924 Owens Lake was virtually dry. The farmers and ranchers of Owens Valley, whose produce had once fed the miners of Cerro Gordo—whose work, in turn, built Los Angeles—were driven from their land by man-made drought. Several times, in the 1920s, "Valleyites" attempted to blow up the aqueduct that was draining away their lives. They failed, and land that had once supported orchards was claimed by the desert. Mesquite and sage grew where cattle had once grazed in grass up to their bellies.

The bleakest part of the new desert lay on the western edge of the dry lake, surrounding the old town of Keeler. It is not a ghost town, not yet. Though the road sign claims a population of fifty, there are closer to seventy people living in Keeler today. Folks live in trailers or in homes separated from one another by rows of abandoned ramshackle houses. Keeler is a good, cheap place to buy land and retire in a self-created oasis of lawn and flowers. Some people come to escape something—better not ask what—and others live in Keeler because they are poor and a welfare check lasts longer on the shores of a dry lake than it does in Bakersfield. There are some good artists who live cheaply in Keeler, and their creations are the heart of a dying town.

The soul of Keeler, though, is a woman named "just Annie," of Annie's Keeler Market. It is a small grocery, and it looks more like a home than a store. You have to go around back, to the house behind the store, and knock on the door to get Annie to open up for you. She has lived on the shores of Owens Lake since the 1930s, and nothing much surprises her anymore, least of all a large, sweating man carrying a backpack who wants a raspberry Popsicle with a cold beer chaser.

Annie's store doesn't pay for itself as it once did. The market is really a community service, and though the signs inside say NO CREDIT and DON'T ASK, Annie will generally carry a tab.

For a stranger stumbling in out of the desert heat, Annie has a shower in the back and a washing machine to clean the desert grime off his clothes. In back of the grocery, alongside the house, there is a shady area with several picnic tables, some overstuffed chairs, and a sofa. It is a place for the people of Keeler to meet after work, to drink a beer or a soda and wait for the day to cool into night.

Annie can remember when there was water up to the shores of Keeler. That was back when she first came here, in the 1930s, though the history books say the lake was drained by 1924. Annie is adamant: She recalls mail boats heading south to Olancha.

When what was left of the mines finally closed, when the lake died, Keeler began its slow slide into history. Oh, there was a time when Annie's husband was alive and people from Lone Pine, fifteen miles away, drove to Keeler to buy Annie's meat. Then the desert, like an enemy, closed in around Keeler. People gave up on it, moved away.

Some ecologists argue that the water that might have made Keeler and the Owens Valley fertile was, in truth, best sent to Los Angeles. They say that the uninhabitable desolation of the valley is what saved its wildlife and provided a place for man to live apart from man, if only for a while. Tourism, not agriculture, provides a living for people elsewhere in the Owens Valley. With water, the valley might have become a chaos of tract homes.

There are no tract homes near Keeler, and no tourists to speak of. People like Annie, who watched the lake go dry, feel cheated, though she doesn't address the question directly. She says she hates the "soda ash" that blows off the lake in a high wind. It gets into the house and dirties wall and floors. Just recently, she had to repaint the kitchen. Her late husband's fishing hat had hung beside the refrigerator for years, and she had to take it down, for the first time since he died, to repaint. Because of the soda ash. Blowing in off a lake that has been flushed down the toilets of Los Angeles.

Annie is willing to pose for a picture, but she'd like her prize toy poodle in the photo, too. "Jump up, Fifi," Annie says, patting her lap. "You're a good girl, yes you are. You're all Annie has left now, aren't you?"

She scratches the little dog behind the ears. "Fifi's all Annie has left, yes she is. . . ."

Out beyond Annie's Keeler Market, in the cool indigo of a gathering desert night, a coyote calls. In a land bereft of tract homes and taco stands, a gray fox moves like mercury through the sage.

World-Class Attractions

It is said that as a somewhat deflated George Armstrong Custer lay bleeding in the Montana dirt at the Little Big Horn, he turned his glazed and dimming eyes east and said, "At least we won't have to go back through South Dakota."

These days, Custer might actually enjoy a trip through South Dakota. He could stop at the Badlands and battle the Winnebagos for a look at Mount Rushmore. He could hardly fail to resist those several hundred signs commanding him to visit Wall Drug (TURN WHERE YOU SEE THE 80-FOOT DINOSAUR). Out in eastern South Dakota, in Mitchell, Custer would marvel at the "World's Only Corn Palace," a great one-block square building decorated entirely with colored corncobs. Although it is true that the Incas fashioned replicas of cornstalks out of pure gold, it took South Dakotans to come up with the idea of decorating the outside of a building with corncobs. When I was there last Thanksgiving, birds were feeding on the colored corn face of a mammoth astronaut.

Interstate 90 through South Dakota is, indeed, a paradise of kitsch. By comparison, the more northerly route across the country, I-94 through North Dakota, is bleak, barren, almost entirely lacking in roadside attractions. Those the state does have—like Route 46, the world's straightest road, 121 miles without a curve—seem to emphasize the drawbacks of driving through it.

Even people who love North Dakota end up damning it with faint praise. Teddy Roosevelt arrived there in 1883, at the age of twenty-five, a spindly young fellow wearing thick eyeglasses. The trip west toughened Roosevelt, and after he demolished a local bully in a fair fight, he won the fearsome nickname Old Four Eyes, which is what all the really tough guys in North Dakota are called. North Dakota, Roosevelt wrote, "has a desolate, grim beauty that has a curious fascination for me." The adjectives here tell the story: grim . . . desolate . . . curious.

Recently, I drove through North Dakota on the way to Wisconsin to visit my parents. I hadn't been in the state for more than ten years and was delighted to discover that there is now a genuine tourist attraction along I-94. Just outside the National Grasslands, I was amazed to see, in the distance, a huge cow standing on a ridge. This cow was at least five miles away, and it dwarfed all the other cows that were standing around in little groups talking about the best way to get out of North Dakota.

At eighty miles an hour, which is the only way to drive through North Dakota, you stare at that big cow for quite some time before you get to the sign saying that you have been looking at the world's largest Holstein cow. There is a turnoff and an arrow. You can drive right up to the world's largest Holstein cow. My guess, having missed the turnoff, is that the cow was fashioned from ferroconcrete. Clustered about its hooves were a cafe, a gas station, and perhaps a motel. All else was utter desolation.

I doubt if the businesses under the cow prosper. By the time you get to the sign showing you where to turn off to see the world's largest Holstein cow, you've pretty much already seen it. That brings up the question of the North Dakota mind, which my fellow Montanans do not hold in high regard.

While Montanans are ranchers, NoDaks are farmers: stolid, respectable, churchgoing folk who have difficulty mastering the mechanical intricacies of the dinner table and who can be spotted by the tiny fork-caused craters in their foreheads. Montanans tell NoDak jokes—you can always get a one-armed NoDak out of a tree simply by waving at him—and NoDaks invariably respond with polite bewilderment.

I suppose it is unfair to attribute feeblemindedness to an entire state upon the evidence of one dim-bulb roadside attraction. People from Wisconsin, where I grew up, are known to be beautiful, sexy, and wonderfully intelligent, yet the state has gone to idiotic lengths to publicize a fact that most people already know, namely that cheese is made there. I am thinking specifically of the twelve-foot-high sculpture of a rat named Igor outside the Fennimore cheese factory in Fennimore, Wisconsin. Igor has four feet, is gray with blue eyes, and has whiskers erupting from its snout. Igor appears to be gnawing a huge piece of swiss cheese.

Large as Igor's cheese may be, it is not the world's largest cheese sculpture. The world's largest cheese, indeed the alleged "Largest Cheese in the History of Mankind," is located in Neillsville, Wisconsin. The seventeen-ton cheddar is enclosed in a semitrailer with one glass side for viewing. Jane and Michael Stern, in their book *Amazing America*, unraveled the secret of this monolithic cheese. "We peered closely at the cheese and thought it looked pretty unappetizing, like a block of compressed burlap. We looked closer at the fact sheet: 'This cheese was eaten in 1965, at a cheese convention.'" The Sterns, sticklers for accuracy, suggest a more honest appellation for the thing in the glass truck: "The Largest Piece of Cheeselike Burlap in the History of Mankind."

Out there in Neillsville, next to the truck containing the ersatz cheese, is an attraction that would astound all of North Dakota. It is "Chatty Belle, the World's Largest Talking Cow." Chatty Belle is nowhere near as large as the world's largest cow, but Chatty will, at the touch of a button, tell you about a variety of dairy products. (The NoDak Holstein is, predictably, entirely mute.)

Now, what I suggest is that North Dakota engineers—who have already built the tallest structure known to man, the 2,063-foot-high KTHI-TV tower—install a bank of Woodstock-like speakers in the world's largest Holstein, thereby wresting the locution crown from Chatty Belle as well.

The problem here is just what exactly the new world's largest talking Holstein should say. It could, perhaps, threaten tourists who refuse to turn in to the cafe. This approach might work in Nevada, but NoDaks are nothing if not polite, and I imagine they wouldn't want to threaten interstate travelers. Maybe the cow should say clever things; maybe it should have a script full of aphorisms and bons mots. Of course, the NoDaks would have to hire a Montanan to write such a script. I could do it myself.

I'd have a photoelectric sensing device atop the rise so that even before you could say, "Hey, what's that up there on the ridge?" a great godlike voice would shake the land: "Hi, I'm Igor the Rat."

This single sentence would, in one fell swoop, establish an attraction any American family should want to see: "The Largest Talking Holstein Cow That Thinks It's a Gray 12-Foot-High Fiberglass Rat Outside of a Cheese Factory in Fennimore, Wisconsin, in the History of Mankind."

This is the sort of roadside attraction North Dakotans can point to with pride; then again, maybe not. It takes an awful lot of them to screw in a light bulb.

Fire and Brimstone

on the Volcano Watch

On Friday, March 27, Mount St. Helens, a volcanic mountain in the state of Washington, erupted, spewing forth a plume of steam and gas and ash to a height of some four miles.

There was no causal relationship—none that I know of—but the next day in Montana, snow began to fall, lightly. It fell throughout the next day, driven by high winds. By Sunday the ranch at Poison Creek was buried under three feet of snow. In places, the drifts were piled to six and eight feet. Certain of my neighbors, those in the ranching business, were using snowmobiles to get out to their pastures. Some newly born calves were already dead. Much of next year's income was freezing, suffocating under the blanket of snow.

Down at the lumber mill, 110 people had just been laid off as a result of unpleasant economic trends. Various friends who specialize in carpentry foresaw a bleak and workless summer. In New York, my publisher wasn't willing to advance me any more money on a book I had been writing for the past six months.

I was sitting at my desk, writing an article about scuba diving, and a massive drift was piling up over the window. The whole house seemed to hum in the wind. I was sorry for my neighbors and friends and for myself. And I was depressed unto death about the worms in the water. Little black fellows, about half the size of a fingernail. They swirled out into a glass held under the tap like so many rat droppings, a dozen or more to an eight-ounce glass.

So, of course, I would get a call asking me to go cover the volcano. I was writing about scuba diving while calves froze in the fields and no one wanted to buy my book and everyone was going broke and there were worms in the water—and they wanted me to drive through a cattle-killing blizzard to cover a volcano. The world, clearly, was coming to an end.

666　666　666　666

It was best to pack up everything, typewriter and all, in my backpack and wade through waist-deep snow to the jeep, which was parked a mile away, by the plowed road.

Outside Butte I picked up a hitchhiker, a big twenty-one-year-old fellow named Marty who had just finished his last year as a defensive tackle for a Southern California junior college. Marty didn't think the eruption of Mount St. Helens signaled the end of the world. He had read a number of idiot pseudoscientific tomes and had learned that the world would end in "1984, I think," when all the planets would be arranged in a straight line out from the sun— The Grand Alignment—and gravitational forces on the earth would cause earthquakes and more volcanoes and tidal waves and hurricanes and tornadoes. For his part, Marty figured the next four years would be a good time to "party," and that a party under the volcano would be superior to one held in a Montana blizzard.

666　666　666　666

Just before midnight, in Spokane, the jeep broke down. We would have to wait until morning to fix it, so Marty and I each got a motel room.

The jeep was defective and there were worms in the water and the depression weighed on me so that life seemed to be a process of swimming one's way up through an endless vat of spoiled custard. I picked up the Gideon Bible and read my favorite verse, the epistle in which the apostle Paul advises Timothy, my patron saint, to forsake water and drink wine "for thy stomach's sake and for thine often infirmities."

But Timothy is near the Book of Revelations, and the pages fell open to chapter nine, where I read prophecies of the Apocalypse. The fifth angel, it says, will blow his trumpet and a star will fall to the earth, and to him, the star, will be given the key to the bottomless pit. Smoke will spew from the pit, as though from some great furnace, and the sun and air will be darkened by the smoke.

Out of the smoke will come locusts with the power to sting as scorpions, and these will torture those who have not the mark of God on their heads, torture them with scorpion stings for five months.

In chapter 13, verse 11, I read of the beast who will rise from the earth to enslave men; the Beast, in the Apocalypse of the Blessed Apostle John, shall bear the mark 666.

There is solace to be found in the Bible, but not a whole hell of a lot of it in Revelations. I drifted off to sleep and the depression sat on my chest like a three-hundred-pound toad.

666   666   666   666

The mightiest peaks of the Cascade Range, which stretches from Northern California to southern Canada, are volcanic in origin, part of the Pacific Ring of Fire. The volcanoes of Alaska, Japan, Mexico, and Ecuador are part of the same system, and it is thought that in these spots the plate that forms the ocean floor is being thrust under the plate that forms the continents. This creates cracks, or faults, in the earth's crust.

Such faults allow gas and molten rock—called magma—to rise up out of the bowels of the earth. We know that most of this gas and liquefied rock originates somewhere between twenty-five and two hundred miles below the surface of the earth, and that at those depths, the earth is very hot. Forty miles down, for instance, the temperature is probably twelve hundred degrees centigrade, more than hot enough to liquefy rock. There is gas present in deep magma, but the pressure of the rocks above keeps it in solution. Like bubbles in a bottle of Blitz beer, the gas will stay in solution as long as the cap is kept on. But when the magma rises—as it hawks its way up through the earth and into the throat of the volcano—the pressure lessens. The gas forms bubbles, and bubbles join together. The gas in the bubbles is under pressure still, pressure from the weight of the magma around and under and over it.

When the gas pressure becomes high enough, it explodes out of confining, enclosing liquefied rock, blowing magma onto the surface of the earth. This reduces the pressure of the gases lower down, and they explode, reducing the pressure on lower down, and they explode, reducing the pressure on lower gases and so on.

An eruption, then, is not one huge, cataclysmic explosion, but a series of them, each lasting several seconds or minutes and separated by periods of minutes or hours or even days.

666   666   666   666

I was sitting by my campsite under the volcano, a grassy park on Yale Lake, about two miles west of Cougar, Washington, reading about all this and glancing up at the silent mountain every now and again, when an angry older woman approached and demanded to know "why I can't see it." It was her impression that the volcano was erupting constantly and that great rivers of molten lava were roaring off down the wrong side of the hill, simply to spite her.

There were thousands of people in the park, most of them in cars and campers, all lined up and facing the mountain, which rose in the distance. The drivers had politely aligned their vehicles so as not to obstruct the view of those behind them. It was a drive-in volcano.

The woman who was mad at the mountain poked me in the shoulder. "What's the matter with it? What does it say in those books you're reading? Why's it just sitting there?"

I began explaining about magma and gas and intermittent eruptions and was about to show her a diagram in one of the books when I was stung, quite painfully, on the side of the neck. It was a wasp of some kind, but the implications were all too clear.

Ash had fallen for days, *tephra*, the scientists call it, and when the wind was right, some had fallen on Cougar, so that there was a fine coating of it on the hoods and roofs of the locals' cars and pickups. These sand-sized fragments of ash or dust couldn't be wiped off the vehicles with a dry rag because they caused scratch marks and marred the finish.

Ash had fallen. And out of this ash had come a wasp—a locust with the sting of a scorpion, if you will—and the little sucker nailed me right in the side of the neck. I explained to the woman that she was on hand for the Big One, that it was Good Friday, noon exactly, and time for the fifth angel to blow his trumpet, for the star to fall from the sky and open the abysmal pit. There would be fire and ash and plague, there would come wars and numberless hosts and rivers would flow with blood and the Beast 666 would rise from the earth and terror would reign over the land.

The woman seemed relatively certain that I hadn't read all this in my copy of *Geological Hazards*, and she wandered off to ask someone else. There were many knowledgeable people there that day, both locals and people who came from thousands of miles away. There were also a number of twenty-year-old cowboy shoe-clerks from Vancouver, Washington, who tipped their Stetsons back on their heads, squinted up at the mountain, and let out with the sort of mystical wisdom that is given only to cowboy shoe-clerks. "Nah, lady, she ain't gonna blow . . . no way."

My tent was out on a promontory over the reservoir called Yale Lake. Marty, the hitchhiking tackle, was still with me, and somewhere along the way we had picked up Ken and Len from Kansas, who'd come to the coast looking for work on the shrimp boats. They had taken acid for the eruption.

If that is what you like to do, I suppose it was a good day for it. The sky was blue, and it was warm enough to sit around drinking beer in your shirtsleeves. A vendor, working out of a van, was doing a brisk business selling "I survived Mount St. Helens" T-shirts. Other people were wearing shirts reading, "Mount St. Helens, Lava or Leave Her." One woman wore a button reading, "They laughed at Pompeii."

666   666   666   666

Mount St. Helens stood white against the blue sky. It was a gorgeous mountain, curved, symmetrical, somehow more feminine in appearance than the more pyramidal, ice-carved summits of Mount Hood or Mount Adams. In geological terms, St. Helens is a youthful volcano, and its top section was formed a scant twenty-five hundred years ago. Hood and Adams were present in the ice age of ten thousand years ago, and glaciers have carved great cirques and valleys in them. The summit of St. Helens had never suffered the erosive scraping of the Pleistocene's great glaciers.

The rounded summit was perfectly white. I had heard that there was ash on the snow, on the present glaciers, but a snowfall the previous evening had renewed her, made her shine against the sun, virginal and glittering.

At 12:20 by my watch, a great plume of steam billowed up out of the top of the mountain, out of the crater there, and it was carried north and west by the wind. Ken and Len watched with spinning eyes, and Len whispered that it was "bad." Three minutes later, a black cloud rose under the steam, and two minutes after that an even denser black cloud followed. These clouds rose several thousand feet over the mountain, and the heaviest black ash was spread along a line by the wind, like a curtain. The ash fell along the northwest slopes like rain from a thunderhead. The eruption was visible from Portland, nearly fifty miles away.

There was no noise, no sound at all, and it looked almost too perfect, like a diorama of the Jurassic period in some museum. There was a sudden sense of the Dawn of Time: the placid lake, the blue sky and green grass, and all that steam and ash rising soundlessly, eerily, from the summit of the most appealing mountain in America.

"There should be dinosaurs," I said. Ken and Len took up the thought. They wanted to see pterodactyls—great, fire-blackened flying reptiles—come belching up out of the crater. They wanted a brontosaurus to break the surface of Yale Lake. That would be "bad," the taloned pterodactyls screaming down on all these people, thunderous bellows from the brontosaurus, oh God, that would be bad.

At 12:31 the eruption came to an end. The whole northwest side of the mountain was covered with black ash. The Beast was still confined to the pit.

666　666　666　666

There isn't much to do between minor eruptions on the volcano watch, and I spent hours reading, computing my chances of survival in case of a major cataclysmic event, a worst-possible-case scenario.

Lava flows weren't going to be much of a problem. Lava, the term for magma when it reaches the surface of the earth, advances quite slowly, and it is easy to outrun. One schematic drawing in *Fire and Ice*, a book about Cascade volcanoes by Stephen L. Harris, showed that lava flows during the past four thousand years had advanced almost to the town of Cougar. I was camped two miles farther on down the road. In four thousand years lava flows had never hit my campsite, but in a worst-case scenario, they might.

The flow would look like a slowly moving heap of coal. By the time it reached the camp, the surface of the flow might even be cool enough to walk upon, but that would be somewhat foolhardy, because if one did fall through the upper crust, he'd find himself standing waist deep in a thick river of incandescent rock. Also, the heat of the flow thins the air above it so that a person working his way across the sharp, jagged clinkers of the crusted surface would possibly faint from lack of oxygen.

(It is worth noting that one lava flow on St. Helens formed the Ape Caves. Located near the base of the mountain, the Ape Caves are actually a unitary lava tube some 11,215 feet long. Such tubes are formed when less-viscous lava, called *pahoehoe*, congeals on the surface, but a river of molten rock continues underneath, finally emptying out, leaving a smooth, often ovoid tube.

The caves were discovered by a logger in 1946 and explored by a group of cavers who called themselves "the St. Helens Apes." That is the official explanation for the name. But the Cascade Range is Bigfoot country. There have been numerous sightings in nearby areas: in The Dalles, in Kelso, even on St. Helens herself. On a summer's night, so say some locals, you can hear them, the congregated ape things, howling and gibbering in the coolness of the caves.)

Tephra falls—thick rains of black, glassy ash—would cause more deaths than the biggest lava flow. In a major eruption, exploding gases can throw up bombs—semimolten rock—and blocks—angular pieces of older, solid rock. Bombs and blocks would land somewhere on the slopes of the mountain. The problems at my campsite would be caused by sand-sized fragments of wind-carried ash and dust, and by light, gas-saturated stone, or pumice.

In 79 A.D., two thousand people lost their lives in an ash fall when Mount Vesuvius erupted. In that year, on August 24, just after noon, ash and pumice began falling on Pompeii. The ash fell throughout the day. The darkness was so intense that a lantern held at arm's length could hardly be seen. Pompeii was being buried. The ash reached a depth of nearly nine feet. Most of the twenty thousand people fled, but some of those who stayed were crushed when their roofs collapsed. Others took refuge in cellars and were literally buried alive. Some bodies have been found with pieces of cloth held to their faces, suggesting that gas given off by the pumice as it solidified might have filled the air with toxic fumes.

Pompeii was about five miles from the vent of Vesuvius. I was about ten miles from St. Helens. The ash fall, in a worst possible case, might be expected to pile to eight or nine feet. The winds on Good Friday would have carried the ash to the east, but if they changed, and a major tephra fall developed, it seemed likely that many lives could be lost. Most of the people at Yale Lake would want out, fast. They'd highball it on down Route 503, a perpetually wet, winding road that follows the Lewis River valley. Headlights would not penetrate the darkness. Dozens would die in accidents.

If ash and pumice fell on the campsite in any volume, I intended to go back to the jeep and wait it out. I was unintentionally prepared. A snow-shovel is a necessary tool for any Montana driver, and I had one in my car. I would simply step out of the jeep every once in a while and shovel the light ash and pumice from the roof and sides. Likely it would be no more heavy than wet snow.

That left the remote problem of choking gases given off by cooling pumice. One book I read suggested the use of industrial gas masks. Lacking them, it said, a wet cloth might remove some harmful gases. A cloth saturated with a weak acid such as vinegar or urine would be even more effective.

I read this section to Marty, the hitchhiking tackle. "Buddy," I said, "when that ash starts to fall, we're going to have to piss in our shirts."

"I'm buying vinegar," he said.

"What happens if the ash fall lasts twenty hours? You could run out of vinegar. I have enough beer stashed in the car that we won't have to worry about running out of urine."

"No way," Marty said. He vowed that he'd choke to death on toxic gases before he'd piss in his shirt.

We could survive a tephra fall, but mud flows seemed to be a more significant danger. Mount St. Helens was mantled in snow, and there were a number of young glaciers on her flanks. Great clouds of burning volcanic debris, ejected during a major eruption, could cause rapid melting and then flooding at the top of the mountain. The flood would resemble a high-altitude tidal wave, and would be propelled down the steep slopes of St. Helens by gravity. The speed of a mud flow depends on the steepness of the slope and the viscosity of the mud. A mud flow would contain boulders, uprooted trees, shattered homes, cars, cattle, and men.

In a worst-case scenario, a major mud flow would scour St. Helens and move at speeds in excess of sixty miles an hour on the upper slopes. The flow would be largely confined to the drainages.

There is evidence that about three thousand years ago mud flows made their way down the Lewis River canyon, a distance of some forty miles. I checked my map. We were a little more than ten air miles from the vent, and fifteen miles from it by way of the drainages.

The mud flow I envisioned on our side of the mountain—it was actually much more likely on the other side—would sweep down over Ape Caves and pour into Swift Reservoir, just above Yale Lake. The water level in Swift had been lowered thirty feet to accommodate a possible flow, but nothing could hold back a really big one. It would tear through the dam and inundate Yale Lake and, incidentally, the place where I happened to be camped.

On this lower, more level land, the flow would lose velocity and begin piling up.

I looked out from my tent perched on the promontory. There was a ridge before the mountain, and St. Helens was perfectly framed by a pass in the ridge. Yale Lake swept around a bend to the right and passed out of sight, obscured by the canyon walls.

The mud flow would arrive with the roar of a hundred snow avalanches, and the ground would tremble beneath it. It would come rolling around the bend in the canyon, carrying tons of debris—a thick, dirty tidal wave perhaps twenty feet high moving at the rate of, say, twenty miles an hour.

I wasn't going to try to drive out from under anything like that, not with hundreds of cars clogging 503. You could barely do forty on that road anyway. The wall of mud would simply roll over the crawling cars, and it would set like cement. No, when the mud came, I'd run for the high ground and watch my jeep and a thousand dollars' worth of my camping gear roll on down the Lewis River valley another thirty-five miles.

So, in case of tephra falls, it was piss in your shirt and get out the shovel. In the event of a mud flow, it was a quick sprint to the high ground. That left one last, terrifying hazard, the glowing avalanche. Clouds of incandescent gas and ash and other debris can burst from the vent and travel down the slopes of the mountain at speeds of nearly one hundred miles an hour. The superheated mass of a glowing avalanche can be particularly deadly when an obstruction in the throat of the crater causes an explosive eruption to blow a hole in the side of the crater. A glowing cloud is aimed directly down the slope. Sometimes the explosion is a vertical one, and the hot ash and gas simply falls back onto the area around the crater and rolls down all sides of the mountain.

666   666   666   666

This last is what happened during the eruption of Mount Pelee, on the island of Martinique on May 8, 1902. The huge cloud belched up out of the mountain, and at first it seemed totally black. But as its darkness blotted out the sun and the light failed, the cloud could be seen to glow purple and red. It howled down the mountain at a hundred miles an hour, uprooting trees and shattering buildings. In less than two minutes, the burning avalanche hit the city of St. Pierre, killing some thirty thousand persons.

Many died from inhaling the hot gases; others were horribly burned. The cloud emerged from the crater at a temperature of about a thousand degrees centigrade. As it moved, bubbles of gas continued to ignite, so that it hit St. Pierre not much cooler, about eight hundred degrees centigrade. The heat lasted only a few minutes, and the cloud cooled rapidly so that there was not much damage from fire. The blast was not hot enough, nor was it of sufficient duration, to ignite cotton, and many corpses were found fully clothed. The heat did, however, turn body water to steam, so that the fully clothed bodies were hideously distended. In some cases, sutures in the skull had cracked open, like the shell of an overboiled egg.

Mount St. Helens had spewed out a number of glowing avalanches in its readable geological history. Could such a cloud reach the campground on Yale Lake? I checked the distance from Mount Pelee to St. Pierre in *Geological Hazards*, by Bolt, Horn, MacDonald, and Scott. It appeared to be about four or five miles. We were double that distance from St. Helens, three times the distance by way of the drainages. And the glowing avalanche, like a mud flow, would follow the drainage.

It seemed a safe enough distance, but not in a truly catastrophic situation. Then there would be a mighty eruption, and the inky black cloud would hide the mountain from us, then blot out the sun. Minutes later, in the gritty midnight, we'd see it rounding the bend in Yale Lake, a huge cloud, a hundred feet high, glowing purple-red, like a burning bruise.

The glowing avalanche would follow the river valley like a mud flow, but because of its greater speed, it would climb ridges hundreds of feet high. Gas bubbles, separating the particles of glowing ash, reduce friction and allow the burning cloud to move at such great speeds.

The nearest ridge appeared to be 150 feet high, and it was situated in such a way that a glowing avalanche, rounding the bend in the canyon, would be propelled directly up its slope. There was a higher ridge across the lake, but it was a hopeless distance away. And there would be no refuge in the lake itself; in seconds the surface would become a thick mass of scalding mud.

In a minute, maybe two, the cloud would pass and no one on the campground would be left alive. Those not stripped of their clothes by the force of the blast would still be wearing their "I survived Mount St. Helens" T-shirts, and the buttons reading "They laughed at Pompeii" would be only slightly warped.

666   666   666   666

On March 20, a week before the first eruption of Mount St. Helens in 123 years, seismologists began detecting earthquakes in the vicinity. Three weeks later, there had been a total of 105 quakes registering over 4.0 on the Richter scale. Almost all volcanic eruptions of major significance are preceded by a series of earthquakes.

On April 2, the University of Washington seismic lab detected a "harmonic tremor," a rhythmic expanding and contracting of the ground quite unlike the sharp crack of a conventional quake. Harmonic tremors are caused by the movement of magma and gases within the volcano and, even more than conventional quakes, signal the possible onset of a major eruption.

Forest Service workers on the lower slopes had already been evacuated, and loggers were banned from job sites deemed dangerous.

The scenarios I had been so assiduously frightening myself with seemed unlikely, but that night, Good Friday, at the Wildwood Inn, a bar in Cougar, I heard that there had been, that day, a thirty-five-minute harmonic tremor, the longest yet recorded. Rumors flew. The roadblock would be moved down the mountain several miles. The National Guard would be called in. The Big Blow was imminent.

I woke to an ominous rumbling at 5:00 A.M. on Saturday morning, but it was only a convoy of green National Guard trucks moving on up toward Cougar.

Local folks were allowed to move through the roadblocks. Guardsmen handed them slips of paper which read: "Hazardous Area—Volcano—Enter at your own risk."

At the Wildwood Inn there were stacks of a single-page bulletin from the U.S. Geological Survey entitled "What to Do When a Volcano Erupts." Readers were advised to get indoors during ash falls, to shovel accumulated ash from their roofs, to breathe through a damp cloth, to keep their eyes closed as much as possible "when the air is full of ash," and not to drive cars because "the chance of accident will be increased by poor visibility."

Mud flows, the bulletin said, would resemble wet, flowing concrete. They "move faster than you can walk or run, but you can drive a car down a valley faster than a mud flow will travel." The bulletin advised drivers to check upstream for mud flows before crossing any bridges and said that pedestrians should move to high ground.

In big, screaming capital letters, the bulletin said, "MOST IMPORTANT—Don't panic, keep calm."

This was all good advice, and the last sentence, which was underlined for emphasis, was the best advice of all, even if it was somewhat self-evident: *"During an eruption, move away from a volcano, not toward it."*

The bulletin didn't mention glowing avalanches. Either the Geological Survey didn't think them likely, or it felt that since there was nothing to be done about them, the damn things were better left unmentioned. The very idea could cause a panic.

666   666   666   666

It rained all day Saturday, and I spent the dreary hours at the Wildwood, drinking beer and playing pool. The rumor was that they were going to tighten up the roadblock. The media would no longer have access. Marty and Ken and Len and I took Paul's advice to Timothy to heart, and among us we killed a half-gallon of rot-gut bourbon.

On Easter Sunday there was rain mixed with snow. I drove down to the roadblock and found it was true; the road was closed to the media. An ABC network television crew had gotten in under the wire and interviewed Ken, who had had a great deal of trouble getting out of his sleeping bag that morning. The acid and the bourbon and the beer had caught up with him and he had spent most of the night on his hands and knees, vomiting. The TV crew found him lying in his tent with his dog, Guy.

"Are you excited when the volcano shoots out plumes?" Ken was asked.

"Not particularly," Ken said. He wanted to die.

The TV people decided that it would be best just to get some interesting shots of a man and his dog, living in a tent under the volcano. "Don't talk," they told Ken. "Just pretend we're not here and do what you'd be doing otherwise." Ken zipped up his tent and went back to sleep.

666   666   666   666

I like to think there is an underlying mystical logic to events, a mathematics of catastrophe, a symmetry to the Apocalypse. It was Easter Sunday afternoon, and a cold rain mixed with snow fell on the all-but-deserted campground. It was one of those soul-chilling, incessant, Pacific Northwest drizzles: a steady, endless, timeless rain.

I looked out over the gray surface of the lake. On the ridges, frosted trees gleamed dully in the leaden light. St. Helens was shrouded in fog. Everyone was gone: the press, the sightseers, everyone. The only people left on the campground were a group of geology students from Montreal and myself and the three hitchhikers. Symmetry demanded that Easter Sunday be the day of The Big Blow.

Ash would fall, stinking of brimstone. The day would drown in gritty night and no light would show. Out of the sudden blackness would come the high whine of wasps and locusts and scorpions. In the distance, howling and hissing and steaming, there would be seen a tortured light, the burning bruise of a glowing avalanche, moving at unholy speed. The incandescent cloud would melt the mountain itself, and the rumble of a mighty mud flow would shake the land. It would be over us then, all of us, everywhere; this great wall of mud, stinking of the bowels of the earth.

Only a few survivors would hear it: the demonic howl, the gibbering, the inhuman laughter as the Beast emerged from the Ape Caves to take possession of his newly born kingdom. The Beast had waited long for this time. We always knew he was there, but we could never see him, nor find him, nor kill him, nor even film him. He would stride boldly over the broken, burning land, through the stench of sulfur, and the thing we called Sasquatch or Bigfoot or Yeti would have the number 666 on his forehead.

666   666   666   666

It rained, and sometimes it snowed; other than that, nothing much happened on Easter Sunday. No ash, no fire, no mud, no Apocalypse.

On Monday morning we broke camp, but at 11:00 the clouds cleared and the mountain sent up a great mushroom-shaped black plume. There was a faint rumbling, and on the northwest slope, near the crater, we could see a sizable snow avalanche. The mountain erupted four more times in two hours. Through my binoculars I could see boulders being thrown for what looked to be several hundred yards.

Ken and Len were going on down to Texas where they had lined up a construction job. Marty thought he'd tag along with them and see if he could find work in the oil fields. They were all going to hitchhike together: three tough-looking guys, three big backpacks, and one wet dog. Anyone would pick them up.

I dropped them all off in Portland. That fat, dreary depression came back and sat on my heart.

The next day, at the Forest Service press conference in Vancouver, Washington, geologists said they thought the volcano had entered "a constant mode of activity." It could, they said, continue ejecting steam and ash in minor quantities as it had done for twenty-five years the last time it erupted. Instruments had been placed near the flanks of the mountain, and they showed no significant lift or tilting of the ground. "All these observations," the geologists said, "imply that there is no indication that a major eruption of molten rock will occur in the near future." The monitoring system would provide advance indications of changing conditions that might lead to an eruption.

Roadblocks were moved back up the road, east of Cougar, and loggers went back to their job sites after signing disclaimers. Fishing season would open as scheduled.

On Thursday there was no volcano photo on the front page of *The Oregonian*. The lead photo and story came from San Bernardino, California. It was about a sixteen-year-old who sold his five-year-old cousin to a convicted sex offender who wanted to "teach the young girl things." The sixteen-year-old bargained the buyer up from an initial offer of $50 to $230. The girl was rescued after four days, and the sixteen-year-old was arrested. He had $6 in his pocket. He told police that he had plunked $150 into pinball machines and bought his girl a corsage.

The story had its own hellish smell of brimstone. When the toad is sitting on your heart, you don't have to look very far to see the Apocalypse coming. The mountain, as of this writing, is still steaming up north of Portland, but there are any number of ways to bring it all to an end.

Author's Note:
This article appeared in print two weeks before the cataclysmic eruption of Mount St. Helens. It had been a tough story to write: what can you say about a bunch of people watching an occasional puff of smoke emerge from a pretty white mountain? In order to give the story a little drama, I went and spoke to geologists who had studied the mountain for decades and asked them to help me draw up a worst-possible-case scenario.
At Mount St. Helens, two days after the eruption, reporters from across America were walking around carrying copies of Outside *containing the article. The worst-case scenario I had elicited from the geologists was eerily*

accurate: there had been intermittent blasts, massive mud slides, pyroclastic flows, and they had all occurred on the Spirit Lake side of the mountain.

One reporter even confirmed a fact I didn't want to know: at least one victim had died wearing an "I survived Mount St. Helens" T-shirt. So the article had been prophetic and, since I was there, working on a follow-up story for the late lamented GEO, I was interviewed a few times by my colleagues. It was, I told them, the geologists and vulcanologists, not me, who had predicted what might happen. In retrospect, it was only the tone of the article, the sense of dread and depression I felt under the volcano, that seemed somehow clairvoyant.

Eruption

The ashfall was light in south central Montana, where I live, and it hung in the air all around, like a brittle yellow fog. A thin layer settled on my car. It was like face powder, and I knew people were dead. The news was sparse. I couldn't even get a phone line to Cougar, to Vancouver, to anywhere I'd been in the state of Washington only a month before.

It was Monday, May 19, the day after the cataclysmic eruption of Mount St. Helens. I had visited the mountain shortly after March 27, when it began to vent ash and steam after a silence of 123 years. On April 22, the mountain abruptly stopped venting. In those few weeks, I met many people who lived and worked on or near the mountain. Some of them had become my friends. I had no way of knowing how many were dead.

All planes were grounded due to airborne ash. Accumulations near ground level often reduced visibility to only a few feet, and the roads were closed. The governor had declared a state of emergency.

There was an eerie, almost palpable silence, and it hung heavily over my town of Livingston, like the ash itself. All the gaudy honky-tonks opposite the train station were silent, locked up tight, and there were no cars or people on the streets. The mountains were hidden behind the yellowish haze.

I stood on the corner, and ash scratched my throat as I breathed. The sun was beginning to set. It was barely visible, low in the haze, and the disk was an alien crimson color. It set the drifting ash aglow, and the air itself glimmered with a color out of time.

I stood there thinking about death—about ash and gas, about hellfire and boiling mud—and I knew I'd find some way to get back to the mountain within the day.

The Army, Air Force, and National Guard run their search and rescue operation out of the tiny one-runway airstrip at Toledo, Washington. There are press lines, and the media are not allowed into the Army camp where the bodies are unloaded. The helicopters—the Chinooks and the Hueys—come and go constantly, setting up that chopping, staccato sound, the clatter of war and remote tragedy.

I am sitting in a UH-1 Huey with a crew of four out of the 54th Medical Detachment, Fort Lewis, Washington. There is a medic aboard. Stowed under my seat are a shovel and several rubber body bags.

The Huey lifts off, and its insect eye is splattered by a glittering drizzle. We turn up the North Fork of the Toutle River and begin rising toward the mountain. I see whole forests that have been washed down the river, as well as the major debris flow of the eruption. The riverbed appears to be scoured and widened several times over. Farther on, the river runs over the mud flats in several thin, choked channels, like varicose veins, and the water is a jaundiced yellow-brown.

There are paved roads running down to the flats on either side, but no sign of the bridges that must have spanned the river at those points. There is a collapsed hay barn. Several houses are buried in mud to the roof line. Farther on, a big steel bridge is down, its twisted girders half-buried in the sick, yellow-brown mud.

Here, twenty miles from the mountain, there apparently was escape. The forest still stands on either side. But as we rise higher, the mud flats expand—two hundred yards, five hundred yards—until, past Camp Baker, a vast valley perhaps one and a half miles across has been reduced to mud flats. The river here has not yet found its new channel, and it runs in thin yellowish dribbles, like bile.

Now the high ridges on either side of the river appear to have been scoured, and we are into the devastated area, where all trees are down and stripped of their limbs. The blast area extends about thirteen miles north of the mountain and is almost eighteen miles wide. At the outer edges the trees lie across hillsides, and you can follow the lines of the blast by the way they lie.

The mind simply refuses to comprehend the force of the blast that tore over the land. It is one thing to imagine something capable of stripping the limbs from a hundred-foot Douglas fir and instantaneously snapping it off at the roots. It is another thing entirely to realize that whole forests of these giants were sheared and shattered and ripped from the earth.

The color below is constant, a combination of the brown of the mud and of the black and the yellow-white of the ash. It is like no other color on the face of the earth, and it stretches, constant, from horizon to horizon. It insults the eyes, this color, and it will not allow the mind to fasten upon it. The color excites a sense of horror: it is like looking at the carcass of a skinned animal.

We follow what is left of the Toutle to the remains of Spirit Lake. The lake is yellow-green, like a thick cesspool. The water itself was set aboil by a literal mountain of boiling mud and glowing rock. Everything in the lake is dead. You can smell the death from three hundred feet.

There is a new vent just west of the lake, and it is spewing up a cloud of steam and dark ash to a height of about one hundred feet. The steam is the same color as several drifting pockets of fog, only thicker.

Between the lake and the mountain is a hummocky mud flat. There are bilious standing ponds down there; jaundiced streams run aimlessly through the flat, searching for a new drainage. From three hundred feet up, the flat looks like the Canyonlands of Utah seen from thirty thousand feet.

Soldiers who have searched this area on foot tell me that it is like walking on a water bed. The layers of water and mud and ash have turned the earth into a moldy poison pudding. Bubbles the size of a man's head rise up out of the mud, and when they burst, there is a sudden stench of brimstone.

Everywhere there are great dirty white humps sunk partially into the mud and surrounded by bile-colored puddles. These are sections of glaciers thrown from the flanks of the mountain by the blast.

The Huey moves toward the base of the mountain, and I can just barely make out the crater through the mist: it is shaped like a horseshoe, the open end canted down to the north. There is the smell of smoke, of a choked, closed-in fire. Below, hundreds of logs, sunk in the mud and covered with ash, are still smoldering: these are the remnants of the dozens of forest fires ignited by the volcano. Dirty gray smoke rises to meet the leaden clouds.

We skirt the base of the mountain and drop down over the South Fork of the Toutle in order to search the drainages just up from Disappointment Creek. The crew chief spots something angular in the mud along a steep slope, and our pilot wheels the bird around. We hover over the object, and the helicopter bucks like a skittish horse held tight.

It is a toppled logging crane, the tower pointing downhill, a muddy logjam behind its threads. Gray ash billows around us as we land. The mud clutches our boots ankle-deep, and there is a cold, funereal wind whipping off the ridge. We find no body in the cab, no body in the vicinity. The crew chief marks the spot with a yellow smoke bomb: the vehicle has been searched.

We lift off in a storm of ash and pass over the ridge, where we spot a small blue car. Two bodies were recovered there yesterday. In another drainage, we set down beside a small red car, an import. A sleeping bag is humped in the back seat. The crew chief breaks the window with a rock. There is nothing under the bag. On the front seat of the car there is a wallet with a driver's license in it. The crew chief will see to it that it gets to the next of kin. There is some camera gear scattered on the front seat, but the camera body is missing. We trudge through the deep ash and mud to the top of the ridge, looking for anything that protrudes: an arm, a foot, anything. We guess that the occupant of the car ran to the top of the ridge to shoot some pictures. We find nothing.

Farther down the South Fork, we come upon a logging-company truck. It is badly burned. The cab is crushed, and a mudslide has pushed it into the twisted roots of an overturned tree. We cannot get into the cab. It is partially buried in the mud and entangled in the roots. There is another odor here: something worse than the smell of ooze and sulfur and ash and fire. It is very faint, this odor, and it emanates from the vicinity of the truck. It will take a crane or bulldozer to get the truck out of the roots and mud. The helicopter crew marks the truck for further search.

This mission is over. We rise up off the tortured land, and rain streaks race across the Huey's insect eye.

Weeks before the big blast, a sort of blister had been observed forming on the north flank of the mountain. The bulge was growing outward at the rate of five feet per day. It was an ominous development.

On Saturday, May 17, the day before the eruption, Frank Valenzuela, twenty-three, was camped due west of Mount St. Helens, near Goat Mountain and just off N820, an all-weather road. He was about five miles from the base of the mountain. A naturalist for the St. Helens Ranger District, Frank had recently been evacuated, and everything he owned was piled in the back of his white Ford Maverick. On Sunday, he intended to hike into the Goat Marsh area. Near his campsite, Frank ran into Robert, a friend of his. Also camped nearby was Ty Kearney, an amateur radio operator who had volunteered to spend a week monitoring the volcano for the Washington Department of Emergency Services.

Frank and Robert got up before dawn on Sunday morning and hiked down near the South Fork of the Toutle. They returned to the N820 campsite about 8:00 A.M. Kearney was talking to a second radio operator about three miles to the northeast.

"There are two vents," the second operator said.

"Yeah." Kearney sounded bored. "I see them clearly."

Frank was sitting on a stump, eating an orange. The stump began to sway under him. It was 8:31 and 31 seconds, according to various seismic stations, and the earthquake that rocked the land was centered some three miles under Mount St. Helens. It measured over 5.0 on the Richter scale.

The ground wobbled like Jell-O, and Frank turned toward the mountain. Immediately, the north flank began to slide into the Spirit Lake basin. There was no sound.

"I see the face moving," the second operator told Kearney.

As the north flank dropped away from the mountain, almost

simultaneously, Frank saw a white cloud with pink and yellowish tinges burst out of the lower north side of the shattered mountain. It moved in a lateral direction, to the north, and Frank could see into it but not through it.

At precisely the same time, two dark plumes shot out of the upper slope of the north flank. They were as black as sheets of heavy construction paper. Both the upper and lower blasts seemed to be moving at incredible speeds.

The lower, white blast spread out to the north. It seemed to Frank, from his high vantage point, that the cloud was at least fifty yards high.

Kearney's radio crackled. "It's coming toward me," the second operator said. There was panic in his voice. He mumbled something, perhaps his call letters. There was the sound of a revving engine, then sudden silence. *My God*, Frank thought, *he's dead*.

The north flank slid into the basin toward Spirit Lake. At first it stayed together as one huge plate. Then it began to ripple, and finally it broke apart and became an avalanche.

A white, cloudy substance appeared around the summit, and it seemed to Frank that the entire top of the mountain had caved in. St. Helens lost at least thirteen hundred feet in those few seconds.

Frank wasn't checking his watch, but he felt perhaps thirty seconds had passed. It took that long for the sound to reach him. It was an incredible roar, like a jet engine at close range, and he could feel its vibration in his chest.

To understand the mechanics of that initial blast, it is necessary to start at least sixty miles below the surface of the earth, where the temperature is thought to be about twenty-two hundred degrees Fahrenheit. Though this is more than hot enough to melt rock, the weight of the earth above keeps the rock from melting.

Any crack or fissure allows the rock to expand, to melt and to move toward the surface of the earth. Great quantities of water and gases of carbon and sulfur are contained in the molten rock, and as it moves upward and the pressure lessens, these substances begin to form gas bubbles, which expand and coalesce as they push the superheated rock, called magma, upward with ever greater force.

A pool of magma fed St. Helens for months. The upward movement of magma heated the very rocks that composed the mountain. Snowfields and glaciers began to melt, liberating enormous quantities of water. Some of this water found its way into the various drainages, but much of it dropped into cracks and fissures and sank into the mountain. As the water seeped deeper, it came into contact with even hotter rock, and its temperature was raised well above the boiling point. Even before the major explosion, bursts of steam and ash had erupted from several vents within the old crater.

The big explosion, when it finally came, is thought to have been at least five hundred times more powerful than the atomic blast that leveled Hiroshima. Huge boulders and great chunks of glacial ice were thrown for miles. A hurricane of fragmented rock and steam literally shattered trees on the ridge above Spirit Lake; small slivers of wood can be found everywhere beneath the ash and mud on those hills. Other trees were sheared off at ground level or simply uprooted. A low volcanic cloud limbed and leveled 156 square miles of forest.

The upper section of the blast pulverized the old rock above it. Tiny fragments of this rock gave the cloud its dark color. The lethal lower section of the blast did not carry as much fragmental material, which accounts for the lighter color of its cloud.

It was a searing explosion, the temperature of the lower cloud probably near 390 degrees Fahrenheit. It spread like a white blanket below Frank. The roar was deafening, a massive composite of various cataclysms: the slide and avalanche, the collapse of the rock summit, the explosion, the hurricane of steam and pulverized rock, the shattering of forests.

Frank thinks that it was somewhere near the thirty-second mark, just after the roar started, when he could no longer differentiate between the upper and lower components of the blast. A heavy black cloud began rising, billowing, moving toward him with frightening speed.

The initial blast tore away much of the mountain. Magma had been rising toward the vents, rising slowly, but now there was almost no downward pressure on it at all. Steam and gases in the magma ripped upward through the molten rock. It was a continuous process: as magma was hurled into the sky by the gases, pressure was reduced on deeper magma, causing more explosions. The force of the continuous blast reduced the magma to tiny fragments that eventually fell to earth as ash. The ash was blasted ten miles into the air.

The great black cloud was expanding in all directions, and it was moving toward Frank. It was so huge, its speed so rapid, that Frank found he simply didn't comprehend it. The black cloud opened like some great, poison black flower in a time-lapse film.

Other clouds, white ones, were forming somewhere in the new crater, and they were bubbling up out of that awful hole like vapor out of a beaker of dry ice. These clouds, called pyroclastic flows, are gas-charged mixtures of small glassy fragments of cooling magma combined with larger hunks of cooling molten rock saturated with gas bubbles and called pumice. The explosions that propelled the pyroclastic flows were not strong enough to send them into the atmosphere. Instead, the flows rolled out of the crater and, since they were denser than air, then rolled down into the drainages like a series of searing avalanches. Such flows are hot—392 degrees Fahrenheit by some estimates—and because the fragmental material is separated by gas, they are not substantially slowed by friction. The pyroclastic flows were rolling up out of the crater constantly and moving at speeds of nearly one hundred miles an hour. They were accompanied by the sound of hundreds of separate explosions, as closely spaced as popcorn popping or violently boiling tar. This burning material may have been forming its own clouds in the cool mountain air, and one of these white clouds rolled down the slopes of the mountain. Its momentum carried it up and over a nearby ridge where Frank knew a family was camped.

"Those poor people," Robert said.

Ty Kearney said, "I'm getting out of here."

The eruption cloud was billowing toward them. Frank and Robert, suddenly afraid, decided to drive out, too. There followed a series of events that might have been comic if they had not been so nearly deadly.

Frank's car was stuck in some mud. A logger came speeding down the road in his pickup. Frank flagged him down. The logger, a big, burly man, was terrified: his face was white and his eyes bulged in his head. "The gas," the logger screamed, "the gas is coming." He sped away without offering any assistance. It was almost funny, Frank thought, that sweating, comic-book caricature of fear on the man's face.

Frank and Robert got the Maverick out of the muck and raced up to a high ridge near Goat Mountain. Only a few minutes had passed, and Frank knew his emotions had been erratic. He had first felt great awe—as if his heart were expanding in his chest—and then the pyroclastic flow rolled over the ridge and down to where the family was camped. He had been ashamed that he didn't go down and offer help, but he knew they were dead, they had to be dead, he would die in any attempt to find them. Then came the fear, and the logger, whose. fear made Frank laugh at himself.

And now, once again, the mountain held him in thrall. There was a vast, obscene beauty to it all, something mystical, perhaps even holy. The cloud, which now had the appearance of being black with a glowing purple tinge, rose above him and around him and it was so high he could no longer see the top of the ridge. There were billows within billows: it was a great, heaving, convoluted thing. The particles within the cloud rubbed against one another and charged the air with static electricity. Long streaks of orange-white lightning shot from cloud to cloud. Thunder rolled continuously.

One bolt dropped out of a billow and struck a spot on the next ridge. The lightning seemed to hang there for several seconds, stationary in the cloud, stationary on the ground. But the body of the bolt wavered back and forth, striking several trees, which immediately burst into flame. There were forest fires everywhere. Frank could see at least five of them.

The black cloud was on them then. The heat was oppressive, the heavy stench of sulfur was sickening, and there seemed to be no oxygen in the air.

Robert had left some precious possessions back at the N820 campsite, and the two men got back into their cars and tried to drive back. Their headlights couldn't pierce the blackness, and they got lost. Finally, they got back to the campsite. They sat in their cars, the air-conditioning going full blast to equalize the atmospheric pressure. The darkness was complete but for the slightly larger pieces of glowing ash that fell through the gritty midnight like drunken falling stars.

Within an hour or so, a stiff wind out of the west sprang up and began pushing the cloud to the east. Light dawned over the N820 campsite. Frank wrapped a T-shirt over his face and stepped out into the cloud. Lighter ash fell like fog, a tired yellow fog. To the north, thick ash was falling out of the penetrating black cloud like rain from a thunderhead. Frank had felt at least a dozen earthquakes, and the ground continued to roll under his feet like pudding. Lightning was still striking within the cloud, and fires howled under the roll of thunder. The explosions rumbled on, and those deadly white clouds kept boiling up out of the crater and floating on down the drainages with hideous and graceful speed.

By 1:30 P.M., five hours after the initial blast, Frank and Robert thought it was clear enough to drive out. They reached the town of Cougar a little after 3:00 P.M. and reported to the sheriff.

Of the scores dead and missing, the only one I knew was Reid Blackburn, a photographer for the *Vancouver Columbian*. I had met him once, very briefly, sometime in early April in the town of Cougar, on the south flank of the mountain. They found him in his car, ash piled to the windows.

A coroner who had personally examined five of the victims told me that all had died from "mechanical obstruction of the air passages." Ash had simply clogged their throats and lungs. "Aside from those who suffered trauma—who had trees fall on them, for instance—this is the way most of the victims died." The coroner couldn't tell me if death came quickly. We both hoped so.

Harry Truman, the tough-talking eighty-three-year-old who had refused to leave his lodge near Spirit Lake, was probably buried when the north flank of the mountain rolled over him. The avalanche carried glowing rock and boiling mud all the way across Spirit Lake. The water probably ran several hundred feet up the ridge behind the lake, gathering in the shattered trees, until it spilled back into the basin and began flowing down the North Fork of the Toutle River. This debris flow—which contained much of the north flank—may have been twenty feet high or more; it may have moved as fast as thirty miles per hour. It leveled the forests before it and carried them down the drainage.

The mudflow on the South Fork of the Toutle was fueled by melting glaciers. These high floods of boiling mud and water scoured the slopes of the mountain and may have moved as fast as sixty miles an hour. As they hit flatter ground, they slowed and piled up, forming a great, thunderous tidal wall of mud.

Both the mudflow and debris flow set like cement. Many of the missing must be buried there, somewhere along the banks of the North and South forks of the Toutle River. Others lie under fallen trees, under the debris from pyroclastic flows, under a thick blanket of ash somewhere in that steaming, trackless devastation.

I thought a lot about the missing and about a conversation I overheard outside the press information office in Toledo. An army colonel was talking to a young man.

"We have eighteen we are going through the process of identification with," the colonel said.

"I guess . . . I guess some will never be found."

The colonel did not like what he had to say. "Yes." He paused. "How old was your father?"

"Forty-eight."

"He was a young man."

"Yes."

There was a strange, helpless expression on the colonel's face. "I'm sorry," he said.

"It's not your fault," the young man said.

The Killing Season

The bars in Montana are like the families of China: Millions upon millions of them, with only a few names. In China, you've got your Hongs and Wongs, and, aside from an occasional Sun Yat-sen and Mao Tse-tung, that's about it. In the same way, thirsty individuals throughout Montana are confined to places called the Mint, the Longbranch, and the Stockman. You've got to go out of your way to drink in a classy joint like the Owl Casino or Trixie's Antler Saloon.

Long about mid-March, you want to avoid bars of any name in Montana. Even in the genteel and marginally famous Livingston Bar and Grille, one notices an alarming increase in the rascalur density (defined as the number of bona fide sons of bitches per square foot). Brothers punch one another in the Longbranch for no apparent reason. Previously married individuals mope about the Mint, where they are heard to mutter things like, "Left me a note, said she couldn't take it anymore, she was going to California."

What she couldn't take was winter's last blast. Nobody can. There may be two feet of new powder in the mountains, but they'll have closed the ski hill for want of business. Something in the body's internal clock makes us pack the Rossignols away, informs us that this is the season of resurrection, and suggests a naked romp through fields of blooming wildflowers. Mid-March ought to be spring, dammit, but in Montana that season is at least another month or two away—an eternity of cracked engine blocks, broken spirits, and the animal longing for warmth. Jimmy Buffett encapsulated the psychological malady in a single telling line: "This morning I shot six holes in my freezer. I think I've got cabin fever."

Here's a word of advice: When you start thinking about stomping your toaster, stay out of the Stockman. Better to face the enemy in the domain of her harshest fury. Think Nietzsche: If winter hasn't killed you yet, another bitter month of it is only going to make you stronger.

Toward the shank end of the month, when cabin fever descends like a sickly sad syrup of regret, I like to go cross-country skiing in Yellowstone Park. Up at the eight-thousand-foot level, in the caldera of that vast and ancient volcano, there are only two seasons anyway, August and winter. Even in March, temperatures can drop to the forty-below mark. In dry cold like that, snow crystals refuse to clump up and form stars. The glittering crystalline "diamond dust" of Yellowstone is light and ephemeral, and does not fall but floats on currents of air, where it bends the light of the sun and forms boreal rainbows that reflect off the rolling surface of the snow below.

Plodding through these polar rainbows are the denizens of the park, more pitiful and bedraggled than any patron of the Long-branch. The elk, the buffalo, the mule deer and coyotes, the bighorn sheep all congregate in a few very specific winter ranges. During the summer, they have more than two million protected acres in which to roam, but as high-country snow begins to pile up belly high on an elk—when feed is buried under layers of ice and simple walking takes dangerous amounts of energy—the animals are driven down into the geyser basins and the relative warmth of the low northern fringe of the park. During a summer's drive through these areas, a tourist is likely to see a dozen or more animals; the visitor in winter can expect to multiply that number by two hundred, by three hundred.

Along the geyser-fed stretches of the upper Firehole River,

steam rises in purely expressionistic clouds, and great beasts—thousand-pound elk, fifteen-hundred-pound buffalo—emerge out of the fog. A skier gliding along the bank is presented with the sight of a bull elk in midstream, feeding on aquatic plants. Mule deer haunt the area around Old Faithful, where there is warmth but no feed. The geyser basins have been methodically picked over by winter-ravaged beasts, and herds of buffalo grunt over the few dandelions that bloom in February at the edge of thermal pools.

The winter range I know best is an hour's drive from my house, via the north entrance road, just outside Gardiner, Montana. This is the only road in the park that remains open all winter, and it presents the motorist with problems not covered in basic driver's-education classes. With plowed snow sometimes piled to the eight-foot level on either side of the road, it is disconcerting to round a bend and encounter some belligerent half-ton animal who does not want to climb back up over the snow or yield the right-of-way. In a confrontation between a small Japanese car and large American moose, bet on the moose every time. Best to back up fast, crimp the wheels, pull on the emergency brake, and let the momentum and the slick surface of the snow spin you around in a reverse bootlegger's turn. The moose drops her head, and the ruff around her neck bristles like fur on a hissing cat. Hit the gas before she charges and—please God—don't spin out.

Moose hazards, however, are no great hindrance to the intrepid. There are places to ski everywhere along the north road. My favorite is a great, open plain, the Lamar Valley. March weather rumbles into the valley in absurd abundance; in a single day, you may ski through pellets of stinging spring snow, a ground blizzard, a display of diamond dust, and yet finish out the day badly sunburned. Rolling clouds soar overhead, and broken shafts of sunlight fall in obtuse angles throughout the expanse of the valley. Several small thermal pools flank the river. Steam rises into the still air through the shafts of sun, so that gentle pastels color the snow; the land itself seems to float and sway.

Wintering along the banks of the Lamar River is a staggering concentration of extremely large animals. In March, when the high-country snow is as deep as it will get all year, when the animals have all finally come down, the Lamar Valley is America's Serengeti Plain. Herds of elk move through the slanting shafts of light. They stand stolidly, starving in the glowing pastel steam. Buffalo, singly and in herds, feed by clearing away patches of snow with their massive heads. They glance up at the touring skiers—nothing to eat there—and return to their meal, the humped back muscles rolling in the effort it takes to work through the snow.

A thoughtful skier, who doesn't want to kill or be killed, keeps 250 yards between himself and any of the animals. All of them— buffalo and elk, mule deer and antelope, even the bighorn sheep— are starving. Their instincts are dulled by the proximity of death, so that it is quite possible to touch them. This is foolish, even suicidal. An enraged buffalo can run through deep snow faster than a man can ski, and not so long ago a French photographer was gored to death by a park buffalo. Mostly, however, the buffalo and elk of March are docile, in the manner of all starving creatures. Approaching too close is an unforgivable brutality. Should the beasts run from you, they may be using the very calories that will sustain them until true spring. Touch an elk, kill an elk.

Hundreds of the animals alive on a mid-March day will not last until summer. They have reached the edge of their tolerance, and a late spring blizzard or a brutal cold snap will kill them in droves. The skier marks those who will not survive: a yearling elk, a venerable and grizzled buffalo. It is a drama of real life, real death, and no one can ski the valley without feeling the truth of it building like unbidden tears, and without somehow celebrating the brutality, and the strength, of life. It is a thought to take back to the Longbranch or the Stockman or the Mint: One more storm won't kill me.

A Camp at the End of Time

T he Missouri Breaks is a stretch of high prairie in northern Montana. Not too far from the town of Roy, which is difficult to find on most maps, an obscure road cuts into the heart of the Breaks: thirty-seven miles of rutted dirt, a morass of muddy potholes in the wet seasons, a treacherous iced-over washboard in the cold.

At its outer expanse, before the land begins its gradual run down to the Missouri River, the Breaks is a simple shortgrass prairie, a high, windblown, sage-littered flatland, seldom visited. Prairie dog colonies along the road look like little areas of atomic desolation. The grass there is cropped right down to dark earth, and at least one of the stout, burrowing rodents will be standing atop his mound, barking out a warning, his short, black-tipped tail vibrating rapidly.

As the road begins to slope down to the Missouri, there are small, stunted stands of ponderosa pine, and the land begins to fold in on itself, all the tree-lined drainages meandering endlessly down to the river. Mule deer and whitetail bed down in the tall grasses of the dry creek beds, and an occasional elk can be seen.

I am driving down the road in a four-wheel-drive pickup with my sometime racquetball partner, one Blasius Bauer. We have driven down out of the mountains where we live to this strange, broken flatland because Blasius thinks I ought to see the Breaks. From what I can gather, it is a land that speaks to him spiritually.

About halfway to the river, just where the expanse of sage (antelope country) gives way to the pines (deer habitat) there is a ramshackle, weatherbeaten settler's cabin. Photographers win prizes taking shots of such abandoned cabins. They use telephoto lenses and frame the cabin in the lower third of the picture, with the sky stretching away forever above and the prairie rolling into infinity beyond, so that the impression you get is that the vastness of the land itself defeated the people who lived there.

"I have," Blasius says, "a recurring dream about that cabin." In his dream Blasius is on foot, inexplicably wandering the prairie. He comes upon the cabin and knows instinctively the woman who lives there and why he has come. But she is not there, and he can't say the words he needs to speak: an explanation, an apology. The cabin is entirely empty except for hundreds of dolls scattered about—sitting against the walls, propped up on the bare wooden table—and they stare at him with cold, ice-blue marble eyes.

Some land has the power to do that, to snap the thread of linear thought so that the mind spins free.

It is late November, the last full weekend of deer-hunting season, but a sudden cold snap has hit the Breaks. It is nearly fifteen degrees below zero, and the deer are huddled in the hollows, staying out of the wind, so that the prairie seems entirely devoid of life. We pass a few hunters. They are cruising in four-wheel-drive vehicles much like ours, rifles on the rack in the back window, two or three men in the front seat. They wear blaze-orange vests and hats, and they stare out into the land with forlorn, hungry eyes. These are the unlucky ones, the late hunters, the patently unsuccessful.

We camp at the mouth of Soda Creek on a sloping black expanse of earth that forms the bank of the Missouri. The river is frozen solid all the way across, and it is partially covered with swirling patterns of wind-scattered snow. An occasional gust of wind whistles down Soda Creek Canyon and spills out onto the ice. It is a lonely, short-lived sound, resonant, empty, and cold. Blasius and I take turns trying to describe the sound, and the barehanded work of setting up the tent has left us chilled and has colored our imaginations to a purple pitch. "It is," I say, "the sound of the last frozen god, blowing across the last empty beer bottle in the universe."

We tromp along the bleak banks of the river, kicking among the rocks until we come to a series of mounds Blasius wants to show me. The rocks have been exposed by the rise and fall of the river, and one formation looks like a monstrous kangaroo: There are the same short forelegs, a heavy pair of hind legs, and a long, curved-back tail. The head is ovoid, longer than it is high, and about the size of a large watermelon. The entire rock formation is thirty feet long from tip of tail to end of snout.

Blasius thinks the formation is a fossilized dinosaur. I am not so sure, but he shows me three more nearby rock piles, all in the same formation. Blasius once dug a bone out of one of these piles. It looked like a section of spine, and he took it to the Rocky Mountain Museum in Bozeman, where they told him it was somewhere between 70 and 120 million years old, which would place it in the Cretaceous period of the Mesozoic era: the age of the last dinosaurs. "I can't figure out why they all laid down to die together," Blasius says.

I am walking off the pile, measuring the distance of forelegs from head, the length of the spine, and I am thinking, *flesh eater*. The herbivores, such as the brontosaurus, were great long-necked beasts set on four pillarlike legs; and though they weighed in excess of thirty tons, their heads weren't much larger than ours. The carnivores—Tyrannosaurus, for example—were smaller and somewhat more agile. They carried their short forelegs close to the chest and must have walked with a bobbing, side-to-side motion, rather like chickens. The head was massive and shaped like the one outlined in rock at the bottom of the Breaks.

We kneel to clear some fine, powdery snow off the rocks, and the incongruity of clearing snow off the remains of a dinosaur snaps the linear thread. I am imagining a time-lapse film of the world, two or three frames every million years or so. There is a long, long run of bare, mud-brown hills and rolling sand dunes from pre-Cambrian times, and it is a world without life. Half a billion years ago we see the first marine invertebrates, and 100 millions years later the first plants invade the land, followed by lobe-finned fishes and amphibians. Vast jungles of fern cover the land, and fin-backed reptiles move through the coal forests in company with small, mammal-like reptiles.

Then, in the Triassic period of the Mesozoic, about 225 million years ago, the first dinosaurs burst upon the land, and they rule for 140 million years. The Missouri Breaks is a vast swamp, steaming, humid, choked with vegetation, rather like today's Amazon basin. The largest animals ever to walk the earth dominate the swamp, and then, in a span of only 10 million years—sometime between 70 and 60 million years ago—they all lay down to die.

No one knows why. There may have been too much CO_2 in the atmosphere or too little. Volcanic activity may have cooled the earth, or solar eruptions may have baked it. The animals may have become vastly overspecialized, or there may simply be a kind of racial life span that the dinosaurs outlived.

Pieces of the dinosaur, this creature of rock, crumble in my hands. Above, high cirrus clouds blow across a sun you could stare into without squinting. It is a feeble silver sun, without warmth, and its glow is that of a cold, imperfect gem. Sparse snow, fine as talc, drifts down out of glacial skies.

H. G. Wells wrote about such a world in *The Time Machine*. "So I traveled, stopping over and over again, in great strides of a thousand years or more, drawn on by the mystery of earth's fate . . . then I stopped once more . . . and the red beach, save for its livid green liverworts and lichens, seemed lifeless. And now it was flecked with white. A bitter cold assailed me. Rare white flakes ever and again came eddying down . . . a certain indefinable apprehension still kept me in the saddle of the machine. But I saw nothing moving, in earth or sky . . . I fancied I saw some black object flopping about on this bank, but it became motionless as I looked at it, and I judged my eye had been deceived, and that the black object was merely a rock. The stars in the sky were intensely bright and seemed to me to twinkle very little."

The banks of the Missouri were black where I stood, and I felt as if we had set up camp at the end of time. In a few billion years the sun will go nova, and it will fill the sky and blister the land. Then it will slowly die. If there are still men alive—if we haven't left the dying planet, if we haven't killed ourselves, if there is not too much CO_2 in the atmosphere or too little, if there is no racial life span— then the last of us will lumber over the land, lumpish creatures bundled in layers against the cold. Some few hunters, the late and luckless ones, will walk the earth with hungry, hopeless eyes. Others of us may squat in the dirt, scrabbling among the rocks and bones, finding evidence of a warm, forgotten time.

The traces of our life here will lie cold and still, dreaming, like the brittle eyes of dolls in an abandoned cabin, and the last men will look to them for explanations, or apologies.

ALSO BY Tim Cahill

"Tim Cahill is one of those rare types whose fun quotient seems to increase in direct proportion to the diceyness of the situation."
—*San Francisco Examiner*

PECKED TO DEATH BY DUCKS

Intrepid traveler Tim Cahill sleeps with grizzly bears, treks with llamas, inches his way through the deepest cave in America, and assesses the cuteness quotient of giant clams in the South Pacific—all in the service of some of the most lively, nerve-wracking, and outrageous travel writing of our time.

Travel/Adventure/0-679-74929-2

ROAD FEVER

Engine trouble in Patagonia. Sadistic troopers in Peru. Document hell in Colombia. These are just some of the perils that Cahill braved in the course of a 15,000-mile road trip from Tierra del Fuego to Prudhoe Bay in a record-breaking twenty and a half days.

Travel/Adventure/0-394-75837-4

A WOLVERINE IS EATING MY LEG

Tim Cahill brings 'em back alive. Not only has he survived fantastic journeys through the Himalayan rapids, the Grand Terror of Montana, and Dian Fossey's forbidden zone, he writes about them, too. He dares readers to follow him wherever danger and craziness lurk—and to laugh as he prevails.

Travel/Adventure/0-679-72026-X

Available at your local bookstore, or call toll-free to order:
1-800-793-2665 (credit cards only).